THE TRIUMPH OF ELOHIM

The Triumph of Elohim

From Yahwisms to Judaisms

Edited by

Diana Vikander Edelman

William B. Eerdmans Publishing Company
Grand Rapids, Michigan

© 1995 Kok Pharos Publishing House
Kampen, the Netherlands

This edition published 1996
through special arrangement with Kok Pharos by
Wm. B. Eerdmans Publishing Co.
255 Jefferson Ave. S.E., Grand Rapids, Michigan 49503
All rights reserved

Printed in the United States of America

00 99 98 97 96   7 6 5 4 3 2 1

Library of Congress Cataloging-in-Publication Data

The triumph of Elohim: from Yahwisms to Judaisms /
  edited by Diana Vikander Edelman.
      p.   cm.
  Includes bibliographical references and index.
  ISBN 0-8028-4161-9 (paper: alk. paper)
  1. God — Biblical teaching. 2. Bible. O.T. — Theology.
3. God (Judaism) — History of doctrines. 4. Judaism — History —
586 B.C.-210 A.D. 5. Monotheism — Middle East — History.
I. Edelman, Diana Vikander, 1954-
BS1192.6.T75   1996
296'.09'01 — dc20   95-49398
                                                       CIP

Table of Contents

Editor's Note

For the sake of consistency among the seven essays contained within this volume, I have standardized the use of the following terms: Judah, Judahite, Yehud, Judean, Judea, Jew, Yahwism and Judaism. "Judah" designates the state that existed from ca. 960 BCE-587 BCE and "Judahite" a citizen of that state. "Yehud" refers to the territory that became the Persian province, whose citizens were "Judeans," while "Judea" designates this same province under the Greeks, whose citizens were also "Judeans." The term "Jew" is reserved for use to describe citizens of the Hasmonean state. "Yahwism" is used to describe various forms of religious expression centered on the deity Yahweh that existed from the foundation of the state of Judah through the end of Judea as a Greek province and "Judaism" is used to designate various forms of exclusive monotheistic belief systems centered on Yahweh that existed during the Hasmonean state.

In the introduction I propose a subdivision of the Yahwistic religions that existed over the time span indicated into the following categories: "national" or "first temple Yahwism" to describe the religion of the state of Judah, "intertemple Yahwisms" to describe the different forms of religion that developed inside and outside the territory of the former state after its destruction among people who had been citizens, and "second temple Yahwism" to describe the official religion of the province of Yehud and Judea. "Judaism" is reserved for use to describe the official state religion of the Hasmoneans as well as other, contemporaneous belief systems that were also exclusively monotheistic. Just as there were multiple Yahwisms, there were multiple Judaisms, a fact that has been reflected in the subtitle of the present volume.

I have also standardized the collection by using American spellings, idioms, punctuation style and biblical citation style. I have not, however, enforced the consistent use of BCE and CE vs. BC and AD; I feel that one's choice of one of abbreviations over the other reflects a personal, conscious decision about the importance of avoiding christocentric terms in biblical scholarship and that an individual's decision on this matter needs to be respected.

October 15, 1994   Diana Edelman

List of Abbreviations

AB	Anchor Bible
ADPV	Abhandlungen des Deutschen Palästina-Vereins
ÄAT	Ägypten und Altes Testament
AJT	*American Journal of Theology*
ANET	*Ancient Near Eastern Texts Relating to the Old Testament*. Edited by J.B. Pritchard. 3rd edition. New Haven: Yale University Press, 1969.
AOAT	Alter Orient und Altes Testament
BA	*Biblical Archaeologist*
BAR	*Biblical Archaeology Review*
BBB	Bonner biblische Beiträge
Ber	*Berytus*
BETL	Bibliotheca ephemeridum theologicarum lovaniensium
Bib	*Biblica*
BibB	Biblische Beiträge
BJRL	*Bulletin of the John Rylands Library*
BN	*Biblische Notizen*
BR	*Biblical Research*
BWANT	Beiträge zur Wissenschaft vom Alten und Neuen Testament
BZ	*Biblische Zeitschrift*
BZAW	Beihefte zur *Zeitschrift für die altestamentliche Wissenschaft*
CBC	Cambridge Bible Commentary on the New English Bible
CBQ	*Catholic Biblical Quarterly*
ConBOT	Coniectanea biblica, Old Testament
DBAT	*Dielheimer Blätter zum Alten Testament*
DTT	Dansk Teologisk Tidsskrift
EstBib	Estudios Bíblicos
FAT	Forschungen zum Alten Testament
FBBS	Facet Books, Biblical Series
FRLANT	Forschungen zur Religion und Literatur des Alten und Neuen Testaments

HSM	Harvard Semitic Monographs
HUCA	*Hebrew Union College Annual*
ICC	International Critical Commentary
INJ	*Israel Numismatic Journal*
JAOS	*Journal of the American Oriental Society*
JARCE	*Journal of the American Research Center in Egypt*
JBL	*Journal of Biblical Studies*
JBTh	*Jahrbuch für Biblische Theologie*
JEA	*Journal of Egyptian Archaeology*
JJS	*Journal of Jewish Studies*
JNES	*Journal of Near Eastern Studies*
JNSL	*Journal of Northwest Semitic Languages*
JQR	*Jewish Quarterly Review*
JSNTSup	Journal for the Study of the New Testament Supplement Series
JSOT	*Journal for the Study of the Old Testament*
JSOTSup	Journal for the Study of the Old Testament Supplement Series
JSS	*Journal of Semitic Studies*
NTS	*New Testament Studies*
OBO	Orbis biblicus et orientalis
OLA	Orientalia Lovaniensia Analecta
OTL	Old Testament Library
OTS	*Oudtestamentische Studiën*
PEQ	*Palestine Exploration Quarterly*
PSAS	*Proceedings of the Seminar for Arabian Studies*
QD	Quaestiones diputatae
RAI	Rencontre Assyriologique Internationale
RB	*Revue biblique*
RevArch	*Revue Archéologique*
SBLDS	Society of Biblical Literature Dissertation Series
SBLMS	Society of Biblical Literature Monograph Series
SBS	Stuttgarter Bibelstudien
SBT	Studies in Biblical Theology
SHANE	Studies in the History of the Ancient Near East
SJOT	*Scandinavian Journal of the Old Testament*
StOr	Studia Orientalia
StTh	*Studia Theologica*
StudPhoen	Studia Phoenicia

SUNT	Studien zur Umwelt des Neuen Testaments
SWBAS	Social World of Biblical Antiquity Series
ThRu	*Theologische Rundschau*
TZ	*Theologisches Zeitschrift*
UF	*Ugarit Forschungen*
VT	*Vetus Testamentum*
VTSup	Vetus Testamentum Supplements
WBC	Word Bible Commentary
WMANT	Wissenschaftlichen Monographien zum Alten und Neuen Testament
ZAH	*Zeitschrift für Althebräistic*
ZAW	*Zeitschrift für die alttestamentliche Wissenschaft*
ZDPV	*Zeitschrift des deutschen Palästina-Vereins*

List of Contributors

Thomas M. Bolin   Department of Theology, St. Mary's University

Philip R. Davies   Department of Biblical Studies, University of Sheffield

Diana V. Edelman   Department of Philosophy and Religion, James Madison University

Lowell K. Handy   American Theological Library Association

Herbert Niehr   Theologicarum, University of Tübingen

Brian B. Schmidt   Department of Near Eastern Languages and Literature, University of Michigan

Thomas L. Thompson   Institute of Biblical Exegesis, Copenhagen University

Introduction
Diana V. Edelman

The process leading to the emergence of monotheistic belief systems in the ancient Near East and the time frame in which this development took place continue to be topics of debate and concern. The present volume is dedicated to a fresh look at both issues by a group of scholars who do not espouse standard views and answers. The collection of seven essays is designed to help the reader reassess the issues in light of recent developments in biblical studies, Jewish studies, ancient Near Eastern history, the history of religions, archaeology, and numismatics. Newer evidence that has only been known for a decade or so as well as evidence that has been around for a long time but which has not been brought to bear on the two issues will be incorporated into the argumentation in the various essays. All readers who approach the volume with an open mind should not be disappointed; they will find a set of challenging ideas and proposals that are not easily dismissed, which call for the rethinking of the standard views and answers.

The present volume grew out of a long conversation I had with Philip Davies and Tom Thompson one afternoon in the fall of 1991 about the late origin of monotheism in general, the need to recognize a new, early form of monotheism that Tom has coined "inclusive monotheism," the meaning and possible late date of the term אלהים, and the multiplicity of monotheistic beliefs in early Judaism. The ideas we discussed were so exciting that I decided on the spot to organize a symposium for the 1992 SBL/ASOR Meeting in which they could be put before a larger group of colleagues for consideration and debate. The essays by Lowell Handy, Tom Thompson, and Philip Davies are revised forms of papers they presented in the symposium sponsored by the Hebrew Bible, History and Archaeology Section at the SBL/ASOR Meeting in San Francisco. A fourth paper, which was to deal with early Persian imperial religion and early Zoroastrianism, was scheduled to be part of the symposium but was not delivered, due to a sudden family crisis. It was never written and so has not been included in the present volume.

The collection has been rounded out by the addition of the four essays by Herbert Niehr, Tom Bolin, Brian Schmidt, and myself. All the essays have been written specifically for the volume, although the contributions by Tom Bolin and Brian Schmidt are based on previously written material that has been revised and expanded for inclusion within the present framework. As a whole, the seven essays look at issues and developments in the religious belief systems associated with the deity named Yahweh from the late monarchic period through the Hellenistic period. The volume is not an exhaustive exploration of all the relevant points and issues; rather, it is a collection of individual essays that rethink standard positions on a number of selected points associated with the two larger issues of the development of monotheistic beliefs in the ancient Near East and the chronological framework in which these changes took place. The volume is intended to spark debate and a reexamination of these two topics, in the hopes of engaging a larger group in a new, systematic analysis of the evidence and the generation of the best set of working hypotheses about the issues in light of the evidence.

Study of the development of monotheism is easily colored by personal religious beliefs and often, investigators slip into a faith perspective when evaluating certain biblical texts instead of their usual academic perspective. This can be a subconscious move of which individuals are not even aware; they think they are continuing their customary, critical approach, yet their results and conclusions lack intellectual and argumentative rigor. It is particularly important that anyone working on issues relating to the development of monotheism be deliberately cognizant of how his or her religious beliefs might be influencing conclusions being drawn; this effort can provide a modicum of control that can help produce a well reasoned and critical analysis of the available data.

It is important to realize that the text of the Hebrew Bible is the product of a long, editorial process. Its final shapers were monotheistic and they wanted the inherited traditions to reflect their own religious beliefs in a single creator deity, Yahweh, who had at his command various lesser divine beings who also populated heaven, the angels.[1] Had they created the texts themselves, they almost certainly would not have included the scattered references to Asherah, Nehushtan, Plague, Pestilence, Death, Sun, Moon and other lesser deities, which they have gone out of their way to turn into cultic objects used in the worship of Yahweh or turn into mere abstract qualities. Having inherited sources that were used to create the texts, if not some of the texts themselves, they apparently felt constrained to maintain these references, yet obligated at the same time to neutralize them in a way that would make them acceptable within their own, later religious world view. This suggests that some texts already enjoyed the status of "classics" and so could not be discarded wholesale. Earlier generations may have had more freedom to edit such texts more extensively and delete direct references to deities other than Yahweh that were not easily understood within an emerging monotheistic framework, before certain texts became "classics." It is unknown, then, how much information about the cult of Yahweh during the period that the state of Judah existed from ca. 960-586 BCE has been deliberately excised from the books that make up the Hebrew Bible through the centuries. We are extremely fortunate to have the few remnants that remain, even though they have been altered from their original meanings and referents in the vast majority of cases.

It is imperative that any study of the development of monotheism be conducted in full recognition that changes have been made to the current biblical texts. In this way, arguments that claim that religion during the period of the state of Judah is accurately reflected in the final form of the text can be dismissed as naive, as can assertions that monotheism must have been the dominant form

---

[1]   Here I probably differ in degree from Philip Davies, who in his essay suggests a late Persian and Hellenistic date for the generation of most of the biblical books. Philip does not explicitly address what percentage of the competing ideologies that are being generated to define early Judaisms are derived from earlier, inherited tradition. He acknowledges that ben Sira is educated through the rote study of a set of "classic" texts and discusses the content of some of these works, but does not comment further on their possible dates or what made them "classics." Tom Thompson tends also to lean toward a late date for the creation of the biblical texts, although he explicitly acknowledges that they contain some material that can be dated to the Assyrian period (*Early History of the Israelite People from the Written and Archaeological Sources* [SHANE 4; Leiden: Brill, 1992] 383-99).

of Yahwism in this period because there are so few indications in the biblical texts that gods other than Yahweh ever existed in Judah. Lists of deities worshipped in neighboring regions over a wide span of time[2] provide a base from which to understand various concepts of pantheons and categories of deity in the larger world of which Judah became a part. A careful reading of the biblical texts discloses a number of these same deities lurking in obscure references or in statements that make no logical sense in spite of their constructions that are grammatically correct. Take, for example, the statement in 1 Kgs 15:13 that Maacah the queen mother had made an image of the asherah; if "the asherah" is some sort of cultic image or object used in the worship of Yahweh, as asserted by some because of the grammar,[3] what does it mean to have made an image of an image or object? While most references to the goddess Asherah were able to be whitewashed by adding the definite article to her name, thereby turning her into a common noun, a few did not work,[4] allowing us to understand the true nature of this term in earlier, premonotheistic contexts within Judah.

The predominance of names in the biblical texts that use Yahweh or El as their theophoric element virtually to the exclusion of other deities except possibly Baal should be seen to be the result of the same process of "monotheizing" inherited tradition. A number of personal names have appeared in the small corpus of inscriptions that have been recovered from various sites that have been

---

[2]   Here it should be noted that I agree in principle with the argument that Herbert Niehr makes in his essay in this volume that Iron Age texts and material cultural remains should be used as the primary data pool for understanding the national Yahwism of the state of Judah (45-6). I think the Ugaritic texts, as well as other earlier texts, can be used profitably to determine the range of deities worshipped in the ancient Near East over time and the length of popularity of certain of prominent gods and goddesses.

[3]   So, for example, A. Lemaire, "Who or What was Yahweh's Asherah?," *BAR* 10 (1984) 42-51, esp. 50-1; P.K. McCarter, Jr., "Aspects of Religion of the Israelite Monarchy: Biblical and Epigraphic Evidence," in *Ancient Israelite Religion: Essays in Honor of Frank Moore Cross* (ed. P.D. Miller, Jr., P.D. Hanson, and S.D. McBride; Philadelphia: Fortress, 1987) 137-56, esp. 146-7; and M.S. Smith, *The Early History of God: Yahweh and the Other Deities in Ancient Israel* (San Francisco: Harper & Row, 1990) 16.

[4]   In addition to 1 Kgs 15:13, 1 Kgs 18:4; 2 Kgs 21:7; 23:4, 7.

excavated in the area of ancient Judah.[5] The preponderance of the use of Yahweh as the theophoric element to date merely indicates that the worship of Yahweh was particularly strong among the upper class of the state at the end of the monarchy; a person who wanted his son to advance in the governmental bureaucracy named him after the head male deity of the state pantheon, Yahweh. The individuals who appear in these inscriptions tend to be associated with the military, the civil administration, or with the cult, the spheres of influence especially considered the domain of the head of a national pantheon.[6]

Monotheism does not appear to have sprung up, full-blown, overnight. The emergence of various forms of monotheistic Judaisms by the 2nd century BCE, as described by Josephus,[7] would seem to be the culmination of a long process that began during the Persian empire as inclusive monotheism and evolved slowly into exclusive monotheism during the Hellenistic period. The following is a brief sketch of a working hypothesis that describes major steps in this process.

During the period when Judah existed as a state, from ca. 960-586 BCE, it seems to have had a national pantheon headed by the divine couple, Yahweh and Asherah. As the title Yahweh Sebaot

---

[5]   For a convenient presentation of the data, see G.I. Davies, *Ancient Hebrew Inscriptions: Corpus and Concordance* (New York/Cambridge: Cambridge University, 1991).

[6]   For the opinion that the epigraphic evidence indicates that exclusive monotheism was the norm in the state of Judah by the late 8th and early 7th century, see e.g. N. Avigad, "The Contribution of Hebrew Seals to an Understanding of Israelite Religion and Society," in *Ancient Israelite Religion: Essays in Honor of Frank Moore Cross* (ed. P.D. Miller, Jr., P.D. Hanson and S.D. McBride; Philadelphia: Fortress, 1987) 195-208, esp. 196-7. J. H. Tigay is more cautious in his conclusions, recognizing a monotheizing of the biblical texts, but tends to see the epigraphic evidence to support some sort of monotheism by the last decades of the state also. See his "Israelite Religion: The Onomastic and Epigraphic Evidence," in *Ancient Israelite Religion: Essays in Honor of Frank Moore Cross* (ed. P.D. Miller, Jr., P.D. Hanson and S.D. McBride; Philadelphia: Westminster, 1987) 157-94. For a response similar to mine, see E.A. Knauf, "'You Shall Have No Other Gods.' Eine notwendige Notiz zu einrer überflüssigen Diskussion," *DBAT* 26 (1989/1990) 238-45.

[7]   See his four philosophies in T.E. Page *et al.*, *Josephus* (9 vols.; Loeb Classical Library; Cambridge: Harvard University, 1960-1967) 7.311-3, 375-7; 9.9-23.

would suggest, Yahweh was king of a whole heavenly host that included lesser deities who did his bidding, having various degrees of
autonomy depending upon their status within the larger hierarchy.
The names of most of these various lesser deities and their functions
are no longer known, due to editing by later monotheists, but a few
have survived: Nehushtan, Mot, Shemesh, Yareah, Deber and Re-
phesh. The essays by Lowell Handy and Herbert Niehr discuss the
nature of this form of religion that might aptly be called national
Yahwism or first temple Yahwism and the evidence that exists
about it. The essay by Brian Schmidt explores competing systems of
representative imagery for Yahweh that were in use during the
monarchy through an analysis of the Second Commandment.

In the Neo-Assyrian empire, the national gods of conquered
states were demoted in status from being heads of their own pantheons to becoming what Lowell Handy characterizes in his essay
as second-tier major active gods of the Assyrian empire pantheon.
The empire god Ashur is referred to in several texts by the title,
"king of the gods,"[8] leaving defeated national gods to hold a rank
somewhere lower than the most important cluster of local Assyrian
Major Active gods, often designated collectively as "the great gods":
Sin, Shamash, Adad and Ishtar, as well as the Babylonian gods Marduk, Bel and Nebo. This demotion is perhaps most clearly expressed in the prologue to Sargon's account of the battle of Musasir, but
is implicit in all the royal texts:

> Ashur, father of the gods, lord of all countries, king of all
> heaven and earth, progenitor [of all], lord of lords, to whom
> Marduk, the foremost of the gods, has granted from olden
> times the gods of lowlands and mountains, from the four
> quarters of the world, that they, with no exceptions, might
> even honor him, bringing their heaped treasures into [the
> temple] Ehursaggalkurkurra.[9]

Yahweh of Israel would have been so demoted after 721 BCE.

Assyrian propaganda told conquered territories that their gods
had been defeated and were now subservient to Ashur or that their

---

[8]   See conveniently, *ANET*, 278, 283, 285, 288, 295, 297, 298.
[9]   Quoted from the translation in M. Cogan, *Imperialism and Religion: Assyria,
Judah and Israel in the Eighth and Seventh Centuries B.C.E.* (SBLMS 19; Missoula,
MT: SBL and Scholars, 1974) 20.

gods had abandoned them either out of anger or in submission to the superior might of Ashur.[10] Statues of various former national gods were routinely removed as booty[11] and often damaged in the process, while those of less important gods apparently were destroyed or converted to raw materials for reuse.[12] During Esarhaddon's reign, images of the gods of the Arab ruler Haza'il were returned to him at his request, but only after they had been repaired and inscribed with a proclamation of the might of Ashur and the name of Esarhaddon to make it clear that the gods and their followers were now the servants of Ashur and Esarhaddon, respectively.[13] He followed the same procedure before returning the defeated god statues of Yadi to Layale, king of that region.[14]

The Neo-Babylonians appear to have maintained this same understanding of the status of the head deities of conquered states. Marduk bears the same title that Ashur had, "king of the gods,"[15] and both Sennacherib and Nabopolassar report that they carried away gods of conquered territories.[16] By implication, the removed gods were demoted in status, having been conquered by Marduk and the other great gods of the empire pantheon. When Nabonidus temporarily replaced Marduk with Sin as the supreme god of the Neo-Babylonian empire, he continued to use the title "king of the gods" to designate Sin's status the head of the pantheon.[17]

---

[10] For a convenient presentation of the various texts and a discussion of their meanings, see *ibid.*, 9-41.

[11] See e.g. statements in texts in *ANET*, 286, 287, 293, 299. For a compilation of all relevant royal inscriptions from the Middle Assyrian and Neo-Assyrian periods, see Cogan, *Imperialism and Religion*, 119-21.

[12] For this dual approach to dealing with god images of conquered areas, see Cogan, *Imperialism and Religion*, 22-41.

[13] For the text, see *ANET*, 291.

[14] For the text, see conveniently, Cogan, *Imperialism and Religion*, 37.

[15] See *ANET*, 307, 310.

[16] *ANET*, 302, 304.

[17] *ANET*, 311-2. Here then I would differ with T. Thompson, who suggests that Nabonidus identified Sin "with the God of Heaven, the ultimate spiritual representative of all that is divine in the Neobabylonian world" (*Early History of the Israelite People*, 417). To my knowledge, the title אלהי השמים is not attested in Neo-Babylonian texts, but is first used in Persian-era texts as an abstracted category of supreme deity. Thus, "inclusive monotheism," which Thompson has defined in large part in terms of the development of the concept אלהי השמים, only began un-

It is under the Persians that a shift in conceptualization of the empire pantheon becomes apparent. Instead of demoting the state gods of conquered regions to a lower level of the pantheon, they seem to have been equated with the new empire god, Ahura Mazda, through the use of a new abstract title, אלהי השמים. In this new system, head deities of national pantheons all became manifestations of a single category of deity, אלהי השמים, which served as a general descriptive designation for the head of the empire pantheon. Ahura Mazda no longer bears the title "king of the gods," but instead, is called "the great god who gave [us] this earth, who gave us this sky, who gave us humanity and who gave his worshipers prosperity."[18]

Tom Thompson has coined this new theological development "inclusive monotheism"[19] and discusses it in his essay. Tom Bolin explores the use of this new term in the Elephantine correspondence in his essay.

As a result of the adoption of the new category "godhead of the heavens," אלהי השמים, the major active gods and goddesses tended to be collapsed into the couple that constituted the highest authority; the two upper tiers of the pantheon came to be merged into one. The title אלהי השמים was used to designate the male head of the pantheon, who was now especially conceptualized as the creator of the universe. The plural form of the word for god in this new title might well be a deliberate attempt to express the multiple specific manifestations that the abstract category of head of pantheon could take. In biblical literature, the texts of 2 and 3 Isaiah particularly emphasize this new single category, creator-god theology, even though the title אלהי השמים is not explicitly used. Note, however, the statement in Isa 54:5 (ET 54:4): אלהי כל־הארץ he will be called, which is consistent with the Persian conception mentioned above. The title אלהי השמים appears in biblical texts in Gen 24:3 (in the form "God of the heavens and the earth"), Jer 10:11 (in its Aramaic form), Jon 1:9; Ezr 1:2, Neh 1:5; 2:4 and 2 Chron 36:22-23. I would propose that the use of the designation "Elohim" as an alternative to the deity name Yahweh in the biblical texts

---

der the Persians, not with Nabonidus at the end of the Neo-Babylonian period, as he claims.

[18] See conveniently, *ANET*, 316.

[19] *Early History of the Israelite People*, 422.

reflects the theology of inclusive monotheism and therefore, cannot predate the Persian period.

With the introduction of Zoroastrianism as the offical religion of the Persian empire in place of the former, pantheon-based Persian imperial religion, the female half of the divine couple may have been lost in favor of a single, male creator deity. It was probably also during the course of the Persian empire that the two lower level of deities, the specialist gods and the messengers, were collapsed into a single category of messenger beings who were converted from lesser deities into abstractions or non-divine heavenly life forms, perhaps again under the impetus of Zoroastrian conceptualization.

It was at some point during the Hellenistic period that inclusive monotheism seems to have given way to forms of exclusive monotheism. The new monotheisms maintained the abstract concept of a head creator deity but rejected the existence of multiple manifestations of such a deity in favor of a single manifestation: Yahweh. Had she not already lost her position in the later part of the Persian period, the female half of the couple that had constituted the highest authority now faded into oblivion and heaven became the exclusive domain of a single male creator deity who had a host of lesser divine beings without any autonomous power to do his bidding. The exact place where this shift in conceptualization first took place and the time it emerged cannot be pinpointed, but it seems to find full expression in the official religion endorsed by the Hasmonean state. Philip Davies explores the process by which the Hasmoneans came to impose one type of exclusive monotheism over competing ones in his essay. My essay uses numismatic evidence to track the changing systems of representative imagery for Yahweh that were used in Yehud and Judea from the Persian period to the end of the Hasmonean dynasty, as inclusive monotheisms gave way to exlusive monotheisms.

In light of the foregoing sketch, it would be prudent to develop a set of labels to describe various phases that the official religion of the people living within the territory that went from being the independent state of Judah to the Persian province of Yehud to the Hellenistic province of Judea to the short-lived independent state of Judea under the Hasmoneans went through. I would propose the following set of terms: "national Yahwism" or "First Temple Yahwism" for the religion of the state of Judah from ca. 960-587 BCE, "intertemple Yahwisms" for the religions practiced by those in exile and those who remained in the land from 587-515 BCE, "Second Temple Yahwism" for the cult that was established under the Persians in 515 and which lasted through the rise of the Hasmonean state, and "early Judaism" for the official religion that began with the latter state in 143 BCE and ended with the destruction of the temple.[20] It should be noted that there was more than one form of early Judaism and that these new belief systems developed during the period when "Second Temple Yahwism" was still the official cult of the province. In addition, types of "intertemple Yahwisms" would have continued outside of Yehud alongside "Second Temple Yahwism." At this point, virtually nothing is known about "intertemple Yahwisms," except possibly for the cult at Elephantine, if it is to be so classified. Nevertheless, it is clear that such religions were practiced, so some sort of designation needs to be included to acknowledge their historical existence.

These labels correlate with the more general categories of inclusive and exclusive monotheism in the following way: "Second Temple Yahwism" was an expression of inclusive monotheism, while early Judaisms were expressions of exclusive monotheism. The Elephantine papyri make it clear that at least one form of intertemple Yahwism developed into "inclusive monotheism" under

---

[20] N. Gottwald has proposed the use of the term "Jewish colonialism" to describe all forms of religion practised by former subjects of the states of Israel and Judah both inside and outside of Cisjordan from 586-63 BCE (*The Hebrew Bible: A Socio-Literary Introduction* [Philadelphia: Fortress, 1985] 421-2). While this term acknowledges the important impact that foreign domination had on the shaping of the various Yahweh-centered religions practised by descendants of the state of Judah, it overlooks a number of crucial distinctions. First, it uses the term "Jew" anachronistically to denote anyone of Judahite descent beginning in 586 BCE and so does not take the monotheistic connotations usually associated with this label seriously. Second, it does not acknowledge the important distinction between Yahwisms and Judaisms on the one hand, and inclusive and exclusive monotheisms on the other hand. Third, it does not allow a distinction to be drawn between intertemple forms of Yahwism and the official cult of Yahweh that was established with the building of the second temple. In light of these major weaknesses, it seems better to adopt a more explicit set of descriptive terms that can allow the important distinctions mentioned above to be emphasized.

the impact of this new theology of the Persian empire. It is quite possible that other types did as well.

The proposed model needs testing and undoubtedly, further refining. I would invite anyone interested in the development of monotheistic belief systems to help investigate the various ramifications of the points that have been explored within the seven essays contained in this volume. It is hoped that such research will engender scholarly debate that will lead eventually to the creation of a new model that will replace the one that has been widely accepted for many years, which espouses the development of exclusive monotheism during the period of the state of Judah. It is time to rethink the process that led to the emergence of monotheism by consciously removing both inherited and personal faith-based filters that have obscured much of the vision in the past.

The Appearance of Pantheon in Judah

Lowell K. Handy

It is fairly well established by now that the narrative of the book of Kings cannot be taken as an accurate reflection of the religious world of the nations of Judah and Israel.[1] The cults of Jerusalem and Samaria appear therein as respectively, the repository of a proper religious tradition with lapses into heterodoxy and the fiendish creation of a sacrilegious traitor. This heterodoxy is portrayed by means of presenting those, wished to be denigrated by the author, as being worshippers of a pantheon rather than being loyal devotees of the one "true" God. As it is clear that the authors of the present material have a theological ax to grind, this picture should be seen as the product of an exilic or postexilic theology rather than a reflection of a real religious past. On the other hand, it is impossible to dismiss the picture of a religious world based on a pantheon totally; sufficient artifactual material has been excavated from the regions of the two petty states of Israel and Judah to support the notion that the populace revered more than just the

---

[1]   The historicity of certain sections of the narrative has been questioned for a long time within scholarly circles, even though the majority of the text is accepted to be historically trustworthy; this is particularly true of aspects of the depiction of the northern kingdom, Israel. See J.A. Montgomery, *A Critical and Exegetical Commentary of the Book of Kings* (ed. H.S. Gehman; ICC 10; Edinburgh: T. & T. Clark, 1951) 24-45. On the problem of accepting religious aspects of the narrative to reflect actual practice, see, among others, J. Van Seters, *In Search of History: Historiography in the Ancient World and the Origins of Biblical History* (New Haven: Yale University, 1983) 315-21; P.K. McCarter, Jr., "Aspects of the Religion of the Israelite Monarchy: Biblical and Epigraphic Data," in *Ancient Israelite Religion: Essays in Honor of Frank Moore Cross* (ed. P.D. Miller, Jr., P.D. Hanson, and S.D. McBride; Philadelphia: Fortress, 1987) 138; G. Savran, "1 and 2 Kings," in *The Literary Guide to the Bible* (ed. R. Alter and F. Kermode; Cambridge, MA: Belknap, 1987) 146-7, 149-55, 159-60; S.W. Holloway, "Kings, Book of 1-2," in *Anchor Bible Dictionary* (6 vols.; ed. D.N. Freedman; New York: Doubleday, 1992) 4.79-80.

single deity that now is posited in the texts as the sole legitimate object of worship.[2]

There is no reason to assume, though it often is, that the people, prophets, priests, or rulers of these two kingdoms in the first half of the first millennium BCE were essentially monotheists.[3] A series of works have recently appeared that conclude that there was, at least, a goddess in the cults of Israel and Judah in the heydays of their independence, and it has long been maintained that several gods were both recognized and worshipped in Judah at least at

---

[2] See surveys by T.A. Holland, "A Study of Iron Age Baked Clay Figurines, with Special Reference to Jerusalem: Cave 1," *Levant* 9 (1977) 121-55; G.W. Ahlström, *An Archaeological Picture of Iron Age Religions in Ancient Palestine* (StOr 55/3; Helsinki: Finnish Oriental Society, 1984) 115-45; H. Weippert, *Palästina in vorhellenistischer Zeit* (Munich: C.H. Beck, 1988) 620-31; and most recently, O. Keel and C. Uehlinger, *Göttinnen, Götter und Gottessymbole: Neue Erkenntnisse zur Religionsgeschichte Kanaans und Israels aufgrund bislang unerschlossener ikonographischer Quellen* (QD 134; Freiburg: Herder, 1992) 149-452. The latter covers the period of the monarchies in Judah and Israel. Keel and Uehlinger are primarily interested in Egyptian and Mesopotamian influences on the area, but their data clearly shows a continuing pantheistic theology in the areas of Israel and Judah.

[3] The position that Israelites, meaning usually Judahites, were always essentially monotheists was popularized within Jewish scholarly circles in the mid-20th century by Y. Kaufmann (*The Religion of Israel: From its Beginnings to the Babylonian Exile* [ed. and tr. M. Greenburg, Chicago: University of Chicago, 1960] 132). See, in the same tradition, I. Zeitlin, *Ancient Judaism: Biblical Critcism from Max Weber to the Present* (Cambridge: Polity, 1984) 222, 236, 252. The continued modern contrast of the monotheistic "Israelites" with polytheistic "Canaanites" in Protestant and Catholic scholarship owes much of its current argumentation to the influential works of W.F. Albright (*From the Stone Age to Christianity: Monotheism and the Historical Prcess* [Baltimore: Johns Hopkins University, 1940] and *Yahweh and the Gods of Canaan: A Historical Analysis of Two Contrasting Faiths* [Garden City, NJ: Doubleday, 1968]) as well as to the numerous works by his students and their pupils. The idea that Judah was a "monotheistic" nation continues to appear in various works, though it has been noted that it is only with the so-called Babylonian Exile that any form of religion that might be called true monotheism appears in the extant texts; so M. Smith, *Palestine Parties and Politics that Shaped the Old Testament* (New York: Columbia University, 1971) 29-30. Note the survey of possibilities in F. Stolz, "Monotheismus in Israel," in *Monotheismus im Alten Israel und seiner Umwelt* (ed. O. Keel; BibB 14; Freiburg: Schweizerisches Katholisches Bibelwerk, 1980) 163-82.

various times in the nation's religious history.[4] Though not original insights with them, Susan Ackerman and Elizabeth Bloch-Smith have provided documentation in two very recent works that highlights the anachronistic, academic nature of the scholarly distinction made between official and popular religions, on the one hand, and the notion of a "syncretistic" religious tradition on the other, in either of these kingdoms. These notions reflect the theories of modern scholars much more than they reflect the religious life of the states under consideration.[5] It is quite unlikely that the devotees of pantheon in either of the two ancient countries would have perceived themselves as properly described by such terms, nor is it likely that anyone in ancient Judah would have seen those persons who believed in numerous deities as odd, evil, unnatural, or substantially different from themselves solely on that ground.

If the text of Kings were trustworthy, it would have to be acknowledged that the religion of Jerusalem centered on a series of temples built to a group of deities; a religious world that the biblical narrative presents as having existed from the end of the reign of Solomon to well into the reign of Josiah.[6] This was the real cult,

---

[4] See the excellent survey of scholarship on the goddess Asherah to the date of his article by J. Day, "Asherah in the Hebrew Bible and Northwest Semitic Literature," *JBL* 105 (1986) 385-408, and S.M. Olyan, *Asherah and the Cult of Yahweh in Israel* (SBLMS 34; Atlanta: Scholars, 1988). The first modern popularization of the notion of a goddess in the official cult of Judah or Israel, despite its now being clearly dated by more recent scholarship and archaeological discoveries, can be traced to the work of R. Patai, *The Hebrew Goddess* (New York: Avon Books, 1978) 12-58, which was first published by KTAV Press in 1967. This work insisted that Asherah and Anat, along with several other goddessess, were part of the Judahite religious world and that the influence of these goddesses continued into later Judaism. On the general question of other deities in the Israelite cult, see the essay by Stoltz ("Monotheismus in Israel," 144-84).

[5] S. Ackerman, *Under Every Green Tree: Popular Religion in Sixth-Century Judah* (HSM 46; Atlanta: Scholars, 1992) 214; E. Bloch-Smith, *Judahite Burial Practices and Beliefs about the Dead* (JSOTSup 123; Sheffield: JSOT, 1992) 150.

[6] L.K. Handy, "Dissenting Deities or Obedient Angels: Divine Hierarchies in Ugarit and the Bible," *BR* 35 (1990) 27; one need only take notice of the connected narratives in 1 Kgs 11:5-8 and 2 Kgs 23:13 that are clearly motivated by theological concerns. If Solomon was the founder of the "apostate" sanctuaries, as he was of the sanctuary to Yahweh, and if these structures remained in operation throughout the monarchy down to the time of Josiah, then they were part of the official, royally patronized religion of Jerusalem, if not of all the people in the larger na-

according to Kings, in addition to the religious apostasies attributed to the so-called evil behavior of such rulers as Athaliah and Manasseh. However, the pervasive religious world of pantheon in Judah is also a standard feature of the prophetic texts. These speakers, in the name of God, condemn the behavior of the rulers and people alike for their disloyalty to the one true Lord; if the texts have not been edited beyond recapture of the historical events that first produced them, these messengers give a picture of a polytheistic religious world.[7] However, the prophetic texts may well have been edited beyond our capacity to use them for reconstructing an accurate view of the religious world of the nation of Judah.[8] On the other hand, the Psalms also convey a belief in the existence of other deities in the divine realm and, if these poems did indeed derive from the cult, then it would have to be argued that the Judahite

---

tion. That Solomon is recorded as the founder of the temples (built for his wives, according to the text) would mean that they had royal sanction and were official religious sites. See A.S. Kapelrud (*God and His Friends in the Old Testament* [Oslo: Universitetsforlaget, 1979] 184-90) on the role of the king in temple-building, keeping in mind that the biblical narrative emphasizes the divine call for the "true" temple of Yahweh and the human call for what the author considered to be false temples for the other deities; such a distinction would not have been made at the time of the construction itself. That Solomon founded a polytheistic cult for Judah has been noted, since it is hard to miss the passage in 1 Kgs 11:1-10, but this point has not traditionally been emphasized in scholarly histories of Judahite religion; see, for example, T.C. Vriezen, *The Religion of Ancient Israel* (tr. H. Hoskins; Philadelphia: Westminster, 1967) 185-6, and G. Fohrer, *History of Israelite Religion* (tr. D.E. Green; Nashville: Abingdon, 1972) 130.

[7] A few of the "classic" texts: Isa 2:18-20; Jer 1:4-6; 7:9-19, 30-31; Ezek 8:10-16; Hos 2:15; 11:2; 13:1-4. For a proposed historical reconstruction of the relation between the prophets and the religious practices of Judah and Israel, see the earlier work of A. Lods (*Israël des origines au milieu du 8e siècle* [Paris: Renaissance du Livre, 1930]) or the more recent essay by B. Lang ("The Yahweh-Alone Movement and the Making of Jewish Monotheism," in *Monotheism and the Prophetic Minority* [SWBAS 1; Sheffield: Almond, 1983] 13-56).

[8] See, for example, the discussion concerning the problems of using Jeremiah for recording historical events by R.P. Carroll (*From Chaos to Covenant: Prophecy in the Book of Jeremiah* [New York: Crossroad, 1981] 5-30).

cult recognized several deities.[9] This seems the most reasonable conclusion from the biblical texts.

What the religious vision of a heavenly realm, populated with myriads of deities, was for the populace of the first half of the first millennium Judah needs to be asked if the ancient Judahites are to be understood and not simply the religion of a select small section of their historians. These people clearly saw control of the cosmos in terms of a group of deities, but how did such a cosmos function and what did it mean to those devotees? It can safely be said that they were not simply perversely and intentionally evil in their own eyes, but that they had a theology for the pantheon in which they believed that satisfactorily explained the cosmos to them and fulfilled their basic religious needs. It was also most reasonably the

---

[9]   Ps 8:6; 29:1; 82; 86:8; 89:7; 95:3; 97:7; 135:5; 138:1; 148 all simply assume the existence of other deities in the heavenly sphere. Since the work of H. Gunkel in the early 20th century (*The Psalms: A Form-Critical Introduction* [tr. T.H. Horner; FBBS 19; Philadelphia: Fortress, 1967] 5-9 [which is a translation of a text from 1930]), it has generally been assumed that the poems in the book of Psalms derive from the official religious circles of Judah, if not necessarily from the temple worship service. S. Mowinckel (*The Psalms in Israel's Worship* [Nashville: Abingdon, 1962] 29-41) extended Gunkel's theory to assume that the vast majority of the psalms derived, in fact, from the temple cult of Judah. This position has remained the dominant theory; see, for example, H.H. Guthrie, Jr., *Israel's Sacred Songs: A Study of Dominant Themes* (New York: Seabury, 1966) 14-25, and L.A. Schökel, *Treinta Salmos: Poesia y Oracion* (2nd ed.; Madrid: Ediciones Cristiandad, 1986) 13-33. There is no overwhelming reason to doubt the substantial correctness of this assumption; most recently, J. Limburg, ("Psalms, Book of," in *Anchor Bible Dictionary* [6 vols.; ed. D.N. Freedman; New York: Doubleday, 1992] 5.524-5), has asserted that they derive from public religious songs related to the temple worship. However, it needs to be remembered that the current content of the book of Psalms is a highly edited sampling of the songs from the temple cult, not a complete liturgical rendition of the religion of Yahweh; see E. Sellin and G. Fohrer, *Introduction to the Old Testament* (tr. D.E. Green; Nashville: Abingdon, 1968) 295. Moreover, the collection is clearly from the second temple and not necessarily representative of the psalms that would have made up the service in the first temple, leaving open the possibility that the earlier temple hymnic texts not only recognized other deities in the cult but may well have included songs to the other deities that are now lost. The full liturgy of the nation of Judah is simply not available and is not able to be retrieved from the biblical texts or any known archaeological data. Since the remains of the first temple have been totally removed from the temple site, it is not likely that new evidence will be uncovered in the future.

case that the diversity of devotees for the pantheon in Judah ranged from the "blindly," if devoutly pious (those who would believe without asking any questions about the theology of the deities in which they believed) to the Machiavellian agnostic (who could manipulate the faith of the devout for increasing a personal store of goods or picking up sexual favors); in short, it contained the same range of levels of belief and opportunism as found in any religious (or political, or academic) system at any time.

Unfortunately, the artifacts that have been uncovered reflecting Iron Age "goddesses" (if they are sacred and not secular figures) and other emblems of divine character do not reveal much about the theology of the people who worshipped the deities to which they refer and nothing at all about the personal devotion of those who made or used them. The biblical texts do not provide large amounts of pantheon mythology that would elucidate the theology of those who believed in the array of divinities and certainly do not themselves intend to reflect the piety of the Judahites who believed in the pantheon. Thus, it appears that the personal piety of the Judahites within the sphere of a pantheon theology necessarily eludes the modern scholar. However, the Ugaritic texts have presented the modern scholar with a pantheon and the manner in which these deities were seen to have interacted. This same pantheon structure can be seen in those biblical texts that reflect Judahite religious thought. This allows a certain amount of reconstruction of the theological vision of pantheon in ancient Judah, if not an understanding of the personal piety of that time and place.

In a short article published in 1984, Mark Smith noted that the narratives recovered from Ugarit reflected, in their representations of the behavior of the gods, a four-tiered pantheon.[10] I had at that time just finished the chapter of my dissertation in which I had demonstrated from anthropological and sociological approaches the same four-tiered hierarchy.[11] The hierarchy at Ugarit seems quite certain and there is sufficient literary material from the site to

---

[10]   M.S. Smith, "Divine Travel as a Token of Divine Rank," *UF* 16 (1984) 359.
[11]   L.K. Handy, "A Realignment in Heaven: An Investigation into the Ideology of the Josianic Reform" (Ph.D. dissertation, University of Chicago, 1987) 47-166; Smith's article was one page long while my chapter was 120 pages, telling us something about who is capable of being concise.

demonstrate the levels. What I suggest here is the reasonableness of believing that the pantheon of Judah had a similar four-tiered structure and that at least a minimal amount of data remains in the biblical texts to demonstrate the knowledge of such a cosmic vision on the part of the Judahite scribes and, probably, the populace in general.

To begin, then, it should be recounted what the levels were and what they represented.[12] First, at the top, was the royal couple, what I call "highest authority." At Ugarit, this was El and Asherah, who together constituted a divine ruling pair. They owned the heavens and the earth and so were entitled to appoint and establish the various rulers of their cosmic world. They did these things together, as a unit.[13] Here I diverge from Smith's levels, for it appears clear that Asherah was seen to be on a par with El as far as the divine levels were concerned. El's decisions may have been the final appeal, but Asherah's choices for a deity to hold a particular position certainly are presented in the surviving myths to outrank El's. This is evident when El establishes Asherah's choice for the replacement of Baal, even with his own misgivings about Athtar.[14] At Ugarit, El was the highest king of a series of deities who were kings over various aspects of the universe, while Asherah was neither a "fertility goddess" nor a "mother goddess" but the divine Queen Mother, with both authority and power.[15]

---

[12] See Smith, "Divine Travel," 359 and Handy, "Dissenting Deities," 19-26, for short presentations of these levels. A full description of the hierarchy appears in L.K. Handy, *Among the Host of Heaven: The Syro-Palestinian Pantheon as Bureaucracy* (Winona Lake, IN: Eisenbrauns, 1993) 65-167.

[13] On the meaning of *qny/h*, see P. Katz, "The Meaning of the Root קנה," *JJS* 5 (1954) 126-31, and B. Vawter, "Yahweh: Lord of the Heavens and the Earth," *CBQ* 48 (1986) 461-7.

[14] *KTU* 1.6.I.43-65. The speeches by each deity in this scene are revealing; both El and Asherah are shown to be interested in the intelligence of the proposed replacement deity, but El has a further requisite, which is that the god be tough enough for the job. El does not think this is the case with Athtar.

[15] On the hierarchy of deities all known as *mlk*, see L.K. Handy, "A Solution for Many *mlkm*," *UF* 20 (1988) 57-9; on the impropriety of describing all goddesses with the adjective "fertility" see, regarding Anat, both N.H. Walls, Jr. ("The Goddess Anat in Ugaritic Myth" [Ph.D. dissertation, Johns Hopkins University, 1991] 19-20) and P.L. Day ("Anat: Ugarit's 'Mistress of Animals,'" *JNES* 51 [1992] 181-90). The use of "Mother Goddess" should, likewise, be discontinued as a desig-

El and Asherah are portrayed as wise and lofty rulers, knowing
how to regulate the cosmos and capable of appointing other deities
to do the actual governing under their control. They act within the
extant mythological narratives as corulers of their universe, each
with their own sphere of regulatory activity. This does not mean
that they would agree on everything or that their rule ought to
have been without conflict. Like other divine couples from the
ancient world known through extant myths from Mesopotamia,
Egypt, and Greece, El and Asherah are not expected to live together
or without friction between them on a personal or governing level.
They are quite distinct deities but together, form the highest level
of the cosmos as a divine couple. This does not diminish their
mutual status at the head of the pantheon. It means, however, that
even at the highest level of cosmic authority, the possibility of
rancor is omnipresent.

Second, under the level of the highest authority, were the major
active deities. These are those famous gods and goddesses who take
center stage in the myths. Baal, the virile dim-bulb, Anat, the berserker warrioress, Shapshu, the arbitrator, Mot, the lord of all (in
time), and many others.[16] These deities are the functional rulers of
the universe, since El and Asherah have placed them in their respective positions to take care of the cosmos under their dual wills
as gods of highest authority. The authority of the major active
deities is directly dependent upon the will of the deities of highest
authority. The gods of the second level are very like extremely
powerful rulers on the human level: filled with their self-importance
and assured that they can get away with anything — and that they
deserve to do so. The level of highest authority puts up with a lot
of selfishness and misrule on the part of these divinities since they

nation of any female divinity one happens to be describing. This is true especially
in the cases of Asherah and Anat, neither of whom is particularly described in
terms of motherliness, though the "mother goddess" title was attached to Asherah
already by Patai (*Hebrew Goddess*, 20).

[16] The characteristics of these particular deities have been chosen from the extant
narratives derived from Ugarit; whether the devotees worshipped their divinities
for reasons other than the obvious characteristics displayed in the literature is
unknown. If the Ugaritic narratives reflect the religious world of the cult of Baal,
the possibility arises that all the named deities were seen from a different perspective by devotees of those various divinities that appear in the narratives.

are thought to be needed to keep the world functioning properly. They basically have free dominion in their rules, which allows them to fight among themselves, argue with their superiors, abuse their power to thwart others (both divine and human), and even kill each other (not to mention humans). In all of this, however, they remain answerable for their behavior and can be called up in judgment before El if their infractions are too severe. In such a situation their thrones may be taken away from them if it pleases El so to do, leaving them no longer deities of the second level, but with diminished authority and less leeway in their behavior. It is precisely the fact that they can and do display all that is best and worst in characterization that makes them the center of the mythological narratives; they are the most exciting of the divinities in the hierarchy.

Beneath them in importance were the craft-deities, who formed the third level. The most famous of these was Kothar-wa-Hasis,[17] but the goddess Shatiqatu and the "Technogony" in the History of Philo of Byblos would seem to demonstrate that there were others on the same level.[18] These deities were specialists whose expertise was appreciated by those above them but who had to take orders, often from deities who did not really know what they were doing. The deities of this level are presented as knowing exactly what they are doing within their own sphere; they are experts and are left to their own devices to complete their occupations. Since they are so skilled, they are allowed to talk back to their superiors and argue with them, even to make fun of them. They are, however, never given as much leeway as those of the divine level above them and they obey orders even when they know them to be ill-advised.

At the bottom of the heavenly hierarchy were the slaves of the divine realm, the messengers. These deities (and the Ugaritic texts

[17]   On the description of the level and an investigation into the deity Kothar-wa-Hasis, see M.S. Smith, "Kothar wa-Hasis, the Ugaritic Craftsman God" (Ph.D. dissertation, Yale University, 1985) 22-6.

[18]   Technogony is a term suggested by J. Barr ("Philo of Byblos and his 'Phoenician History,'" *BJRL* 57 [1974] 22). The problems of determining the origins of the narratives now found in Philo are extremely complicated and this section of inventors of various useful items may not originate in mythological circles, but rather, in the antiquarian interests of the author; see J. Van Seters, *Prologue to History: The Yahwist as Historian in Genesis* (Louisville: Westminster/John Knox, 1992) 85-6.

call them deities: ilm[19] were not allowed any personal volition; they simply took orders, delivered messages, and behaved themselves. Indeed, in the Ugaritic narratives they are written about in terms of being living letters, with the same epistle vocabulary as a missive. Thus, the hierarchy decreased in personal volition as it descended from highest authority to the messengers, a parallel to the theoretical digression in power from king to slave in the human world. The cosmos was seen to have been governed by a hierarchy that extended upward from human rulers into the divine realm, the human king being the point at which divine and human levels of administration met. This explains why rulers had so many divine qualities attributed to them and could be called the children of the gods.

The Bible reflects a knowledge of this four-tiered system and even provides examples of the divine hierarchy itself.[20] At the low-

---

[19] A status noted by K.M. Alomia, "Lesser Gods of the Ancient Near East and Some Comparisons with Heavenly Beings of the Old Testament" (Ph.D. dissertation, Andrews University, 1987) 237. In the texts from Ugarit these messengers appear as deities in both narrative and liturgical literature. See: *KTU* 1.3.III.32 and 1.123.26.

[20] It should also be pointed out that the social hierarchy of the divine realm represented in the myths can also be seen in Judahite traditions on the human level. It is quite clear that the idea that the nation was ruled by a king, with one queen, or by an equivalent figure like Moses, Joshua or the judges was understood to have existed since the emergence of the nation frcm Egypt. In the narratives, the royal family appears to have formed a singular institution that could be treated as a unit. In this political system, it may have been the case that the Queen Mother held a particular position of importance, though the data is sparse and the reality is highly debated. For the queen's priviledged political status, see G. Molin, "Die Stellung der Gebira im Staate Juda," *TZ* 10 (1954) 161-75, and for the authority of particular queens in the political realm being gained by their own initiative, see Z. Ben-Barak, "The Queen Consort and the Struggle for Succession to the Throne," in *La femme dans le proche-orient antique* (ed. J.-M. Durand; RAI 33; Paris: Éditions Recherche sur les Civilisations, 1987) 33-40. The administrative districts of the nation reflect, on a small scale, the division of the "owned" property of the divine ruler among those who will actually carry out the directives of the central authority on the mundane human plane. See E.W. Heaton, *Solomon's New Men: The Emergence of Ancient Israel as a National State* (New York: Pica, 1974) 50-5. Like the deities of the second level, the ranks of the local administrators of Judah may have been filled by members of the royal family who may well have been at odds with the local populace over which they ruled (R. de Vaux,

est end of the pantheon, there is the notion of the king as a child of
the divine world, a bridge between the heavenly and the human
realms.[21] But, to remain within the realm of the pantheon, it may
be pointed out that two of the four levels are unabashedly retained
even in the biblical record. The lowest level of deities is presented,
not only in certain restricted passages that might have slipped past
an editor, but throughout the biblical texts and into Judaism, Christianity, and Islam. The "angels" of the Bible are the same characters
as the messengers of the Ugaritic texts. They are the low level deities who have no volition, but who merely take orders from above.
The word of the angel is understood to be the word of God; indeed, the presence of the angel is the presence of God. That is because the angel cannot do anything but what it is ordered.

Unlike the Ugaritic messengers, it might be noted, the biblical
messengers were sent on various errands in addition to delivering
messages for the higher authority, but as with the Ugaritic messengers, they acted only as extensions of Yahweh in whatever activity
in which they engaged, as good human messengers act only as an
extension of the person who sends them. The relatively late notion
of "fallen angels" is a theological development from a period well
after the nation of Judah and probably would have been absurd to
the Judahite populace. The texts in the Hebrew Bible that had been
used and occasionally still are used to show to existence of disobedient angels are in fact passages about gods of the higher three levels;
the notion that בני אלים or אלהים means angels is a position es-

---

Ancient Israel [2 vols.; New York: McGraw-Hill, 1965] 1.68-70). That there were
honored specialists in any number of professions is without question; Exodus 35-39
reflects specialists and the skilled workers who fashion the tabernacle under their
control. This level also would include the scribes of the temple and palace (de
Vaux, *Ancient Israel*, 1.76-8). Legal texts and narratives alike assume the existence
of slaves, who form the bottom level of the social hierarchy and were, in theory,
bound to the orders of their owners; a great deal is recorded in the biblical texts
about this lowest level as a social level (*ibid*, 80-90). See also C.A. Fontela, "La
esclavitud a través de la Biblia," *EstBib* 43 (1985) 99-104. He describes slavery in
fairly optimistic terms, but notes both the various manners in which one became
a slave and the numerous varieties of slaves held in Judah and Israel (104-24, 238-56
[extensive citation of patristic and talmudic commentary on the narratives concerned with slavery demonstrate how the texts were viewed in later tradition, but the
institution is clearly established as the low level of society]).
[21] Psalm 2, 89, and 110 provide examples of this relationship.

poused within the later traditions of Judaism and Christianity but most certainly does not reflect the reality of the texts as they appear. Gen 6:1-4 does not have a single reference to the מלאכים but contains information about deities as they were understood to have existed before the flood.[22] Psalm 82 deals solely with the deities of the higher orders and conforms to the understanding of those deities; it makes no comment about the lowly angels.[23] In the cult of Judah, the מלאכים clearly behaved in the same servile manner as the *malakim* in the Ugaritic narratives. The possibility exists that in Judahite theology there were messengers sent by deities of unsavory character, who, in obeying orders from their superiors, would have done evil things, but their status as mere pawns to other deities would have remained the same. They would have been comparable to the messengers of Yam in the Baal myths of Ugarit.

At the other end of the hierarchy, Judah had a level of highest authority. In the biblical texts this position is retained solely by Yahweh. From creation to future judgment, the course of the entire world is presented as having been directed by this single deity. It has long been recognized that the deities El and Yahweh were understood by the Judahites, or at least the biblical heirs to the Judahites, to be the same god. Indeed, the names are interchangeable in the Hebrew Bible, and for the Judahite religious world, Yahweh is the highest authority. No one, I suspect, would argue against Yahweh having been the authoritative god in Judah. It was this god who created the world, who owns it and all in it, and who even owns all that exists beyond the world. He is the one who places persons of importance in their postions to rule; indeed, this is the deity who may remove rulers from such positions if they do not behave as they are supposed to act.

On the other hand, the authors of Kings were aware that there was a goddess named Asherah in the cult of Jerusalem. It is reasonable to assume that Asherah was understood as the Queen Mother

---

[22] See now, succinctly, Van Seters, *Prologue to History*, 149-58; a general survey of the relevant verse is presented in C. Westermann, *Genesis 1-11: A Commentary* (tr. J.J. Scullion; Minneapolis: Augsburg, 1984) 365-73.
[23] On the original meaning of this psalm, see A. Schökel, *Treinta Psalmos*, 290-7 and L.K. Handy, "Sounds, Words and Meanings in Psalm 82," *JSOT* 47 (1990) 51-66.

of the Judahite cult, just as she was viewed in the pantheon of Ugarit. It is interesting that this goddess is associated with the Judahite queen mother Maacah, whom Asa is said to have removed from her position after she did something for the goddess.[24] A series of biblical references would seem to make it clear that the goddess was popular and her devotees widespread in Judah.[25] Inscriptions unearthed through excavation, however enigmatic to modern scholars, reflect the presence of Asherah in the religious world of independent Judah. When taken together, the Bible and the inscriptions prove fairly conclusively that the Judahites worshipped a goddess who was associated with the god Yahweh. Since the biblical text insists that the goddess should not ever have been considered a deity, it gives no narratives about her activity in the mythology of those who adored her. It may be inferred, however, that the goddess was sufficiently important that she terrified the biblical authors, and the inscriptions that link Yahweh and Asherah suggest, if not prove, that this was the divine couple of highest authority in the area.

As for the other two levels of divine populace, they also can been discerned in the biblical texts, though their existence is generally discounted by the authors. At the same time, the very presentation of the existence of devotees for these gods demonstrates that they did indeed exist as deities in the religious realm. The prophetic admonitions against priests, prophets, and rulers who preferred these deities to Yahweh, particularly those by Ezekiel, Jeremiah, Zephaniah, and Isaiah of Jerusalem, though there are others, also demonstrate that these deities were established in the official religion as it was practiced at the time and not some bizarre aberration easily discounted as irrelevant to the cult. Those who are mentioned in the texts include Baal, Shemesh, Yareah, Mot, and, perhaps, Astarte. If the name Shamgar son of Anat reflects a real person, and there is no real reason to assume it does not, then it may have to be assumed that there was a devotee of the Berserker Goddess who rose to a position of authority at some time in the Israelite period,

---

[24]   2 Chron 15:16.
[25]   See Olyan, *Asherah and the Cult of Yahweh*, or R.J. Petty, "Asherah: Goddess of Israel?" (Ph.D. dissertation, Marquette University, 1985).

even if it is not known when or where.[26] It needs to be pointed
out that Shemesh and Yareah, who are deities commonly found in
the second level in the west Semitic world, are directly addressed in
the poetic fragment quoted from the so-called ספר הישר in Josh
10:12.[27] The cult of the sun god (or goddess) finds representation
in the temple in Jerusalem in Ezekiel 8 as well. The deity of death,
Mot, appears to make his appearance in the prophecies of both Hosea and Jeremiah as an actual deity to whom Yahweh could and
would turn over the land of Judah as punishment for the populace's
believing in, or, more accurately, worshipping, other deities.[28]

The notion that these gods controlled sections of the cosmos
under the jurisdiction of Yahweh is clearly spelled out in the prologue to Job and the Psalms.[29] Job is clearly a literary wisdom text,
however, and so may only be used to demonstrate that the Judahite
scribes understood the divine world of west Semitic pantheon hierarchy. Since the story of Job is set in Edom, it is possible that the
vision of heaven presented in the text reflects only perceptions
within Judahite wisdom circles of Edomite cosmolgy and may not
portray the "real" cosmic world as understood in Jerusalemite scribal theology. Such is not the case with the psalms, however, which
played a part in the the Judahite cult liturgy. Some songs within
this corpus presume the existence of deities that take part in praising Yahweh, in the same manner that contemporary religious pantheons assumed gods praised other deities on their respective feast
days. Psalm 82, on the other hand, which refers to "gods"
(אלהים, בני עליון) and not "angels," "rulers," "judges," or "tenured
professors," assumes the existence of deities who rule aspects of the

---

[26] Judg 3:31; see P.C. Craigie, "A Reconsideration of Shamgar ben Anath (Judg
3:31 and 5:6)," *JBL* 91 (1972) 239-40.
[27] The quote reads: "Shemesh, in Gibeon do not move, and, Yareah, in the Valley
of Aijalon!" The source of the quotation is given in 10:13; as it now appears, however, the quotation is supposed to have been related to Yahweh, even though the
sun and moon are clearly the addressees.
[28] Hos 13:14 appears to be a reference to the deity Mot, from which Yahweh
could save one, while Jer 9:20 presents a quite anthropomorphic Mot seeking out
those to slay despite attempts to stay his progress.
[29] This passage is discussed in relation to the structure of pantheon by L.K.
Handy ("The Authorization of Divine Power and the Guilt of God in the Book
of Job: Useful Ugaritic Parallels," *JSOT* 60 [1993] 107-18).

cosmos independent of, but under the jurisdiction of, the head deity. They have become corrupt and now are condemned to oblivion for their misbehavior. The lesser gods are answerable to the highest authority in the pantheon, the twosome who have the right, and perhaps the duty, to condemn these deities, removing them from their positions for improper behavior.[30] If the psalms derive from the cult, then they provide clear evidence of a cult with a hierarchically structured pantheon in which deities are capable of misbehavior and the loss of their ruling positions at the discretion of their superiors; that is to say, there are gods of the second level.

As for the third level, the historical books are the only source of information about these deities. The most famous god of this level would have to be Baal Zebub, who, however, is not a deity of the Judahite or even Israelite pantheon. He is presented as only having been believed in by King Ahaziah of Israel.[31] There is, however, a third-level deity that can be identified within the pantheon of Judah. The name of this god of snake-bite-cure is unknown because the text provides only a pun playing on its shape and the metal from which it was constructed, not the actual name. The level of specialist deities is, however, certainly represented by the god of snake-bite-cure, called by Hezekiah, we are told, Nehushtan.[32] Ac-

---

[30] See G.E. Wright, *The Old Testament against Its Environment* (SBT 2; London: SCM, 1950) 30-41; the highly influential J.S. Ackerman, "An Exegetical Study of Psalm 82" (Th.D. dissertation, Harvard University, 1966); and H.W. Jüngling, *Der Tod der Götter: Eine Untersuchung zu Psalm 82* (SBS 38; Stuttgart: Katholisches Bibelwerk, 1969).

[31] 2 Kgs 1:2-6; see A. Tångberg, "A Note on Ba῾al Zebub in 2 Kgs 1,2.3.6.16," *SJOT* 6 (1992) 296; or W.A. Maier, "Baal-Zebub," in *Anchor Bible Dictionary* (6 vols.; ed. D.N. Freedman; New York: Doubleday, 1992) 1.554.

[32] 2 Kgs 18:4; on the object being the symbol of a deity that was actively worshipped, see L.K. Handy, "Hezekiah's Unlikely Reform," *ZAW* 100 (1988) 114-5. That the object was the representation or symbol of a divine being other than Yahweh has long been supposed; see, for example, R. Kittel, *Die Bücher der Könige: übersetzt und erklärt* (Göttingen: Vandenhoeck & Ruprecht, 1900) 278-9; J. Hehn, *Die biblische und babylonische Gottesidee: Die israelitische Gottesauffassung im Lichte der altorientalischen Religionsgeschichte* (Leipzig: J.C. Hinrich, 1913) 314-5; H.H. Rowley, "Zadok and Nahushtan," *JBL* 58 (1939) 136-7; J. Gray, *I & II Kings: A Commentary* (2nd ed.; OTL; Philadelphia: Westminster, 1970) 670-1; or J. Robinson, *The Second book of Kings* (CBC 11; Cambridge: Cambridge University, 1976) 166.

cording to the story told in Num 21:8-9, Moses was ordered to make the symbol of this deity to cure people of venomous serpent bites that Yahweh himself had imposed upon them. This character has a number of parallels to the Ugaritic goddess Shatiqatu and needs to be understood as the same type of deity: highly specialized, created by the higher levels of the divine realm (in both of these cases the highest authority) for a particular emergency as a healing deity.[33] This god was revered in the Judahite cult, where sacrifices were made to it until, according to the text, Hezekiah, for reasons unknown, removed it from the official pantheon. Nonetheless, Nehushtan provides an example of the third and final level of the west Semitic pantheon hierarchy. The religious vision of the state of Judah was of a piece with that of her neighbors and must be understood as having had a hierarchical, bureaucratic vision of the divine realm.

It has long been accepted that absolute monotheism first appeared in the prophetic traditions during the Exile, most notably with Deutero-Isaiah, but how the previous pantheon of Judah was understood to have functioned has not been seriously considered. I think we can say that the universe was understood to be under the control of a hierarchy ranging from the human realm upward into a divine ultimate authority. Like the human realm, the gods behaved in ways that reflected rulers on the human level with resepective amounts of power and self-aggrandizement. This belief would explain a universe seemingly at odds with itself and the occurrence of events clearly at odds with the theology of the devotee of any single divinity. It is unlikely that the ancient Judahites ever sat around and contemplated the meaning of having myriads of deities as opposed to having one. That they would have contemplated what it meant to have a myriad of deities with individual volition under the control of an even higher divine authority is clear from the biblical narratives themselves. The postexilic world was a different matter, for then the pantheon was reduced to only two levels: that of the one highest authority and that of the totally subservient messengers, leaving only one power actively running the universe. Remember, the messengers, unlike the middle two divine

[33] B.A. Levine and J.-M. de Tarragon, "'Shapshu Cries out in Heaven': Dealing with Snake-Bites at Ugarit (KTU 1.100, 1.107)," *RB* 95 (1988) 518.

levels, could only do as they were ordered. Chances for variance with the desires of the proper rule of the universe, as embodied in the notion of the will of Yahweh, disappear, and with it an entire complicated theology disappears from the cult of Judea.

The Rise of YHWH in Judahite and Israelite Religion
Methodological and Religio-Historical Aspects[*]

Herbert Niehr

1. Introduction: Shortcomings of Research

The discovery and excavation of the northwest Syrian city of Ugarit from 1928 onward and the subsequent editing of the Ugaritic texts has changed our understanding of the religious history of Judah and Israel considerably. The clay tablets with mythological contents (*KTU* 1.1 - 1.25) exerted an especially strong impact on attempts to reconstruct YHWH's position as supreme god in Judah and Israel.

Under the influence of Ugaritic mythology a quasi-dogmatic view came into being, according to which YHWH had reached his status as supreme god by taking over traits from the gods El and Baal as they are depicted in Ugaritic mythology. Furthermore, some scholars believed (and still believe) that YHWH was identified with El, one of the supreme gods of Ugarit.[1]

---

[*] I am indebted to Diana Edelman for inviting me to contribute to this volume and for improving my English.

[1] See the references in H. Niehr, *Der höchste Gott: Alttestamentlischer JHWH-Glaube in Kontext syrisch-kanaanäischer Religion des 1. Jahrtausend v. Chr* (BZAW 190; Berlin and New York: Walter de Gruyter, 1990) 1-2.

Yet as early as 1966, R. Rendtorff had demonstrated that for reconstructing Judahite and Israelite religious history, contemporaneous sources of the first millennium BCE should be adduced and
not Ugaritic evidence stemming from Late Bronze north Syria (ca.
1500-1200 BCE). He consequently drew on Phoenician and Aramaic
sources to explore YHWH's status as supreme god.[2]

The history of research since 1966 shows, however, that Rendtorff's article was often quoted but seldom fully understood in its
consequences: it has almost never been taken seriously. As demonstrated by Rendtorff and other authors, neither El nor Baal kept
their status as head of a pantheon or supreme god in the Syro-Palestinian religions of the first millennium BCE.[3] The religion of
Ugarit is not simply identical with "the Syro-Canaanite religion"; it
constitutes one local expression of Late Bronze Age Syrian religion.
Any attempt to correlate Ugaritic religion with Syro-Canaanite religions of the first millennium must investigate the impact that the
transition from the Late Bronze Age to the Iron Age had on religious ideology.[4] For Syro-Canaanite religions of the first millennium, especially for Phoenician religion, which was the heir and
transmitter of Ugaritic culture and religion, there is both continuity
and discontinuity with the religious ideology of Ugarit.[5] Thus, considerations of YHWH's status as supreme god can no longer take
Ugaritic mythology as their unobjectionable starting point. A new
basis for reconstructing YHWH's rise has to be found in sources
from the first millennium BCE.

2. A New Approach

Any further work on the religious history of Judah and Israel has
to take into account certain methodological presuppositions about
and insights into the realm of the religious history of ancient Syria-

---

[2]   R. Rendtorff, "El, Ba'al und Jahwe," *ZAW* 78 (1966) 277-92.
[3]   See the references in Niehr, *Höchste(r) Gott*, 17-21.
[4]   See T.L. Thompson, *Early History of the Israelite People: From the Written and
Archaeological Sources* (SHANE 4; Leiden: Brill, 1992) 216-300.
[5]   See W. Röllig, "On the Origin of the Phoenicians," *Ber* 31 (1983) 79-93; P.
Xella, "Ugarit 3. Culture ugaritique et phénicienne," in *Dictionnaire de la civilisation phénicienne et punique* (ed. E. Lipiński; Turnhout: Brepols, 1992) 482-4.

Palestine. These items cannot be dismissed when looking for an unbiased approach to the religion of Judah and Israel.

2.1 *The Question of Historicity*

When working within the realm of the history of Judah and Israel it is necessary to be aware of the specific peculiarity of the sources used. A distinction between primary and secondary sources or evidence must be made. Primary sources or evidence consist of "those texts that were produced in the course of the events as they were happening"[6] and secondary ones (or tertiary etc.) by "those texts that were produced after the events in an attempt to clarify for future generations how things were thought to have happened."[7]

In applying this basic distinction to historical questions concerning ancient Judah or Israel, it must be admitted immediately that the Hebrew Bible delivers only secondary (or even tertiary) evidence for everything that happened before the exile. Primary sources for the history of ancient Palestine are provided by all kinds of archaeological remains (buildings, artifacts, clay tablets, ostraca, papyri etc.).

Given the nature of primary and secondary sources, it must be judged impossible to write a history of Judah and Israel only on the basis of secondary HB evidence. The HB does not depict the histories of Judah and Israel as they took place, but as they have been reimagined in the mind of the writers.[8] On the other hand, it must also be admitted that in many cases it is only the secondary HB evidence that helps combine and interpret the scattered information obtained from primary evidence.[9]

---

[6] E.A. Knauf, "From History to Interpretation," in *The Fabric of History: Text, Artifact and Israel's Past* (ed. D.V. Edelman; JSOTSup 127; Sheffield: JSOT, 1991) 26-64, esp. 46.

[7] *Ibid.*, 46.

[8] So E.A. Knauf, "King Solomon's Copper Supply," in *Phoenicia and the Bible* (ed. E. Lipiński; StudPhoen 11; OLA 44; Leuven: Peeters, 1991) 167-86, esp. 171; *idem*, "From History to Interpretation," 46, n. 1.

[9] See J.M. Miller, "Is it Possible to Write a History of Israel without Relying on the Hebrew Bible?," in *The Fabric of History: Text, Artifact and Israel's Past* (ed. D.V. Edelman; JSOTSup 127; Sheffield: JSOT, 1991), 93-102; G.W. Ahlström, "The Role of Archaeological and Literary Remains in Reconstructing Israel's History," in *ibid.*, 116-41, esp. 119-41; Thompson, *Early History*, 110-1, 404-5. For

What has been said so far in reference to the history of Judah and Israel is also relevant for any endeavor to reconstruct the religious history of both kingdoms. It is not possible (or even less possible) to write a history of Judahite and Israelite religion on the basis of secondary HB evidence alone. The biblical depiction of the religious history of Judah and Israel is further from reality than its portrayal of historical events. During the past years this has been demonstrated by a significant example that is paramount for our handling the secondary HB evidence. It is the fundamental question of the relationship between Israel and Canaan.

2.2 *Israel and Canaan*

According to the narrative tradition of the HB as especially found in Deuteronomy and in the work of the deuteronomistic historians (Joshua - 2 Kings), the history of Israel is marked throughout by a fundamental opposition between Israel and Canaan. Israel entered the promised land from the desert, bringing with it the uncorrupted cult of YHWH as its only god. Having entered the promised land, Israel came into contact with the gods and goddesses of Canaan, thus perverting its Yahwistic religion. The central implication of this view of Israel's religion is that Israel's religion differs basically from Canaanite religion and that YHWH has nothing to do with the gods of Canaan.

Against this biblical view of the Canaanites and their religions, which impacted on the historical investigations undertaken especially by W.F. Albright and A. Alt and their pupils,[10] new insights have been brought forward. The most important of them is that "Canaan" designates a geographical entity in the Amarna administration of Syria-Palestine but cannot be identified with a real historical *ethnos*. In the second or first millennium BCE, there was

---

guidelines on how to decide about the historicity of OT texts, see K.A.D. Smelik, "The Use of the Hebrew Bible as a Historical Source," in *Converting the Past: Studies in Ancient Israelite and Moabite Historiography* (ed. *idem*; OTS 28; Leiden: Brill, 1992) 1-34, esp. 22-5; D. Edelman, "Doing History in Biblical Studies," in *Fabric of History*, 13-25. For critically established outlines of an early history of Palestine, see Thompson, *Early History*, passim.

[10] So Thompson, *Early History*, 14-6, 22-4, 30-4.

never a people or a political entity that could be understood as Canaan.[11]

In light of the historical nature of Canaan obtained from extrabiblical sources, it must be asked what the biblical writers mean when they speak of "Canaan" and the "Canaanites." "Canaan" is an ideological term coined by Hebrew writers in order to create an "anti-people" in comparison to "Israel."[12] Consequently, the notion of "Israel" needs to be recognized also as an ideological term that serves as the positive answer to "Canaan."[13]

Seen against this background, the religio-historical reality of the religion of ancient Judah and Israel is quite different from a simple "Israel-versus-Canaan-pattern." As a consequence of these insights, M. Coogan's view of "...Israelite religion as a subset of Canaanite religion"[14] can be fully maintained, as well as the logical implications of this position.

> From a historical perspective it is more appropriate, then, to speak of the special development of the religion of ancient Israel, rather than of the ways in which it was influenced by other cultures, as though it were a static, fully formed reality subject only to tangential modification. To be sure, by the beginning of the first millennium B.C.E. Israel, like its neighbors Phoenicia, Ammon, Moab Edom, and Aram, had begun to show distinctive traits in religious as well as in other aspects of its life. But this was a development from a Canaanite matrix and can be understood only by the reconstruction of that matrix from all available evidence and by the analysis of parallel developments in neighboring states.[15]

---

[11]   So N.P. Lemche, *The Canaanites and Their Land: The Tradition of the Canaanites* (JSOTSup 110; Sheffield: JSOT, 1991) 25-62.

[12]   *Ibid.*, 101-21.

[13]   So i.e. P.R. Davies, *In Search of 'Ancient Israel'* (JSOTSup 148; Sheffield: JSOT, 1992), 22-59; Thompson, *Early History*, 310-6.

[14]   M.D. Coogan, "Canaanite Origins and Lineage: Reflections on the Religion of Ancient Israel," in *Ancient Israelite Religion: Essays in Honor of F.M. Cross* (ed. P.D. Miller, Jr., P.D. Hanson, and S.D. McBride; Philadelphia: Fortress, 1987) 115-24, esp. 115.

[15]   *Ibid.*, 115-6. For the religio-historical distortions effected by a biased approach to "Canaanite" religion as opposed to "Israelite" religion, see D.R. Hillers, "Analyzing the Abominable: Our Understanding of Canaanite Religion," *JQR* 75 (1985)

Thus, the religions of Israel and Judah should be viewed as typical northwest Semitic religions of the first millennium.

Comparable to the ideological fiction of an *ethnos* "Israel" as opposed to an *ethnos* "Canaan," it can also be observed that the claim that a pure Israelite religion was imported from outside Canaan is a fiction without historico-religious reality. In addition, the claim of the HB that there once existed a Canaanite religion in opposition to the religion of Israel and Judah is also fictional. All this is not to deny that there was indeed a Judahite and an Israelite religion. Nevertheless, these religions have to be judged as local variants of northwest Semitic religions in Palestine during the first millennium BCE.[16]

2.3 *Guidelines for Reconstructing Ancient Judahite and Israelite Religion*

If the descriptions of Judahite and Israelite religion in the HB cannot be taken at face value, how is insight into the religious life and thought of ancient Palestine to be gained? Some guidelines for reconstructing ancient Israel's religious past need to be established to allow the traps of the HB testimony to be circumvented.

(1) As is the case with all historiographic analyses, history cannot be found simply in the sources. The sources merely provide the material to be exploited. For writing historiography or the history of a religion, it does not suffice to retell the sources. Explicit working hypotheses have to be formulated that are open to subsequent verification or falsification. It is only within the frame of these working hypotheses that the interpretation of the sources finds its place.[17]

253-69.

[16] See also N.P. Lemche, "The Development of the Israelite Religion in the Light of Recent Studies on the Early History of Israel," in J. A. Emerton (ed.), *Congress Volume Leuven 1989* (ed. J.A. Emerton; VTSup 43; Leiden: Brill, 1991) 97-115, esp. 107-15.

[17] E.A. Knauf, *Ismael: Untersuchungen zur Geschichte Palästinas im 1. Jahrtausend v. Chr.* (2nd ed.; ADPV; Wiesbaden: O. Harrassowitz, 1989) 135; *idem*, "From History to Interpretation," 27-34; M. Weippert, "Geschichte Israels am Scheideweg," *ThRu* 58 (1993) 71-103, esp. 71-2.

(2)   With regard to sources, the distinction between primary and secondary evidence is paramount for working out a religious history or aspects of this history of Judah and Israel. Due to the Judean censorship of the texts of the HB during the Second Temple period, the evidence contained in the texts for reconstructing the religious history of Judah and Israel is of secondary or tertiary value. This evidence has to be corroborated, corrected or refuted by primary evidence provided by inscriptions and archaeological findings.

(3)   Texts in the HB that deal with the religious history of Judah and Israel have to be read from the standpoint of the practices and cults denounced in them and thus be turned upside down.[18] What the HB denounces in cultic matters was, in fact, the religious practice in Judah and Israel from preexilic to postexilic times and not apostasy in favor of a pagan Canaanite religion that never existed in this manner.

(4)   The existence of different levels of religion in ancient Syro-Palestine has to be acknowledged and respected. A differentiation must be made between the state cult (official religion) of the temple in the capital, the local religion of sanctuaries all over the country and the private religion of each family.[19] These levels were clearly distinct from one another, so that it is impossible to speak of "the" Judahite or Israelite religion.

(5)   The pertinent evidence of contemporaneous neighboring religions (Phoenicians, Arameans, Ammonites, Moabites, and Edomites) has to be studied and evaluated. These religions are to be seen as the closest analogies to the religions of Judah and Israel, even though each contains its own peculiarities.

With these methodological presuppositions and guidelines in mind, an attempt can now be made to try to reconstruct the outlines of YHWH's rise in Jerusalem and Samaria.

---

[18]   See M. Weippert, "Synkretismus and Monotheismus," in *Kultur und Konflikt* (ed. J. Assmann and D. Harth; Edition Suhrkamp N.S. 612; Frankfurt am Main: Suhrkamp, 1990) 143-79, esp. 151.

[19]   *Ibid.*, 150-60; H.M. Niemann, *Herrschaft, Königtum und Staat: Skizzen zur sociokulturellen Entwicklung im monarchischen Israel* (FAT 6; Tübingen: J.C.B. Mohr, 1993) 227-45.

3. *YHWH's Rise*

A central working hypothesis has already been formulated above in paragraph 2.2: the religions of Judah and Samaria were northwest Semitic religions of the first millennium BCE differing only in local peculiarities from the religions of the surrounding peoples and states. It is only within this set of working hypotheses that the question of YHWH's rise to the position of supreme god can be sufficiently explained.

On the basis of several extrabiblical sources, YHWH's origin can be traced back to the hill country of Midian/Edom, where he was venerated as a local weather god like Hadad or Baal in Syria and Palestine.[20] The exact way in which he entered the panthea of Jerusalem and Samaria can no longer be reconstructed.[21] From the 10th century BCE onwards YHWH appears as a dynastic god in Jerusalem and Samaria. This should not, however, seduce us into believing that YHWH in Jerusalem was identical with YHWH in Samaria. The differences between Judah and Samaria in general[22] and their different cults[23] in particular should not be overlooked.

---

[20]   So, e.g. M. Görg, "Jahwe - ein Toponym," *BN* 1 (1976) 7-14, now in: *idem, Beiträge zur Zeitgeschichte der Anfänge Israels: Dokumente, Materialien, Notizen* (ÄAT 2; Wiesbaden: O. Harrassowitz, 1989) 180-7; M. Weippert, "Jahwe," in *Reallexikon der Assyriologie und vorderasiatischen Archäologie* (8 vols.; ed. E. Ebling and B. Meissner; Berlin/Leipzig: Walter de Gruyter, 1928-) 5.246-53, esp. 252; *idem*, "Synkretismus," 157-8; E.A. Knauf, *Midian: Untersuchungen zur Geschichte Palästinas und Nordarabiens am Ende des 2 Jahrtausends v. Chr.* (ADPV; Wiesbaden: O. Harrassowitz, 1988) 43-63; P.E. Dion, "YHWH as Storm-god and Sun-god. The Double Legacy of Egypt and Canaan as Reflected on Psalm 104," *ZAW* 103 (1991) 43-71, esp. 48-58. To the sources cited and discussed in these articles, inscriptions no. 6 and 7 of Kuntillet 'Ajrud that mention YHWH *tmn*, "YHWH from Teman," have to be added. For comment on the texts, see H.-P. Müller, "Kolloquialsprache und Volksreligion in den Inschriften von *Kuntilled 'Aǧrūd* und *Ḥirbet el-Qōm*," *ZAH* 5 (112) 15-51, esp. 16. For commentary, see *ibid.*, 34-5 and J.A. Emerton, "New Light on Israelite Religion," *ZAW* 94 (1982) 2-20, esp. 9-10.
[21]   In spite of J.C. de Moor (*The Rise of Yahwism: The Roots of Israelite Monotheism* [BETL 91; Leuven: Peeters, 1990]), who only achieves his aim to detect the "roots of Israelite monotheism" by uncritically dating many HB texts much too early.
[22]   See Thompson, *Early History*, 401-15.
[23]   See G.W. Ahlström, *An Archaeological Picture of Iron Age Religions in Ancient Palestine* (StOr 55/3; Helsinki: Finnish Oriental Society, 1984) 10, 20-1; *idem*, "Role of Archaeological and Literary Remains," 128-9; Davies, *In Search of 'Ancient Israel'*, 70-2.

3.1 *In Jerusalem*

In reconstructing the political reality of Jerusalem in the 10th century BCE, the concept of a Davidic-Solomonic empire has to be dismissed.[24] Since Judah became a state only during the 8th century BCE,[25] historians must reckon with the existence of a modest Judahite chiefdom before that time, which was politically and economically dependent on Tyre.[26] This dependence is strongly suggested by the restoration of the first temple, ascribed by tradition to Solomon,[27] which betrays a considerable impact of Phoenician culture on Judah. The Phoenicians not only give architectural advice, as the HB suggests, but strongly influence the kind of YHWH-cult practiced in the Jerusalemite temple beginning with the reign of Solomon.[28]

A main characteristic of the Jerusalemite temple cult in the pre-exilic period is the veneration of YHWH as ישב הכרבים.[29] The reli-

---

[24]   Thus Knauf, "King Solomon," 168-84; J.M. Miller, "Solomon: International Potentate or Local King?," *PEQ* 123 (1991) 28-31; Thompson, *Early History*, 312-3, 406-12.

[25]   So E.A. Knauf, "The Migration of the Script, and the Formation of the State in South Arabia," *PSAS* 19 (1989) 79-91, esp. 79-80, 82-3; D.W. Jamieson-Drake, *Scribes and Scribal Schools in Monarchic Judah* (JSOTSup 109 = SWBAS 9; Sheffield: JSOT, 1991) 138-45; Davies, *In Search of 'Ancient Israel'*, 67-70; Thompson, *Early History*, 409-12.

[26]   See J.K. Kuan, "Third Kingdoms 5.1 and Israelite-Tyrian Relations during the Reign of Solomon," *JSOT* 46 (1990) 31-46. This chiefdom carries even less weight if one accepts the reconstruction of its history by Knauf ("King Solomon") and Thompson (*Early History*, 409-12). A more conservative view is maintained by F. Briquel-Chatonnet, *Les relations entre les cités de la côte phénicienne et les royaumes d'Israël et de Juda* (StudPhoen 12; Leuven: Brill, 1992) 25-58.

[27]   For the restoration of an older Jebusite sanctuary that was still in existence during the time of David (so 2 Sam 12:20) instead of the building of a completely new temple, see K. Rupprecht, *Der Tempel von Jerusalem* (BZAW 144; Berlin/New York: Walter de Gruyter, 1976).

[28]   So Kuan, "Third Kingdoms," 40-1; for Syro-Phoenician traits in the Jerusalemite temple, see O. Keel and C. Uehlinger, *Göttinnen, Götter und Gottessymbole: neue Erkenntnisse zur Religionsgeschichte Kanaans und Israels aufgrund bislang unerschlossener ikonographischer Quellen* (QD 134; Freiburg: Herder, 1992) 189-96; Briquel-Chatonnet, *Relations*, 353-62.

[29]   1 Sam 4:4; 2 Sam 6:2 = 1 Chr 13:6; 2 Kgs 19:15 = Isa 37:16; Ps 80:2; 99:1; See esp. T.N.D. Mettinger, "YHWH SABAOTH — The Heavenly King on the Cherubim Throne," in *Studies in the Period of David and Solomon and Other Essays* (ed. T. Ishida; Winona Lake, IN: Eisenbrauns, 1982) 109-38; *idem, The Dethronement of Sabaoth: Studies in the Shem and Kabod Theologies* (ConBOT 18; Lund: CWK

gio-historical background for YHWH's veneration as ישב הכרבים is
to be found in Phoenician art and iconography, where a sphinx
throne shows the numinous rank of the person enthroned on it.[30]
It appears that in Jerusalem, Yahweh was modelled in the image of
a supreme god of the contemporary Phoenician religion. YHWH's
status as the supreme god in Judahite religion is claimed not only
by HB sources, but also is confirmed by primary sources that provide the pertinent external evidence. The first primary source to be
examined consists of the personal names of Judahite citizens found
on seals dating from the late 8th to the 6th century BCE. The majority of the personal names has "YHWH" or a derivation of this divine
name as a theophoric element. This trait does not indicate the
existence of monotheism, however, but merely betrays which god
held the position of supreme god in Judah during that time.[31]

A second important primary source for YHWH's status in Judah
is one of the Khirbet el-Qom inscriptions dating between 800-750
BCE.[32] It mentions "YHWH and his Asherah," indicating that Judah's supreme god YHWH had a paredra.[33] This indication of the

---

Gleerup, 1982), 19-37; B. Janowski, "Keruben und Zion," in *Ernten, was man sät:
Festschrift K. Koch* (eds. D.R. Daniels *et al.*; Neukirchen-Vluyn: Neukirchener,
1991) 231-64, esp. 235-53.

[30] So Janowski, "Keruben," 248-9, 262-4. The relevant iconographical material is
made available in O. Keel, *Jahwe-Visionen und Siegelkunst: eine neue Deutung der
Majestatsschildungen in Jes 6, Ez 1 und 10 und Sach 4* (SBS 84/85; Stuttgart: Katholisches Bibelwerk, 1977) 18, 20 figs. 4-6; 30, 32 figs. 15-17; M. Metzger, *Königsthron
und Gottesthron: Thronform und Darstellung in Vorderen Orient im dritten und
zweiten Jahrtausend vor Christus und deren Bedeutung für das Verständnis von Aussagen über den Thron im Alten Testament* (AOAT 15/1-2; Kevelaer: Butzon &
Bercker and Neukirchen-Vluyn: Neukirchener, 1985) 1.259-79, 2.236-47; E. Gubel,
Phoenician Furniture (StudPhoen 7; Leuven: Peeters, 1987) 37-84, pls. 1-14.

[31] See the onomastic material gathered in J.H. Tigay, *You Shall Have No Other
Gods: Israelite Religion in the Light of Hebrew Inscriptions* (HSM 31; Atlanta: Scho-
lars, 1986) but see also the pertinent remarks of E.A. Knauf ("'You Shall Have No
Other Gods'. Eine notwendige Notiz zu einer überflüssigen Diskussion," *DBAT* 26
[1989/90] 238-45) regarding the untenable religio-historical conclusions drawn by
Tigay.

[32] For a convenient overview of the range of dates assigned to the inscriptions,
see Keel-Uehlinger, *Göttinnen*, 281.

[33] For the text of the inscription, see Müller, "Kolloquialsprache," 20.

cult of Asherah as paredra of YHWH can be connected with the HB references to the cult of the "Queen of Heaven" in Jerusalem.[34]

A third most informative indicator is tomb inscription A from Khirbet Bet-Lei, situated 8 km east of Lachish. The inscription, which is to be dated for palaeographic reasons around 700 BCE,[35] says:

> "YHWH is the god of the whole country.[36]
> The mountains of Judah belong to the god of Jerusalem."[37]

YHWH's qualification as "the god of Jerusalem" is not an astonishing trait because he was the dynastic god of the monarchy as well as the supreme god of the Jerusalemite pantheon. The text does not imply that YHWH was also regarded as the local god of other Judahite towns. This is clearly shown by the later complaint in Jer 2:28: "For you, Judah, have as many gods as you have towns." In contrast to this complaint, the Khirbet Bet-Lei inscription shows that around 700 BCE there were tendencies to see YHWH as the supreme god of Judah. In the course of time, those tendencies led to the identification of YHWH, the god of the state and the country, with the different local gods of the Judahite towns.

3.2 In Samaria

The HB does not provide detailed information about the worship of YHWH in Samaria. This lack of information stems from the fact that the Jerusalemite redactors of the HB judged Samaria to be an illegi-

---

[34]   As concerns its relationship to 1 Kgs 15:13; 2 Kgs 21:3-7; 23:4-7, 14-15; Jer 7:18; 44:15-25; Ezek 8:3-6, see K. Koch, "Aschera als Himmelskönigin in Jerusalem," *UF* 20 (1988) 97-120, esp. 106-9, 120; Keel-Uehlinger, *Göttinnen*, 386-90. Nevertheless, it cannot be excluded that other goddesses than Asherah were also venerated as "Queen of Heaven"; see the discussion in C. Houtman, *Der Himmel im Alten Testament: Israels Weltbild und Weltanschauung* (OTS 30; Leiden: Brill, 1993) 110-6.

[35]   So A. Lemaire, "Prières en temps de crise: Les inscriptions de Khirbet Beit Lei," *RB* 83 (1976) 558-68, esp. 563-5; S. Mittmann, "A Confessionnal Inscription from the Year 701 BC Praising the Reign of Yahweh," *Acta Academica* 21, (1989) 15-38, esp. 29-32.

[36]   Also possible but less likely is the translation "of all the earth"; see e.g. J.C.L. Gibson, *Textbook of Syrian Semitic Inscriptions* (3 vols.; Oxford: Clarendon, 1971-1982) 1.58; Keel-Uehlinger, *Göttinnen*, 356 and n. 319.

[37]   This is the reading in Lemaire, "Prières," 558; see also Mittmann, "Inscription," 17-23.

mate competitor to the temple in Jerusalem. "It is in harmony with their program that Samaria should not be given any leading position as a center of Yahweh worship because for them only Jerusalem could play such a role."[38] As the capital of the Omride kingdom, however, Samaria must have been the major center of YHWH worship in Israel, especially for the royal court.[39]

In the 9th century BCE the usurper Omri founded the state of Israel according to the standards of his Phoenician overlords.[40] The religious influence exerted by the Phoenicians can be seen in the changes Ahab made to the YHWH temple in the Omride capital of Samaria. The relevant text is 1 Kgs 16:30-32. In v. 32 the MT says: ויקם מזבח לבעל בית הבעל אשר בנה בשמרון. LXX translates בית הבעל with ἐν οἴκῳ τῶν προσοχθισμάτων, a translation that shows that LXX has found בית אלהים in its *Vorlage*.[41] Thus, the MT's incomprehensible statement that Ahab had built a Baal-altar in the temple of Baal disguises an earlier tradition according to which Ahab had erected an altar for Baal in the temple of YHWH.[42]

Does 1 Kgs 16:32 speak of the erection of an altar for an alien god who was to be venerated alongside YHWH in the YHWH-temple of Samaria[43] or does it indicate that YHWH was to be venerated in the shape of a Phoenician state deity from the time of Ahab onward? In the latter case, Phoenician influence would have lead to YHWH's conception as Baalšamem in the royal cult of Samaria.[44]

---

[38] Ahlström, *Picture of Iron Age Religions*, 11; see also *idem, Royal Administration and National Religion in Ancient Palestine* (SHANE 1; Leiden: Brill, 1982) 60-3; *idem*, "Role of Archaeological and Literary Remains," 129-31.

[39] So Ahlström, *Royal Administration*, 17-8, 61-2; Niemann, *Herrschaft*, 213-6.

[40] Knauf, "Migration," 83; *idem*, "King Solomon," 177.

[41] S. Timm, *Die Dynastie Omri: Quellen und Untersuchungen zur Geschichte Israels im 9. Jahrtausend vor Christus* (FRLANT 124; Göttingen: Vandenhoeck & Ruprecht, 1982) 32-3.

[42] *Ibid.*, 35.

[43] See 2 Kgs 16:10-16; 21:3-5 and *ibid.*, 35.

[44] See O. Eissfeldt, "Ba'alšamem und Jahwe," in *Kleine Schriften* (2 vols.; Tübingen: Vandenhoeck & Ruprecht, 1963) 2.171-98, esp. 187-9; H. Niehr, "JHWH in der Rolle des Baalšamem," in *Ein Gott allein? JHWH-Verehung und biblischer Monotheismus im Kontext der israelitischen und altorientalischen Religionsgeschichte* (ed. W. Dietrich and M.A. Klopfenstein; OBO 139; Fribourg: Universitätsverlag & Göttingen: Vandenhoeck & Ruprecht, 1994) 307-26.

As in the case with Judah, there is external evidence concerning the status of YHWH in Samaria. This primary evidence supplements and corrects the data provided by the HB sources. Five sources can be adduced, four direct and one indirect.

The Meša inscription (ca. 850 BCE) clearly states that YHWH was the supreme god of Israel and of the Transjordanian territory occupied by Israel under the Omrides.[45]

The inscription on pithos A from Kuntillet 'Ajrud that reads "YHWH of Samaria and his Asherah" indicates that the royal cult of Israel was centered in Samaria, a situation that had already been deduced from the LXX reading of 1 Kgs 16:32.[46] The reference to his "Asherah" is to be combined with the mention of an Asherah in 1 Kgs 16:32-33, who seems to be the paredra of the dynastic god YHWH being venerated as Baalšamem.[47]

The third primary source for understanding the nature of the Yahwistic cult in Samaria is the Assyrian account of Samaria's fall and its subsequent pillage. The Nimrud-prism of Sargon II says in lines 32-3: "...and the gods, in which they trusted, as spoil counted."[48] This shows clearly the existence of polytheism in Samaria and the deportation of the pertinent divine images.[49] The Assyrian background of deporting divine images has been demonstrated by M. Cogan and H. Spieckermann[50] and there is no argument to

---

[45]   For the text and the evaluation of the Mesha inscription, see the papers collected in A. Dearman (ed.), *Studies in the Mesha Inscription and Moab* (ASOR/SBL Archaeology and Biblical Studies 2; Atlanta: Scholars, 1989).

[46]   See the text in Müller, "Kolloquialsprache," 19 no. 5.

[47]   See S.M. Olyan, *Asherah and the Cult of Yahweh in Israel* (SBLMS 34; Atlanta: Scholars, 1988) 6-8, 32-3; Keel-Uehlinger, *Göttinnen*, 263.

[48]   See the text editions in H. Spieckermann, *Judah unter Assur in der Sargonidenzeit* (FRLANT 129; Göttingen: Vandenhoeck & Ruprecht, 1982) 349-50 and in B. Becking, *The Fall of Samaria: An Historical and Archaeological Investigation* (SHANE 2; Leiden: Brill, 1992) 28-9.

[49]   See C.J. Gadd, "Inscribed Prisms of Sargon II from Nimrud," *Iraq* 16 (1954) 173-201, esp. 181; E.A. Knauf, "Zur Herkunft und Sozialgeschichte Israels," *Bib* 69 (1988) 153-69, esp. 155-6 and n. 13; M. Anbar, "Καὶ ποῦ εἰσὶν οἱ Θεοὶ τῆς χώρας Σαμαρείας: et où sont les dieux du pays de Samarie," *BN* 51 (1990) 7-8; Becking, *Fall of Samaria*, 31.

[50]   M. Cogan, *Imperialism and Religion: Assyria, Judah and Israel in Eighth and Seventh Centuries B.C.E.* (SBLMS 19; Missoula, MT: Scholars, 1974) 22-41; Spieckermann, *Juda*, 347-54.

reduce the deportation of divine images from Samaria to a mere Assyrian *topos* without a historical basis in the religious conditions of Samaria.[51]

The final direct primary source for a study of the preexilic cult of YHWH in Israel consists of the Elephantine papyri that date to the 5th century BCE. In spite of their late date they provide invaluable glimpses of Israelite religion before and after the fall of Samaria.[52] These texts escaped the Judean censorship exercised on the preexilic religious traditions of Judah and Israel. Especially interesting is the occurrence of a goddess Anat-Yahu, a paredra of YHWH who came into being in Samaria as a counterpart to the Aramean goddess Anat-Bethel.[53] Furthermore, the Elephantine texts indicate that in Samaria, YHWH was also venerated as בתאל.[54] In this context, it also becomes clear that YHWH's worship as Baalšamem in Samaria is likewise to be connected with his later designation as "god of heavens" in the Elephantine papyri.

An indirect glimpse of YHWH's status as supreme god in Samaria or Israel is provided by cuneiform evidence from north Syria in the form of royal names from Hamath and Hatarikka/Hazrak that contain YHWH as a theophoric element. These names do not demonstrate, however, that "Yahweh was worshipped in North Syria in the mid to late 8th century";[55] rather, they show only "that the state of Hatarikka probably had a ruler of Israelite descent around 740 B.C.E."[56]

---

[51] So, Becking, *Fall of Samaria*, 31.

[52] So Weippert, "Synkretismus," 156-7, 170-1, n. 36; K. van der Toorn, "Anat-Yahu, some other Deities, and the Jews of Elephantine," *Numen* 39 (1992) 80-101, esp. 92-8.

[53] AP 22,125; 44,3. For Anath-Yahu and Anat-Bethel, see U. Winter, *Frau und Göttin: exegetische und ikonographische Studien zum weiblichen Gottersbild im alten Israel und in dessen Unwelt* (OBO 53; Fribourg: Universitätsverlag & Göttingen: Vandenhoeck & Ruprecht, 1983) 494-508; Weippert, "Synkretismus," 156-7; Van der Toorn, "Anat-Yahu," 80-95.

[54] Weippert, "Synkretismus," 156-7; Van der Toorn, "Anat-Yahu," 94-5.

[55] S. Dalley, "Yahweh in Hamath in the 8th Century BC: Cuneiform Material and Historical Deductions," *VT* 40 (1990) 21-32, esp. 27; see also Z. Zevit, "Yahweh Worship and Worshippers in 8th-Century Syria," *VT* 41 (1991) 363-66 and above all, the cautious remarks in Van der Toorn, "Anat-Yahu," 88-90.

[56] Van der Toorn, "Anat-Yahu," 90.

3.3 *Interim Summary and Outlook*

On the basis of both primary and secondary evidence cited in the preceding pages, it can be assumed that YHWH held the position of supreme god in both Jerusalem and Samaria. In the royal cult of Jerusalem, YHWH was chiefly venerated as ישב הכרבים. According to the inscription of Khirbet el-Qom, the goddess Asherah served as his paredra. In the royal cult of Samaria, YHWH was venerated as Baalšamem. His paredra was Asherah, as indicated by the inscriptions of Kuntillet ʿAjrud. These inscriptions also show that an alternate title for this deity was יהוה שמרן. The Elephantine papyri reveal that YHWH was also venerated as Bethel at Samaria and that the goddess Anat-Yahu was his paredra, too. An identification of the northern and southern local manifestations of the south Palestinian weather god YHWH took place in Jerusalem only after the fall of Samaria in 723 BCE.[57]

Having used the available data to elucidate YHWH's rise in Judahite and Israelite religion, it becomes clear that the religions of Judah and Samaria were Syro-Canaanite religions with a weather god at their top. Yet, contrary to this insight, some HB texts claim that the worship of YHWH differed greatly from Syro-Canaanite religion. This claim, based only on secondary HB evidence and massively contradicted by the primary evidence, is to be explained in light of the religious revolt that took place in the wake of the cult centralization of Josiah.

The historical base of the events narrated in 2 Kings 22 and 23 lies in administrative measures taken by king Josiah. This king tried to strengthen his authority over Judah by several administrative reforms, one of which involved the concentration of all Yahwistic cults in the temple of Jerusalem.[58] It was only in the postexilic wake of the Josianic cult centralization that a "purification" of the Yahwistic worship from foreign i.e. "Canaanite" elements was also ascribed to Josiah.[59]

---

[57]   For this date of the conquest of Samaria, see Becking, *Fall of Samaria*, 47-56.

[58]   So Niemann, *Herrschaft*, 174-84, 203-5, 264-5.

[59]   See C. Levin, "Joschija im deuteronomistischen Geschichtswerk," *ZAW* 96 (1984) 351-71, esp. 356-64; for the religious practice in Judah after Josiah, see S. Ackerman, *Under Every Green Tree: Popular Religion in Sixth-Century Judah* (HSM 46; Atlanta: Scholars, 1992).

This attempt to create a new religion in the wake of Josiah's administrative reforms is responsible for the considerable dichotomy between the image of Judahite religion as a non-Canaanite religion found in many texts of the HB and the image of these religions as typically Syro-Canaanite. Nevertheless, it was not possible to delete all Syro-Canaanite traits from Judahite religion. The motifs used during the postexilic period to categorize YHWH as a supreme god preserved old Syro-Canaanite concepts.

4. *Motif Complexes*

In the preceding paragraphs some distinctive traits of YHWH as supreme god have already been elaborated. Nevertheless, it seems worthwhile to ask explicitly what "equipment" a god needed in order to fulfill the position of supreme god in Syro-Canaanite religion of the first millennium BCE.

4.1 *The Divine Assembly*

The existence of a divine assembly surrounding the supreme god is a distinctive trait of ancient Near Eastern religions that can also be observed in northwest Semitic religions of the first millennium BCE.[60] YHWH's rise to the position of highest god in Judahite and Israelite religion also made him the chief of a divine assembly in Jerusalem and Samaria.[61] Two texts demonstrate that YHWH occupied the position of supreme god within a divine assembly in the royal cult of these two capitals from at least the 8th century BCE onwards. Isaiah 6 is the first HB text to apply the title מלך to YHWH, a title that implies the existence of a divine assembly to

---

[60] Niehr, *Höchste(r) Gott*, 71-8.

[61] For the most important investigations into this subject, see E.T. Mullen, *The Divine Council in Canaanite and Early Hebrew Literature* (HSM 24; Cambridge: Harvard University, 1980); H.-J. Fabry, "swd. Der himmlische Thronrat als ekklesiologisches Modell," in *Bausteine Biblischer Theologie: Festgabe für G. Johannes Botterweck zum 60. Geburtstag dargebr. von seinem Schülern* (ed. *idem*; BBB 50; Köln: Hanstein, 1977) 99-126; *idem*, "Studien zur Ekklesiologie des Alten Testaments und der Qumrangemeinde" (Ph.D. dissertation; University of Bonn, 1979); L.K. Handy, "Dissenting Deities or Obedient Angels: Divine Hierarchies in Ugarit and the Bible," *BR* 35 (1990) 18-35; *idem, Among the Host of Heaven: The Syro-Palestinian Pantheon as Bureaucracy* (Winona Lake, IN: Eisenbrauns, 1993); see also Handy's article in this volume.

surround the king. The presence of such a concept in Isaiah 6 is indicated by the reference to the סרפים (Isa 6:2-4, 6-7), by Yahweh's question to the divine assembly (Isa 6:8), and by Yahweh's title, "lord of hosts" (Isa 6:3, 5). A contemporaneous text, 1 Kgs 22:19-22, describes the pantheon of Samaria as though seen through a rift in the clouds. In a vision Micah ben Jimlah sees "the Lord seated on his throne, with all the host of heavens standing beside him on his right and on his left" (1 Kgs 22:19). This picture is based on terrestrial realities: a king sitting on his throne with his ministers and attendants surrounding him.

Especially interesting is the development of the "host of heavens"[62] in the course of religious history. The "host of heavens" was subject to an astralization that had already taken place in Mesopotamian and other Syro-Canaanite religions. This development is illustrated by texts that understand the "host of heavens" as the sun, the moon and the stars[63] or that set the phrase "host of heavens" in parallelism with the sun and the moon, meaning in this instance the stars alone.[64] The veneration of the "host of heavens" took place on roofs.[65] That this veneration was not confined to popular religion is shown by the fact that even kings were reproached for having exercised this cult.[66] In addition, there were cultic installations for the worship of the "host of heavens" in the temple of Jerusalem that were abolished, together with their priests, in the wake of the concentration of the cult by Josiah.[67] This quashing of the veneration of the "host of heavens" was the result of the rejection of the astralized "host of heavens" by Deuteronomistic circles. Consequently, in Judahite texts dating to the late preexilic and exilic periods, the worship of the "host of heavens," often set in parallelism to the worship of foreign gods,[68] was strictly forbidden to Judahites as anti-Yahwistic idolatry.

---

[62] See H. Niehr, "Host of Heavens," in *Dictionary of Deities and Demons in the Bible* (eds. K. van der Toorn, B. Becking, and P. van der Horst; Leiden: Brill, 1995).

[63] Deut 4:19; compare Ps 148:2-3.

[64] Deut 17:3; 2 Kgs 23:5; Jer 8:2; compare Dan 8:10.

[65] Jer 19:13; Zeph 1:5.

[66] 2 Kgs 21:3, 5=2 Chr 33:3, 5; Jer 8:2; 19:13.

[67] 2 Kgs 21:5; 23:4-5.

[68] Deut 17:3; 2 Kgs 17:16; 21:3; 23:4-5; Jer 19:13; Zeph 1:4-5.

Yet, even through these measures, the concept of a divine assembly could not be removed from Judahite religion and its successor, Judean religion. In postexilic texts the divine assembly appears in the guise of the עדתאל (Ps 82:1), קהל קדשׁים (Ps 89:6), סוד־קדשׁים (Ps 89:8), סוד־אלוה (Job 15:8) and סוד יהוה (Jer 23:18, 22). In other postexilic texts, however, the phrase "host of heavens" has regained its ancient, positive meaning as YHWH's divine assembly.[69]

The divine assembly can also be called אלהים. These אלהים cannot be confused with YHWH because in nearly all the places where the divine assembly is called אלהים, it is stressed that YHWH is higher than the אלהים.[70]

The divine assembly fulfills several tasks on YHWH's behalf: it serves him,[71] gives him advice,[72] glorifies him,[73] mediates between god and humans,[74] protects peoples[75] and human beings,[76] and hears the prayers of humanity.[77]

None of the texts mentioning YHWH's divine assembly claim that YHWH is the father or the begetter of this assembly. YHWH does not seem to have kindred relations to the heavenly beings surrounding him.

In order to clarify why the postexilic texts think that YHWH needs a divine assembly, two explanations can be deduced. The first one has already been mentioned above. The divine assembly is needed to fulfill certain duties towards YHWH and even towards humanity. In other postexilic texts, however, there are several instances where the divine assembly fulfills no precise duty. It just surrounds YHWH, who is described as incomparable and unique within this circle.[78] These references are important in a different way: they show that YHWH needed the divine assembly to maintain

---

[69] Ps 103:19-21; 148:1-5; and Dan 8:9-13. See also Niehr, "Host of Heavens."

[70] Exod 15:11; 18:11; Ps 86:8; 89:7; 95:3; 96:4; 97:9; 135:5; 2 Chr 2:4.

[71] 1 Kgs 22:19; Isa 6:2.

[72] 1 Kgs 22:20; Isa 6:8 and compare Isa 40:13-14, where this function is denied to the divine assembly.

[73] Deut 32:43; Isa 6:3; Job 38:7; Ps 29:1-2, 9; 47:7-8; 103: 20-22.

[74] 1 Kgs 22:20-22; Isa 6:8-9; Jer 23:18, 22; Job 15:8.

[75] Deut 32:8 (LXX version); Dan 12:1.

[76] Ps. 82:3-4; 91:10-13; Tob 3:16-17; 12.

[77] Job 5:1; 33:23.

[78] Exod 15:11; 18:11; Ps 86:8; 89:6-9; 95:3; 96:4; 97:9; 135:5.

his position of supreme god. This same function can also be detected in those places where YHWH is called "God of the gods"[79] or "Lord of the lords."[80] Herein the concept of the divine assembly has been condensed into a Yahwistic title meaning "the supreme god." Thus, in postexilic texts the divine assembly fulfills among other roles the literary function of extolling YHWH as the supreme god.[81]

4.2 The Divine Abode

When YHWH rose to the position of supreme god, his divine abode, Mount Zion, received the trappings of a divine mountain. Ugaritic, Phoenician and Aramaic sources illustrate how a divine mountain was shaped and by what labels it was called.[82] Due to its prestige in the Late Bronze Age, Mount Zaphon to the north of Ugarit[83] became the divine mountain par excellence in northwest Semitic religions and remained so even until the Iron Age. That is why in several Syro-Palestinian religions the weather god or the supreme god was said to have been enthroned on Mount Zaphon.[84] It is not surprising, therefore, to see an impact of this concept also in HB texts.

It is explicitly stated in Ps 48:3 that "Mount Zion is (on) the summit of Zaphon."[85] Jerusalem's sacred mountain is called Zaphon because as supreme god of Judah, YHWH can only be enthroned on the divine mountain par excellence. This aspect also underlies Job 26:7, where "Zaphon" stands for "heaven," meaning

---

[79] Deut 10:17; Josh 22:22; Ps 50:1; Dan 2:47.
[80] Deut 11:7.
[81] Niehr, Höchste(r) Gott, 89-94.
[82] For details, see ibid., 95-101.
[83] For references and literature concerning Zaphon in Ugaritic texts, see H. Niehr, "Zaphon," in Dictionary of Deities and Demons in the Bible (eds. K. van der Toorn, B. Becking, and P. van der Horst; Leiden: Brill, 1995).
[84] See ibid.
[85] For this translation, see also Isa 14:13-14 and Niehr, Höchste(r) Gott, 107-8; M. Dietrich and O. Loretz, "Ugaritisch ṣrrt ṣpn, ṣrry und hebräisch jrktj ṣpwn," UF 22 (1990) 79-86, esp. 83-5.

YHWH's divine abode. Also comparable is Job 37:22, which describes YHWH's epiphany from Zaphon.[86]

Because of the underlying ideology of the sacred mountain, Zion attracted more specific attributes of a divine abode. As the seat of Jerusalem's supreme god, Mount Zion was praised as very high[87] or even as the highest mountain in the world.[88] This Zion ideology had further effects on the sacred geography of the whole land and of the earth. Zion came to be viewed as the navel of the earth.[89] The whole country of Judah could even be designated as a divine mountain.[90] The divine garden is also to be localized on the divine mountain.[91] The waters surrounding the world have their source at the foot of Zion.[92] Zion itself is a place with great rivers and streams,[93] and God gives his salvation by these waters.[94] According to one tradition, YHWH is enthroned on the flood,[95] reflecting the Ugaritic tradition of the divine mountain situated over the waters.[96] As YHWH himself is enthroned on Zion, all enemies and powers of chaos approaching his abode are rejected and defeated[97] and Zion, his seat, is the real divine mountain.[98]

The reason why this ideology of the divine abode was applied to Mount Zion in the HB is twofold. First, Mount Zion, with the temple on top of it, was exalted by mythical means in order to propagate a certain temple theology. According to ancient Near Eastern views, a temple was situated on the place of creation, i.e. of the primeval hillock, which is the cosmic mountain, and the temple is to be seen as the architectural embodiment of this mountain. This

---

[86] So also Ezek 1:4, where YHWH's coming from Zaphon means his coming from the north.
[87] Ps 48:3; Ezek 20:40; Ps 78:68-69.
[88] Isa 2:2-4=Mic 4:1-5; Ezek 17:22.
[89] Ezek 38:12.
[90] Exod 15:17.
[91] Gen 2:10-14; Isa 51:3; Ezek 28:13-14.
[92] Gen 2:10-14; Isa 33:21; Ezek 47:1-12; Joel 4:18; Zech 13:1; 14:8; Ps 87:7.
[93] Isa 33:20-21.
[94] Ps 36:9-10; Zech 13:1.
[95] Ps 29:10; see also Ps 104:3.
[96] Niehr, *Höchste(r) Gott*, 114-5.
[97] Ps 46:2-12; 48:5-9; 76:3-10.
[98] Isa 14:13-14; Ps 46:5; 48:3.

concept also underlies the theology of the temple in Jerusalem, as has been argued convincingly.[99] Secondly, the use of the divine mountain motif serves to praise YHWH in his position as supreme god. YHWH, who is enthroned on his divine abode, is elevated over all gods and human beings.[100] YHWH is the creator of the divine mountain and no other god has achieved this act.[101]

4.3 *Creation and Fight against Chaos*

One of the first indications of a belief in divine creation in Judah is given by a fragmentary ostracon of the early 7th century BCE from Mount Zion in Jerusalem. The text contains the words קן ארץ, to which a divine name of an appellative has to be restored.[102] This ostracon is the only datable evidence revealing a preexilic belief in the creation of the earth by a god. A belief in the creation of heaven is not attested before the exile; the conviction that heaven and earth are created by gods is an insight of Babylonian mythology with which Judah became acquainted only during the exile.[103] In the HB a real theology of creation can only be found in exilic and postexilic texts.[104]

The creation of heaven and earth by YHWH is not told in lengthy mythological narratives, though such also may have existed in Judah and Israel. The HB contains only certain mythological elements of creation stories, which provide glimpses of old Israelite

---

[99] So e.g., B. Janowski, "Temple und Schöpfung," *JBTh* 5 (1990) 37-69; S.W. Holloway, "What Ship Goes There: The Flood Narratives in the Gilgamesh Epic and Genesis Considered in Light of Ancient Near Eastern Temple Ideology," *ZAW* 103 (1991) 328-55.

[100] Isa 14:13-14; Ezek 28:1-10, 11-19; Ps 48:15-16.

[101] Ps 89:13; Job 26:7.

[102] The text is restored in this manner by most commentators. Less probable is the proposal of E. Lipiński ("קנה," in *Theologisches Wörterbuch zum Alten Testament* [8 vols.; ed. G.J. Botterweck and H. Ringgren; Köln: W. Kohlhammer, 1973-1994] 7.69), who adopts the economic sense of קנה, "to buy," for this text.

[103] See W. Herrmann, "Wann wurde Jahwe zum Schöpfer der Welt?," *UF* 23 (1991) 165-80, esp. 167.

[104] Cf. C. Petersen, *Mythos im Alten Testament: Bestimmung des Mythosbegriffs und Untersuchung der mythischen Elemente in dem Psalmen* (BZAW 157; Berlin and New York: Walter de Gruyter, 1982) 265-8; W. Herrmann, "Das Aufleben des Mythos unter den Judäern während des babylonischen Zeitalters," *BN* 40 (1987) 97-129; *idem*, "Jahwe," 168-9; Niehr, *Höchste(r) Gott*, 125-6.

and Judahite concepts of creation.[105] Several functions for the use
of these mythological elements in different contexts can be detected.

(1)   The stability of the earth, which is effected by YHWH's cre-
       ation, is an indicator of YHWH's faithfulness.[106]
(2)   By virtue of his creation, YHWH proves to be higher than the
       gods,[107] almighty[108] and incomparable.[109]
(3)   YHWH is the owner of the creation[110] and full power over
       the natural forces belongs to him.[111]
(4)   As creator of heaven and earth YHWH is also the lord of his-
       tory.[112]

YHWH's fight against the chaos also is to be considered within
the context of creation theology because according to the common
ancient Near Eastern concept, creation is a victory over chaos and
the powers of chaos never refrain from menacing creation.[113] In
HB texts the powers of chaos are personalized in the shape of a sea

---

[105]   For this subject, see M. Metzger, "Eigentumsdeklaration und Schöpfungsaussage," in *"Wenn nicht jetzt, wann dann?" Aufsätze für Hans-Joachim Kraus zum 65 Geburtstag* (ed. H. Geyer; Neukirchen-Vluyn: Neukirchener, 1983) 37-51; Petersen,
Mythos; Herrmann, "Aufleben"; *idem*, "Jahwe"; H. Spieckermann, *Heilsgegenwart:
eine Theologie der Psalmen* (FRLANT 148; Göttingen: Vandenhoeck & Ruprecht,
1989) 21-86; Niehr, *Höchste(r) Gott*, 123-9.

[106]   Ps 90:2; 102:26-27.

[107]   Isa 40:18-26; Jer 10:1-16; Ps 89:7-13; 96:4-5; 135:5-7; 136:2-9.

[108]   Job 26:5-14; Ps 135:6-7.

[109]   Isa 40:25-26; Job 38-39.

[110]   Isa 43:1; Ps 8:4; 29:1-2; 74:16; 89:12; 95:5-7; 100:3; 115:15-16.

[111]   Jer 10:12-13 = 51:15-16; Ps 29; 104; 135:6-7.

[112]   Isa 42:5-8; 44:24-28; 45:1-8, 9-13; 51:9-16; Jer 18:1-12; 27:4-8; Zech 12:1-2; Ps
135:6-12.

[113]   For this subject, see M.K. Wakeman, *God's Battle with the Monster* (Leiden:
Brill, 1973); J. Day, *God's Conflict with the Dragon and the Sea* (University of Cambridge Oriental Publications 35; Cambridge: Cambridge University, 1985); C.
Kloos, *YHWH's Combat with the Sea* (Amsterdam & Leiden: Brill, 1986); Herrmann,
"Aufleben"; G. Fuchs, *Mythos und Hiobdichtung: Aufnahme und Umdeutung alto-
rientalischer Vorstellung* (Stuttgart: W. Kohlhammer, 1993); T. Podella, "Der Chaos-
kampfmythos im Alten Testament. Eine Problemanzeige," in *Mesopotamica-Ugariti-
ca-Biblica. Festschrift für Kurt Bergerhof zur Vollendung seines 70. Lebensjahre am 7.
Mai, 1992* (eds. M. Dietrich and O. Loretz; AOAT 232; Kevelaer: Butzon &
Bercker and Neukirchen-Vluyn: Neukircherner, 1993) 283-329.

dragon or serpent and they occur under the names לִוְיָתָן,[114] רַהַב[115] and תַּנִּין.[116]

Three groups of texts illustrate YHWH's relation to these beings in different ways. To the first group belong those tests that report that YHWH annihilates the powers of chaos that have been personalized as sea monsters.[117] The second group is made up of texts that show that YHWH keeps the sea monsters and the sea itself in check.[118] The third group of texts differs from the first two groups in establishing a positive relation between YHWH and the sea monsters, which are considered his pets and are urged to praise him.[119]

No other divinity is the subject of the processes of creation or the taming of chaos in the HB. YHWH alone is the creator and he alone fights chaos.[120] The HB texts show that he is a universal god having power over everything in heaven and earth and that he is the supreme god by fulfilling deeds other gods cannot fulfill. This theology of creation has even produced an intolerant monotheism in some HB texts.[121]

4.4 Astralization and Solarization

During the first millennium BCE a tendency toward the astralization of religions in Mesopotamia and Syria-Palestine can be observed.[122] This astralization "hängt offensichtlich mit einer verstärkten Zuwendung zu den Mächten am Himmel, insbesondere zu Sonne und Mond, aber auch mit intensiver kosmischer Orientierung

---

114 Isa 27:1; Ps 74:14.
115 Isa 51:9; Job 9:13; 26:12; Ps 89:11; compare Isa 30:7; Ps 40:5; 87:4.
116 Isa 27:1; 51:9; Job 7:12; Ps 74:13.
117 Isa 27:1; 51:9; Job 26:12-13; Ps 74:13-14; 89:11.
118 Gen 1:9-10; Jer 5:22; Job 7:12; 38:8-11; Ps 33:7; 65:8; 104:6-9; Prov 8:29.
119 Ps 104:26; 148:7; cf. Amos 9:3.
120 Isa 51:9-16; Job 26:5-14; Ps 74:12-17; 89:9-13; 104. Contrary to Mettinger (Dethronement, 69-72), it cannot be maintained that the Sitz im Leben of YHWH's chaos battle is the Autumn Festival; see K. van der Toorn, "The Babylonian New Year Festival: New Insights from the Cuneiform Texts and Their Bearing on Old Testament Study," in Congress Volume Leuven 1989 (ed. J.A. Emerton; VTSup 43; Leiden: Brill, 1991) 331-44, esp. 343-4.
121 Jer 10:11; Ps 96:4-5.
122 Koch, "Aschera," 116-20; Keel and Uehlinger, Göttinnen, 322-69.

zusammen."[123] The basis for this astralization lies within Babylonian religion, which turned towards seeing the great gods in astral forms before 1000 BCE.[124] In the case of the northwest Semitic religions, this astralization was connected with the god Baalšamem because this divine name can also be understood as an appellative meaning "lord of heavens."[125]

One of the results of this astralization process was that YHWH, who already was being venerated as Baalšamem in Omride Israel, was seen as "lord of heavens" in Israelite and Judahite religion. The title "lord of heavens" is explicitly conferred upon him in the Elephantine papyri, which mirror an earlier stage of Israelite religion before 723 BCE,[126] and in exilic and postexilic texts of the HB.[127] In tracing the history of this process of astralization the above-mentioned astralization of the divine assembly (4.1) and the existence of YHWH's paredra, the queen of heaven (3.1), serve as important markers.

From the 8th century BCE onward a solarization of YHWH is evident. Two factors can be adduced that are responsible for this solarization: Judahite royal ideology and the common astralization of the northwest Semitic religions.

Important extrabiblical evidence can be adduced from Judah for YHWH's solarization. Working chronologically, the royal jar handle stamps dating back to the reign of Hezekiah provide the earliest evidence.[128] With their motif of the winged sun disc they bear witness to the solarization of the dynastic god, i.e. YHWH.[129] Fur-

---

[123] Koch, "Aschera," 119.

[124] *Ibid.*, 118.

[125] *Ibid.*, 118-9; Niehr, "JHWH," in press; for references to the solarization of the supreme god in Phoenician and Aramaic religions, see Niehr, *Höchste(r) Gott*, 141-7.

[126] See above, sec 3.2.

[127] See the references and discussions in Niehr, *Höchste(r) Gott*, 43-60; *idem*, "JHWH," in press; *idem*, "God of Heavens," in *Dictionary of Deities and Demons in the Bible* (eds. K. van der Toorn, B. Becking, and P. van der Horst; Leiden: Brill) 1995; Houtman, *Himmel*, 98-107.

[128] For the material, see P. Welten, *Die Königs-Stempel: ein Beitrag zur Militärpolitik Judas unter Hiskia und Josia* (ADPV; Wiesbaden: O. Harrasswitz, 1969) 4-46. For its religio-historical evaluation, see H.-P. Stähli, *Solare Elemente im Jahweglauben des Alten Testaments* (OBO 66; Fribourg: Universitätsverlag & Göttingen: Vandenhoeck & Ruprecht, 1985) 10-1; Keel and Uehlinger, *Göttinnen*, 314-7, 464-5.

[129] See Keel and Uehlinger, *Göttinnen*, 314.

ther evidence for YHWH's solarization is provided by two silver amulets that were found in the tombs of Ketef Hinnom in Jerusalem. These texts,[130] which are to be dated to the end of the 7th or the beginning of the 6th century BCE,[131] contain a prayer that also has been preserved in Num 6:24-26: "YHWH make his face shine upon you." It reveals a solarized YHWH.[132]

In the biblical material solar functions are conferred on YHWH in certain contexts. According to Hos 6:5 YHWH says: "My justice dawns like morning light." Here YHWH's justice is portrayed as the gift of the sun god, mirroring a common picture of ancient Near Eastern judicial ideology.[133] Zeph 3:5 draws on the same imagery. The texts says about YHWH: "Every morning he gives his judgment to light." YHWH once again is portrayed as the sun god who rises in the morning to speak justice.[134]

Hos 6:5 and Zeph 3:5 reveal that YHWH moved more and more into the role of the sun god. This can be seen fully in exilic and postexilic HB texts that describe YHWH's theophany in solar terms[135] and ascribe to him the bringing forth of justice.[136]

Since healing of disease was linked closely to the administration of justice in the ancient Near East,[137] the sun god took on healing functions in northwest Semitic religions of the first millennium

---

[130] For the text, see A. Yardeni, "Remarks on the Priestly Blessing on Two Ancient Amulets from Jerusalem," *VT* 41 (1991) 176-85.

[131] See Keel and Uehlinger, *Göttinnen*, 417; Yardeni, "Remarks," 178-80.

[132] Niehr, *Höchste(r) Gott*, 155.

[133] For the motif of "the sun-god as judge," see the literature quoted in H. Niehr, "*spr* V 7/8," in *Theologisches Wörterbuch zum Alten Testament* (8 vols.; ed. G.J. Botterweck, H. Ringgren, and H.J. Fabry; Stuttgart: W. Kohlhammer, 1970-) in press.

[134] For a treatment of this motif in the ancient Near East, see B. Janowski, *Rettungsgewißheit und Epiphanie des Heils 1: das Motiv der Hilfe Gottes "am Morgen" im Alten Orient und im Alten Testament* (WMANT 59; Neukirchen-Vluyn: Neukirchener, 1989).

[135] See references in Niehr, *Höchste(r) Gott*, 151-53 and add to them I. Cornelius, "The Sun Epiphany in Job 38:12-15 and the Iconography of the Gods in the Ancient Near East — The Palestinian Connection," *JNSL* 16 (1990) 25-43.

[136] See the references in Niehr, *Höchste(r) Gott*, 149-55.

[137] See Janowski, *Rettungsgewißheit*, 89-96.

BCE.[138] This feature appears in Judahite religion where YHWH, as healer, has taken over some traits of the healing sun god.[139]

YHWH's solarization left its mark on the cult of the first temple. This is shown by the denunciation of solar worship in Ezek 8:16-18 and by the reference to the "horses of the sun" in 2 Kgs 23:11. Both texts betray Judahite Yahwistic cults and cannot simply be ascribed to Assyrian influences on the religion of Judah.[140] They fit fully into the solarization of YHWH that began already in the 8th century BCE.

In view of YHWH's solarization from the 8th century BCE onward it is not surprising to find him called שמש, "sun (god)." Ps 84:12 calls YHWH שמש ומגן, "sun and shield." The psalm belongs to the group of the Korahite psalms and so can be considered to be a relic of the second temple liturgical texts that still presented YHWH as sun god. Mal 3:20 combines important aspects of solar imagery and applies them to YHWH:

But for you who fear my name,
the sun of righteousness shall rise with healing in his wings.

YHWH is the sun of righteousness rising to those who fear him. This is the only text in the HB where the winged sun disk, known from iconography, is explicitly mentioned. Mal 3:20 adds a further element. This is the abovementioned healing role of the sun god.

Why was it necessary to solarize YHWH in the religions of Judah and Israel? Several different items are to be adduced here. First, the astralization of the northwest Semitic religions in general must be remembered. This trend was then easily applied to YHWH, who already bore the title "lord of heaven."

The roots of YHWH's solarization can be ascertained in this process of astralization. Royal ideology, with its pertinent iconography of the winged sun disk, also impacted on YHWH's solarization. Other important contributing factors include YHWH's conception as

---

[138] See Niehr, *Höchste(r) Gott*, 159-60; *idem*, "JHWH als Arzt," *BZ NF* 35 (1991) 3-17, esp. 8-11.
[139] See Niehr, "JHWH," 8-11.
[140] See M.S. Smith, "The Near Eastern Background of Solar Language for Yahweh," *JBL* 109 (1990) 29-39, esp. 29-34 and G.W. Ahlström, *The History of Ancient Palestine from the Palaeolithic Period to Alexander's Conquest* (JSOTSup 146; Sheffield: JSOT, 1993) 771-2.

judge, an office exercised in Israel and elsewhere in the ancient Near East primarily by the sun god. In Judahite and Israelite iconography and in some biblical texts, traces of an independent sun god have been preserved. Over time, however, YHWH attracted traits of the sun god, especially his judging and healing qualities. When there was no longer a place for a sun god next to YHWH in the postexilic period, YHWH himself became fully solarized and even took on the title "sun" (god).

5. *Summary and Conclusion*

In the foregoing pages a tentative attempt has been made to reconstruct YHWH's rise in the religions of Judah and Samaria by using relevant primary and secondary material. The working hypothesis that has been used to frame the investigation has viewed Judahite and Israelite religions as Syro-Canaanite religions: the history of YHWH's rise has been interpreted within the context of Syro-Canaanite religions of the first millennium BCE, with Phoenician and Aramaic epigraphical sources and archaeological remains providing the bulk of the primary evidence about the beliefs and practices of such religions.

YHWH was seen to be a northwest Semitic weather god from southern Palestine who achieved the position of supreme god in the panthea of Jerusalem and Samaria. In these two capitals YHWH was venerated as the god of the dynasty and the kingdom but not as the local god of the different towns. YHWH's identification with those local deities was the result of a longer historical development that was not completed before the exile.

The process of YHWH's rise began in the early first millennium BCE and did not end until the postexilic period. Since there is only fragmentary primary evidence to document this process and since the secondary HB material underwent a considerable Judean censorship, many religio-historical aspects of YHWH's rise remain unknown to us.

Of special interest are complexes of motifs that illustrate how YHWH was equipped with the traits of a Syro-Canaanite supreme god. He was surrounded by a heavenly assembly, was enthroned on the divine abode, was praised as creator and the fighter of chaos, and underwent a solarization.

The Aniconic Tradition
On Reading Images and Viewing Texts
Brian B. Schmidt

> Words and images seem inevitably to become
> implicated in a "war of signs" (what Leonardo
> called *paragone*) in which the stakes are things
> like nature, truth, reality and the human spirit.

W.J.T. Mitchell, Iconology 1986

Introduction

The subject of aniconism as it developed in ancient Israel has received extensive treatment in recent years and a variety of approaches, issues, and results have been given voice in the secondary
literature. Frequently represented in the scholarship is aniconism's
close ties with monotheism and it is that same association, albeit
loosely construed, that informs the inclusion of the present essay in
a volume devoted to that latter theme.[1] Among the many other
recurring approaches and issues, one can find numerous treatments
exploring the rationale underlying the rise of aniconism and still
others investigating the aniconic cult's impact on ancient Israelite
artistic traditions.

To be sure, various explanations have been offered as the deciding factor(s) contributing to the biblical ban on images[2]: 1) YHWH,

---

[1]   See for recent examples, R. Albertz, *A History of Israelite Religion in the Old
Testament Period* (2 vols.; Louisville: Westminster/John Knox, 1994) 1.664-6 and
W. Dietrich and M.A. Klopfenstein (eds.), *Ein Gott allein? JHWH Verehung und
biblischer Monotheismus im Kontext der israelitischen und altorientalischen Religionsgeschichte.* OBO 139; Freiburg: Universitätsverlag and Göttingen: Vandenhoeck &
Ruprecht, 1994, esp. the article by T.N.D. Mettinger, "Aniconism — a West Semitic Context for the Israelite Phenomenon?," 159-78. That the deuteronomists,
and by extension, most, if not all, biblical writers, did not embrace aniconism is
closely paralleled by the likelihood that they were not monotheistic as the unqualified nature of a passage like 2 Kgs 3:27 suggests.
[2]   See R. Hendel, "The Social Origins of the Aniconic Tradition in Early Israel,"
CBQ 50 (1988) 365-82 for a helpful survey of some modern theories explaining the
rise of aniconism in ancient Israel.

as a hidden and transcendent god, cannot be contained in an image and cannot be manipulated in the cult,[3] 2) he is the god of a nomadic people called Israel over against the gods of the urbanized Canaanites,[4] 3) the imageless cult represents Israel's rational advance over the world view symbolized by the foreign cults that utilize images,[5] or 4) owing to Israel's antimonarchical ideology, YHWH is not to be represented as the typical royal figure of ancient Near Eastern divine symbolism.[6]

The ban on images in the Hebrew Bible has also been cited as the determinative influence in the marginalization of a native artistic tradition in ancient Israel or the relative lack of art altogether.[7] However, Silvia Schroer has made a compelling case for the minimal impact of aniconism on Israelite art, buttressing her argument with extensive archaeological data, a reevaluation of the biblical texts, and what she views as the late and gradual development of the full prohibition against images.[8]

---

[3] So, e.g., C.R. North, "The Essence of Idolatry," in *Von Ugarit nach Qumran: Beiträge zur alttestamentlichen und altorientalischen Forschungen. Otto Eissfeldt zum 1 September 1957* (ed. J. Hempel; BZAW 77; Berlin: A. Topelmann, 1958) 151-60. "Idolatry is the worship of the creature instead of the Creator... Idolatry is the worship of ... the life force ... instead of the Creator ..." (158-9).

[4] So, e.g., O. Keel, *Jahwe-Visionen und Siegelkunst: eine neue Deutung der Majestätsschilderungen in Jes 6, Ez 1 und 10 und Sach 4* (SBS 84/85; Stuttgart: Katholisches Bibelwerk, 1977) 39-40. R.P. Carroll ("The Aniconic God and the Cult of Images," *StTh* 31 [1977] 51-64) entertains a variation on the anti-Canaanite theory by tentatively positing an anti-Egyptian theory: "after an excess of iconic gods a fast is declared" (55).

[5] Carroll (*ibid.*) favors the theory that aniconism can be explained as an ontological conflict of world views in which the idea or word in Israelite religion was a rational advance over the image, for the image was closely related to magic (61-3), but in the end he leaves the matter open.

[6] So, e.g., Hendel, "Social Origins," 365-82 and W.W. Hallo, "Texts, Statues and the Cult of the Divine King," in *Congress Volume 1986* (ed. J.A. Emerton; VTSup 40; Leiden: Brill, 1988) 54-66.

[7] So e.g., W.H. Schmidt, *The Faith of the Old Testament* (Philadelphia: Westminster, 1983) 77.

[8] S. Schroer, *In Israel gab es Bilder. Nachrichten von darstellender Kunst im Alten Testament* (OBO 74; Freiburg: Universitätsverlag and Göttingen: Vandenhoeck & Ruprecht, 1987). For an earlier response, see J. Gutmann, "The 'Second Commandment' and the Image in Judaism," *HUCA* 32 (1961) 161-74. For a series of recent explorations into the social and processual dimensions of artistic creation in the

Given the defining limits of an essay such as this, I can only aim for the modest objective of building upon previous scholarship by suggesting areas for further investigation and offering a tentative interpretive rendition on the topic that, as far as I am aware, has not be previously explicated. As a means toward that goal, I will first consider a representative selection of the central biblical texts and I will then reevaluate a crucial archaeological datum in an effort to interface textual data and material artifact within a theoretical framework that attempts to relate image and text from a semiotic perspective. Against the long held notion that the word is an advance over the image is the argument from general semiotics that although verbal and visual representation do differ as forms of medium, they do not differ essentially from a semantic point of view, for so-called speech acts are not medium specific.[9] Needless to say, the long held assumption that Israel's aniconic tradition stems from her rational advance over the ontology of her neighbors as given expression in the "primitive" use of images hardly suffices as an explanatory model.

Before examining the textual and artifactual evidence, a précis on the meaning of aniconism is in order. Not only does aniconism have multiple applications, but in specific instances the term is not always consistently applied. In what follows, aniconism refers to the imposition of a ban against the use of anthropomorphic, theriomorphic, or physiomorphic images to represent or house the deity as an object of worship in ritual performance. In this sense, aniconism approximates iconoclasm. Tryggve Mettinger labels this *programmatic* aniconism, which he distinguishes from *de facto* aniconism, that is to say, the use of a nonanthropomorphic and nontheriomorphic image of the deity alongside a wide array of iconic images. As Mettinger describes it, *de facto* aniconism is conven-

---

ancient Near East, see the volume edited by A.C. Gunter, *Investigating Artistic Environments in the Ancient Near East* (Washington, DC: Arthur Sackler Gallery/ Smithsonian Institution, 1990).

9   See now W.J.T. Mitchell, *Iconology: Image, Text, Ideology* (Chicago: University of Chicago, 1986) and idem, *Picture Theory: Essays on Verbal and Visual Representation* (Chicago: University of Chicago, 1994) 151-81, esp. 160-2, following E. Gombrich, "The Limits of Convention," in *Image and Code/Ernst H. Gombrich* (ed. W. Steiner; Michigan Studies in the Humanities 2; Ann Arbor: Horace Rackham School of Graduate Studies, 1981) 11-42.

tional, tolerant or indifferent to icons. He has collected an impress-
ive range of data documenting the existence of *de facto* aniconism in
various ancient Near Eastern traditions. Like many before him,
however, he assumes that the biblical traditions give expression to
a *programmatic* aniconism or iconoclasm that is motivated by iconophobia.[10] The present essay not only challenges that consensus, but
it explores ancient Israel's rendering of YHWH as peripherally "vis-
ualized" in the biblical text and as transparently "transcribed" in
material artifact.

The Biblical Traditions

Any investigation into the emergence of aniconism in ancient Israel
must address the issues that arise out of a close study of the so-
called Second Commandment. A detailed analysis of this well-
known proscription entails no small undertaking. One cannot
merely focus on such texts as Deut 5:8-10 and Exod 20:4-6, for the
same or related concerns are reflected in other legal passages (Deut
4:15-19,23,25,28; 27:15; Exod 20:23-24; 34:17) as well as in a host of
narrative (e.g., Judg 17:1-5) and prophetic texts.[11] It is not my aim
here to rehearse the extensive historical and literary critical histories
of interpretation devoted to this commandment or the ten commandments more generally, for others have admirably performed
that service.[12] I should point out, however, that recent studies have
made a forceful case for the relative lateness of the final compilation

---

[10] See his *No graven Image? Israelite Aniconism in Its Ancient Near Eastern Context*
(ConBOT 42; Stockholm: Almqvist & Wiksell, 1995). His invocation of the term
iconophobia is problematic, for if an ideological, propagandistic, or socio-religious
modus operandi should underlay the biblical ban on images, it would severely limit
the usefulness of such a psychologically applied term.

[11] The frequently cited texts in Hosea are here understood to be aimed against
the wrong image of YHWH, in this case, the imagery derived from the Baal cult,
and not imagery *in toto* (3:4; 4:17; 8:1-7; 10:1-8,10; 13:2; 14:4,9). The same applies
in the case of Isa 2:8, Mic 5:12, and Amos 5:26, which also are commonly cited.

[12] R.H. Pfeiffer ("The Polemic against Idolatry in the Old Testament," *JBL* 43
[1924] 229-40) provides a classic application of earlier higher critical approaches in
which all the pentateuchal prohibitions were placed in the Josianic reform. For
recent but divergent treatments of that history, see C. Dohmen, *Das Bilderverbot:
seine Entstehung und Entwicklung im Alten Testament* (BBB 62; Bonn: Hanstein,
1985) 154-80, 237-77 and M. Weinfeld, *Deuteronomy 1-11: A New Translation with
Introduction and Commentary* (AB 5; New York: Doubleday, 1991) 205-7, 242-319.

of the decalogue in the exile or thereafter and for the likely dependence of the Exodus version preserved in 20:3-14 (a priestly tradition?) on that reflected in Deut 5:7-18.[13] My concern is to explore
alternative ways of reading the commandment as it is situated in its
respective literary and (by inference) social contexts.

Deut 5:8-10=Exod 20:4-6

My translation of the First and Second Commandments based on
Deut 5:7-10 [and Exod 20:3-6] is as follows:

> 7[3] You shall have no other gods besides me. 8[4] You shall not make for
> yourself a sculpted image, that is [/or], any likeness of what is in the heavens
> above, or on the earth below, or in the waters under the earth. 9[5] You
> shall not bow down to them or serve them. For I, YHWH your god, am an
> impassioned god, visiting the guilt of the parents upon the children [and[14]]
> unto the third and the fourth generations of those who reject me, 10[6] but
> showing steadfast love to the multitude who love me and keep my com-
> mandments.

The Second Commandment as articulated in Deut 5:8 lacks the
connecting ו on בל תמונה, "any likeness," found in Exod 20:4, "*or
any likeness. ...*" This has led some interpreters to posit an apposi-
tional asyndetic phrase for 5:8: "a sculpted image, *that is*, any likeness of what is in the heavens above ... ."[15] Grammatically speaking, the reference to bowing down "to them" (להם) and serving

---

[13]   See e.g., the discussions and bibliographies in F.L. Hossfeld, *Der Dekalog: seine
späten Fassungen, die originale Komposition und seine Vorstufen* (OBO 45; Freiburg:
Universitätsverlag and Göttingen: Vandenhoeck & Ruprecht, 1982) 21-26;
Dohmen, *Bilderverbot*, 154-80, 237-77; E.W. Nicholson, *God and His People* (Ox-
ford: Oxford University, 1986) 164-78; S. Schroer, *In Israel gab es Bilder*, 12-6; W.
Johnstone, *Exodus* (Old Testament Guides; Sheffield: JSOT, 1990) 76-86, 90-9; L.
Schwienhorst-Schönberger, *Das Bundesbuch (Ex 20,22-23,33): Studien zu seiner Ent-
stehung und Theologie* (BZAW 188; Berlin & New York: Walter de Gruyter, 1990)
287-99; and J. Van Seters, *The Life of Moses: The Yahwist as Historian in Exodus-
Numbers* (Louisville: Westminster/John Knox, 1994) 247-80. In his commentary,
Weinfeld offered a review and critique of Hossfeld, but did not address the works
of Dohmen, Nicholson, Schroer in this regard.

[14]   In Exod 20:6, the connecting ו is lacking on עלשלשים.

[15]   On the relative frequency of apposition and the rarity of asyndeton in biblical
Hebrew, see P. Joüon, *A Grammar of Biblical Hebrew* (Rome: Pontifical Biblical
Institute, 1993) 477-81, 649-53. For these features in the book of Deuteronomy, see
now Weinfeld, *Deuteronomy 1-11*, 290.

"them" (see the suffixed ם- on תעבד-) in 5:9 (=Exod 20:5) would, in this rendering, refer not to the singular image (פסל) or likeness (תמונה) in 5:8, but to the plural gods or אלהים of 5:7. This in turn has resulted in the suggestion that the Second Commandment was originally part of the first: "you shall have no other gods besides me, *that is to say*, you shall not make for yourself a sculpted image, *that is*, any likeness of what is in the heavens above ... you shall not bow down to them or worship them." Thus, in Deut 5:8-10, the worship of other gods is likened to, or equated with, bowing down and serving their images.

However, others conclude that the Exodus tradition makes explicit in 20:4 the distinction between the prohibition against worshipping other gods (that is, the First Commandment) and the (second) commandment against making images and likenesses. The addition of the ו before כל תמונה, "or any likeness," creates the plural number of images and likenesses needed as the antecedent for the acts of bowing down and serving the plural "them" of Exod 20:5. This forms a distinct unit for 20:4 and following thereby separating the two phrases "you shall not make for yourself a sculpted image" and "or any likeness of what is in the heavens ..." from the wording of the First Commandment, "you shall have no other gods besides me." When considered alongside the repeated form of command used to introduce each of the "ten words," the distinction between, and independence of, the First and Second Commandments in Exodus 20 becomes all the more apparent.

While few would dispute that Deut 5 is concerned with the matter of loyalty to YHWH, the reader should not presume that, for the earliest audiences, a monotheistic or an aniconic ideology necessarily informed such a concern. Deut 5:7-10 neither unequivocally denies the existence of other gods nor does it address the making of YHWH images. Instead, it assumes the existence of other gods (see further below) while warning against the total abandonment of YHWH or the diminishing of his importance relative to that of other gods. In other words, if one refrains from reading a monotheistic or an aniconic perspective into these verses, one does not find it present in them. The existence of other gods (and their images) as manifested in Yahwistic religious circles most likely lies behind the prohibition in Exod 20:3, but the clear separation of the commandments in Exod 20 suggests that YHWH images rather than the images of "other" gods are the object of the second prohibition beginning in Exod 20:4. In any case, the divine jealousy referred to in the following verses of both versions of the commandment comprises a jealousy aimed at Israel's preference for other gods and their images on the one hand (Deut 5:9b-10) and for foreign gods and illegitimate Yahweh images on the other (Exod 20:5b-6).[16] That is to say, an ancient reader/hearer of these words might have understood them to convey the following implication: a person could avoid the elevation of other gods (and their images) over YHWH (i.e., obedience to the First Commandment in a monolatrous context), yet stumble by making an image (or as argued here, the *wrong* image) of YHWH (i.e., breaking the Second Commandment).

While in the history of interpretation both versions of the commandment have been understood to encompass all image making, the broader contexts of Deut 5 and Exod 20 suggest otherwise. That is to say, Deut 5:8-10 and Exod 20:4-6 do not provide an inclusive list of what would have constituted conventional images regardless of whether they be images of foreign gods or those of YHWH. Neither the term כל of כל תמונה, "any likeness," nor the phraseology of the immediately following verses hold within their purview the full range of conventionally conceivable images. Not only does the following triad of images — images representative of creatures of the land, air, and sea — delimit the application of the term כל, but the categories themselves include only certain groupings of theriomorphic form namely, those *faunal* forms inhabiting the sky, earth, and sea. They do not encompass the images of other forms of life (i.e., non-faunal life) or inanimate objects.

Excursus: The Triadic Cosmological Schema
A triadic classification system similar to that implemented in the prohibition against images is employed in the priestly account of the creaturely world in Gen 1. There, zoomorphic locomotion is

---

[16] Many scholars view the following verses as a redactional addition: so e.g., T.N.D. Mettinger, "The Veto on Images and the Aniconic God in Ancient Israel," in *Religious Symbols and Their Functions: Based on Papers read at the Symposium on Religious Symbols and their Functions, held at Abo on the 28th-30th of August 1978* (ed. H. Biezais; Scripta Instituti Donneriani Aboensis 10; Stockholm: Almqvist & Wicksell, 1979) 15-29, esp. 25.

divided into the same three spheres: sky, earth, and water. The variation in order between Deut 5 = Exod 20 and Gen 1 is of little consequence; even within the span of thirty-one verses, the order of this triad transposes five or six times in Gen 1 (see also e.g., Deut 4:17 and Jer 8:7). As the wider context of Genesis makes clear, the Gen 1 triad does not hold within its purview flora or the inanimate world. The Genesis classification system used also functions to set these creatures apart from the celestial bodies mentioned in final and prominent position in 1:14-19. In sum, the boundaries of creaturely domain delineated in Gen 1:20-31 confirm that the reference to sky, earth, and water in Deut 5 = Exod 20 does not form a merism inclusive of all conventionally conceivable images. These same boundaries serve to delineate the categories of prohibited images encompassed in that version of the Second Commandment preserved in Deut 4, but more on this to follow.

As applied in other contexts, this same creaturely classification system can take on more restrictive parameters. For example, faunal anomalies do not lie within the boundaries of this system as it is formulated in the book of Leviticus. Anomalous theriomorphic forms fall outside the bounds of the triadic system as it is employed in Leviticus, where it served to identify clean and unclean animals. Those animals that deviated from the culturally determined, conventional or typical creatures of land, sea, and sky creatures are classified as unclean or abnormal and, therefore, taboo for human consumption.[17] What has all this to do with the triadic scheme associated with the Second Commandment? Simply put, images derivative of the inanimate world, floral forms, and *Mischwesen* (composite forms comprising theriomorphic and anthropomorphic elements) do not fall within the confines of the prohibition preserved in Deut 5:8 = Exod 20:4 (on the sun, moon and the stars, see below). They are not prohibited.

---

[17] For the classic statement on the classification scheme underlying the ban against the consumption of certain animals, see M. Douglas "The Abominations in Leviticus," in her *Purity and Danger: An Analysis of Concepts of Pollution and Taboo* (London: Routledge and Kegan Paul, 1966) 41-57. For an insightful response and partial corrective, see J. Milgrom, *Leviticus 1-16: A New Translation with Introduction and Commentary* (AB 3; New York: Doubleday, 1991) 718-36.

An analysis of the phraseology referring to that sector of the triadic world of symbols located in the sky illustrates the restricted scope of the triadic classification scheme shared by Gen 1, Deut 5 and Exod 20. Other passages where the same terminology occurs favor the view that the phrase "... any likeness (תמונה) of what is in the heavens/skies above (שמים ממ על)" refers exclusively to the lower atmosphere; the skies traversed by birds. Another Deuteronomy passage in close proximity, Deut 4:39 to the Second Commandment, depicts YHWH's control over these same skies as embodied in the pillar and cloud theophanies, "YHWH is god in the skies above (שמים ממ על)." These also comprise those skies visible to the naked eye. These skies or שמים ממ על appear in Jer 4:23-28 where they make visible the bird in flight as well as darkness and light. Such phraseology does not have in view the celestial bodies or astral deities. When applied to the variant form of the Second Commandment in Deut 4:15-20, it becomes clear that the triadic scheme encompasses images of flying creatures (cf. vv.15-18), but does not address the appropriateness of the celestial bodies as concrete expressions of YHWH. That is taken up independently of the triadic scheme (i.e., in vv.19-20, see below).

Finally, Gen 1 offers another insight into the ban on images as expressed in Exod 20 where the issue of the appropriate YHWH image is addressed (as opposed to the images of foreign or "other" gods as in Deut 5). On the one hand, Gen 1 identifies living humanity as the suitable, creaturely divine image (see 1:26-27), but in this instance, a *cultic* image of YHWH is not in view. On the other hand, Exod 20 leaves open the identity of an acceptable cultic image of YHWH in its uncompromising ban on crafted theriomorphic forms. In fact both texts leave open the question of an acceptable image of YHWH. To sum up, although typical (i.e., culturally determined) theriomorphic representation, whether animate or inanimate, cultic or non-cultic, was, for these writers, an inadmissable expression of YHWH's image, neither passage actually addresses the possibility of an appropriate image of YHWH!

Deut 4:15-20

Deut 4:1-40 has often been viewed as equating the worship of images with the worship of foreign gods, defining idolatry as syncretism, and requiring that the worship of YHWH be both exclusive and

devoid of any concrete symbol whatsoever. Nevertheless, the immediate context of 4:15-20 and the passage's intertextual connections
suggest otherwise. Although in 4:19-20, the sun (השמש), the moon
(הירח), and the stars (הכוכבים), that is, the whole host of heaven
(כל־צבא השמים) are listed immediately following 4:15-18 where
images made by human hands are condemned, the celestial bodies
are not attributed analogous crafted images.[18] Terms such as פסל,
עצב ,מסכה, or תמונה which typically designate crafted material
icons are entirely lacking in 4:19-20. So, too, are the typical verbs
that refer to their construction like עשׂה "to make," mentioned in
4:16-18. In other words, crafted images are not under consideration
in 4:19-20. The prohibition is aimed at the worship of the luminaries as they can be directly observed with the human eye in their
heavenly positions. This is made explicit in the stated verbal action
of "lifting the eyes" and "seeing the luminaries in the sky" in 4:19.
Perhaps lying behind these actions are rituals enacted in the open
air sanctuaries or roof top altars mentioned elsewhere in biblical
traditions. Job 31:26-28 might assume a similar backdrop wherein
the hero is tempted to revere the moon (or the sun and the moon),
after having gazed upon it (or them). The above considerations
clearly eliminate the celestial bodies from the list of crafted prohibited images of 4:15-18. Nevertheless, as both crafted images and
natural bodies comprise visual symbols or icons, the prohibitions in
4:15-20 are directed at illegitimate (i.e., competing) YHWH symbolism, whether it be crafted theriomorphic forms or the naturally
occurring astral bodies as observed in the open air cults.[19]

The independent status of v.19(a) is further evidenced by the fact
that it parallels v.16 syntactically and semantically. Both verses begin with the particle פן followed by a series of prefixed verbal
forms (and note the conjunctive ו attached to פן in v.19). In other

---

[18] The conceptual equation of the sun, moon, and stars with the phrase "the
whole host of heaven" finds grammatical support in the relative frequency of apposition and the rarity of asyndeton in biblical Hebrew, as noted previously in n.
15; see Joüon, *Grammar of Biblical Hebrew*, 477-81, 649-53.

[19] On YHWH's solar imagery, see J.G. Taylor, *Yahweh and the Sun: Biblical and
Archaeological Evidence for Sun Worship in Ancient Israel* (JSOTSup 111; Sheffield:
JSOT, 1993). For YHWH's lunar associations, see B.B. Schmidt, "The Moon God,"
in *Dictionary of Demons and Deities in the Bible* (ed. K. van der Toorn, B. Becking,
and P. van der Horst; Leiden: Brill, 1995).

words, v.19(a) does not continue the prohibition against making images in 4:16-18, for 4:19-20 is not subordinate to or part of 4:16-18. Rather, v.19(a) stands as one of two subordinate clauses directly dependent upon v.15 (vv.16-18 being the first such clause):

(4:15) For your own sake, therefore, be most careful — since you [= the people] saw no shape (כי לא ראיתם כל־תמונה) when YHWH your god spoke to you at Horeb out of the fire — ...

[פן + prefixed verbal forms]

(4:16) not to act wickedly and make for yourselves a sculpted image in any likeness whatsoever: the form of a man or woman, the form of any beast on earth, the form of any winged bird that flies in the sky, the form of anything that creeps on the ground, the form of any fish that is in the waters below the earth.

[ו + פן + prefixed verbal forms]

(4:19a) and not to look up to the sky and behold the sun and the moon and the stars, all the host of heaven, and be seduced to bow down to them or serve them.

(4:19b) for (אשר) YHWH your god allotted them to all the peoples everywhere under heaven; but you, YHWH took and brought out of that iron blast furnace, Egypt, to be his very own people as is now the case.

The logical development of 4:1-40 confirms the distinction advocated here, for 4:1-40 take a dramatic turn beginning with v.19. With the astral bodies of 4:19-20, the author introduces a category wholly independent of the three theriomorphic worlds catalogued in the preceding verses, that is, the creaturely worlds of land, sea, and air. Although elsewhere in deuteronomistic ideology the luminaries are occasionally described as having taken on specific expression as cultic paraphernalia (e.g., 2 Kgs 23:4,11-12), nowhere are they attributed their own images. To be sure, religious infidelity stands at the forefront of Deut 4:15-20, but there are two distinct aspects of the issue that are addressed in this passage: the worship of YHWH via the wrong man-made images in the crafted form of typical living creatures *and* the equation of YHWH with the astral bodies in their unmediated natural form. In any case, 4:15 establishes the fact that both have to do with symbolizing YHWH, not other gods. However, this is hardly an exhaustive or comprehensive list and so it leaves open the possibility that there was an acceptable cultic image of YHWH in deuteronomistic and related circles.

For the early audiences, the wholesale denial of all material images of YHWH, whether man-made or naturally occurring is nowhere in view. Rather, this passage addresses the nation's ignorance of, or disregard for, YHWH's proper symbolism according to deuteronomistic standards. As 4:11 reiterates, when the Sinai theophany took place, the people did not see, and were therefore ignorant of, YHWH's "genuine" form, for they stood below at the foot of the mountain (Exod 34:3-4). Only Moses saw YHWH's form or תמונה, face to face, as traditions like Num 12:8 and Deut 34:10 make clear.[20] At one level this use of anthropomorphic symbolism flies in the face of the Second Commandment as found in Deut 4 ("the form of a man or a woman"), unless one understands this proscription to encompass only a partial listing of YHWH's anthropomorphic form. More to the point, such passages point to the people's lack of justification in attempting to construct a representation of YHWH other than that revealed to Moses at Sinai (and of course, that known to the deuteronomistic tradition). A passage like 2 Kgs 18:4 further underscores the nation's attempt to (mis)represent YHWH in the cult, for this cryptic account might preserve a once influential tradition that identified (albeit wrongly according to deuteronomistic ideology) the bronze serpent or נחשתן as YHWH's image. The tradition notes that the bronze serpent was removed from the Solomonic temple by king Hezekiah but only after several centuries following its legitimate associations with Moses.

Another assumption underlying Deut 4:16,19 is that the astral bodies and the creatures represent deities whom YHWH long ago appointed as patron gods of the surrounding nations. As made evident in the ancient textual witnesses to Deut 32:8-9, however, the status of the astral bodies as major deities in the pantheon apparently preceded YHWH's rise to prominence in Israelite tradition. The relevant Septuagint and Qumran readings of Deut 32:8-9 describe how the Most High or the Canaanite high god, El (see Gen 14:18-22) had allotted to each of the nations one of the members of

---

[20] Note, however, that in Exod 33:16-20 Moses is only allowed to see YHWH's glory or כבוד and his back or אחור, but not his face or פנים although his hand or כף (33:22-23) and finger or אצבע (31:18) are mentioned as having been seen by Moses.

his pantheon or "sons of El" (בני אל).[21] As the language and thought shared by Deut 4:19 and 32:8-9 indicate, these underlings of El included the moon, the sun and the stars or all the host of heaven. Deut 32:9 also reveals that YHWH was once viewed as an independent, but subordinate, deity to El and was assigned by El to Jacob/Israel. In other words, the tradition suggests that YHWH was once viewed as a deity possessing equal or lower rank and power to that of the astral gods.

While the recognition of the existence of other nations' gods in Deut 4:19-20 may come as somewhat as a surprise, this passage also reveals that their subordination to YHWH in passages like 1 Kgs 22:19 is best understood as a uniquely deuteronomistic ideological strategy. By subordinating them to YHWH, their power and influence were significantly confined: "... I saw YHWH seated upon his throne with all the host of heaven standing in attendance to the right and to the left of him."[22] Perhaps their subordination was implemented to account for their persistence as independent deities in the broader religious milieu. To sum up, Deut 4:16-18 concerns the issue of making the wrong image of YHWH rather than the worship of foreign gods. Deut 4:19-20 outlaws the adoption of the sun, moon, or host of heaven as manifestations of YHWH in contradistinction to what must have stood as a widely accepted convention in non-deuteronomistic circles of Yahwism. Of particular interest is the fact that non-astral inanimate objects are not singled out for censure, just as they are not mentioned in Deuteronomy 5 and Exodus 20. The same applies in the case of mixed or composite forms; 4:16-17 only pertains to conventional anthropomorphic and theriomorphic forms. Such omissions might hint at the nature of the YHWH image that was claimed to have been seen by Moses and

---

[21] On the textual traditions underlying Deut 32:8, see now E. Tov, *Textual Criticism of the Hebrew Bible* (Minneapolis: Fortress and Assen: Van Gorcum, 1992) 269, 365. See also Ps 29:1 and 89:7.

[22] On the host of heaven, see T.N.D. Mettinger, "YHWH SABAOTH — The Heavenly King on the Cherubim Throne," in *Studies in the Period of David and Solomon and Other Essays: Papers read at the International Symposium for Biblical Studies, Tokyo, 5-7 December, 1979* (T. Ishida; Winona Lake, IN: Eisenbrauns, 1982) 109-38, esp. 123-6 and L.K. Handy, *Among the Host of Heaven: The Syro-Palestinian Pantheon as Bureaucracy* (Winona Lake, IN: Eisenbrauns, 1994) esp. 120, 158 n. 30.

the one that was considered acceptable in deuteronomistic and
priestly circles, but more on this to come.

Deut 17:3

Another text, Deut 17:3, presupposes a similar distinction between
the worship of "other gods," אלהים אחרים, (v.3a) and that of the
sun, moon and the stars, or all the host of heaven (v.3b). If the
luminaries were considered merely "other gods" in such circles,
there would have been no need to single them out as a separate
group. In the light of the preceding examination of Deut 4:19, the
mention of the luminaries in Deut 17:3b is best viewed as an
attempt to make a clear distinction between YHWH and the luminaries in their unmediated natural forms. In other words, in its ban
on depicting YHWH with astral images, this passage suggests that
YHWH astral imagery was an indigenous Israelite tradition and not
a product of foreign "syncretism." The use of the phrase "something
which I never commanded ...", אשר לא־צוּיתי in Deut 17:3 supports
the indigenous character of YHWH's astral imagery. The phrase is
used in texts related to deuteronomistic ideology as a rhetorical
means of denying YHWH's culpability in some practice that was
recognized by other biblical writers as a part of the Yahwistic cult.
The relevant traditions concerning child sacrifice illustrate this
development.

Although YHWH's non-participation in the practice of child sacrifice is characterized in Jer 7:31, 19:5, 32:35 as "... something which
I never commanded ...", other considerations suggest that this rite
was performed in at least some versions of the indigenous Yahwistic
cult. Isa 30:33 clearly implicates YHWH in the child sacrifices performed at the Tophet (as מלך–sacrifices or sacrifices dedicated to a
deity named Molek). If no such connection were intended in the
use of this cult language to describe Assyria's total destruction, then
one would have expected some disclaimer to that effect. Moreover,
Ezek 20:25-26 indicates that YHWH gave Israel over to such an
abomination, that is, if one is justified in assuming that the sacrifice
of the firstborn was intimately related to, if not the same as, the
מלך– or Molek sacrifice. If human sacrifice was part of the
Yahwistic cult (and not only of foreign cults), if daughters could be
substituted for sons in matters of primogeniture (see Num 27:1-8
and the texts from Emar and Nuzi), and if, for the biblical writers,

a deity Molek was either a member of YHWH's pantheon or
YHWH's chthonic aspect, then the argument stands for the interpretation of the sacrifices of the firstborn (which would have
included females as well as males) and those offered to Molek as
complementary perspectives on the same cult.

Furthermore, if the phrase "something which I never commanded ..." presupposes that in some circles of Israelite society the YHWH
cult had indeed engaged in the practice in question, worship of the
sun, moon and stars or all the host of heaven was undoubtedly a
Yahwistic rite and, most likely, one directed at YHWH himself. The
language shared by 17:3 and 4:19-20 likewise supports the notion
that 17:3b concerns the ancient adoption of astral imagery for
YHWH in non-deuteronomistic sectors of the Yahwistic cult. This
situation in turn, hints at the competition that existed between
various images or symbols to represent YHWH.

In sum, 17:3a concerns the worship of competing gods (were
these formerly members of the Yahwistic pantheon?), while 17:3b
addresses the adoption of inappropriate symbols of YHWH (not to
be confused with iconoclastic tendencies). Such an abbreviated listing of abominations, all of which are related to the same issue of
improper ritual, is in keeping with the immediate context, for
within the span of just three verses, 16:21-17:1, three other practices
are outlawed. In 16:21 Asherah and her pole are proscribed, in
16:22 the מצבה or stone pillar is banned, and in 17:1 defective sacrifices are forbidden in the cult. There remains one other related
strategy employed by biblical writers that merits attention owing to
the frequency with which modern investigators cite it: the prophetic and psalmic traditions that portray the idols of foreign gods
as lifeless.

"Lifeless Idols"

Within exilic prophetic circles, the images of other gods were from
time to time characterized as "lifeless" (so e.g., Isa 44:9-20; Jer 10:1-
9, 46:6-7; see also Ps 106:28; 115:4-8 and 135:16). This polemic
against "lifeless idols" has been explained as an outgrowth of the
biblical writers' lack of understanding of foreign religions. Accompanying this claim of ignorance is the implicit assumption that
those writers possessed a different "world view," i.e., a more advanced one. Such an explanation does not account for what is

known about the complex relationship that existed between idol
and deity in other ancient Near Eastern societies.[23] Irene Winter
has recently reiterated the thesis that the images of Mesopotamian
rulers as well as those of deities were subjected to a series of ritual
acts with accompanying incantations (e.g., the mouth washing
ritual, the eye opening ritual, processional rites, feeding, clothing,
enthronement, etc.) in order to be given life.[24] Similar rituals were
enacted in ancient Egypt.[25] These rites were designed to animate
the images, resulting in their status as living manifestations of the
rulers or gods. She notes that this tradition spanned two millennia,
lasting well into the mid-first millennium BCE. The point to be
underscored for our purposes is that such images were only perceived to lack a life force or power prior to the enactment of the
animation rituals (or "rituals of constitution"). Without such rituals,
they could not fulfill their intended design.

The biblical writers were familiar with such ritual traditions.
Daniel 3 describes the rituals for animation of a foreign statue while
Exod 32:1-8 might presuppose the animation of the golden calf as
actualized in the pronouncement formula, "This is your god, O
Israel" in response to the request, "Make us a god." However, as a
means of giving expression to their rejection of the efficacious
power of competing cults and of their animation rituals in particular, the biblical writers deliberately misrepresented competing religions in reaction to their potential influence.[26] In making their
claim regarding the lifelessness of idols from competing cults, some
biblical writers focused on the pre-animation stages of the process of
image producing, thereby emphasizing the image as the work of the
artisan to the neglect of the image's status as the animated creation

---

[23] It also does not adequately account for the aniconic aspects of other ancient
Near Eastern religious traditions, for which see now Mettinger, *No Graven Image*
37-197.
[24] I.J. Winter, "'Idols of the King': Royal Images as Recipients of Ritual Action
in Ancient Mesopotamia," *Journal of Ritual Studies* 6 (1992) 13-42.
[25] See A.M. Blackman, "The Rite of Opening the Mouth in Ancient Egypt and
Mesopotamia," *JEA* 10 (1923) 47-59 and S. Morenz, *Egyptian Religion* (Ithaca: Cornell University, 1973) 88, 106, 153, 155-7.
[26] So, similarly, T. Jacobsen, "The Graven Image," in *Ancient Israelite Religion:
Essays in Honor of Frank Moore Cross* (ed P.D. Miller, Jr., P.D. Hanson and S.D.
McBride; Philadelphia: Fortress 1987) 15-32.

of the priest. Such a strategy of omission (or inversion) in reference to the life of an image would have been consistent with the monolatrous outlook of the biblical writers, who elsewhere show their hand in their recognition of the existence and power of foreign deities, as 2 Kgs 3:27 indicates.[27]

It should be pointed out that two passages that are frequently cited as exemplary of the polemic of the "lifeless idol," Isa 44:9-20 and Jer 10:1-9, appear as part of a larger context in which the theme of YHWH's incomparability predominates. For the biblical writers and their early audiences, this theme might well have entailed a distinction at the level of degree, not of kind as it did in other ancient Near Eastern cultures (i.e., there is no denial of the existence of other gods); YHWH is more powerful than the other gods, an argument likewise consistent with a monolatrous outlook. Implicit in this contention is the prior assumption that the specific rituals of constitution so prevalent in Mesopotamia and Egypt were not acceptable in those cults of YHWH embraced by the biblical writers. YHWH's incomparability was therefore given further elaboration through the deliberate separation of the rituals of animation enacted in the cult described by the biblical writers from those enacted in foreign or competing Yahwistic cults.[28] In other words, not only did a legitimate image of YHWH serve as the starting point from which the biblical writers set forth their polemic against competing forms, but both his "legitimate" form and its accompanying rituals of animation were kept distinct from, and viewed as superior to, those of other cults. Two biblical traditions are highly suggestive of acceptable traditions of ritual animation: those related to the wilderness cloud or ענן, and those having to do with the cultic role of incense or קטרת.

In the stories of the nation's wilderness wanderings, the cloud descended on the tabernacle as an indicator of the deity's presence and in anticipation of the divine-human encounter (Exod 24:15-18; 33:9; 40:34-38 and see 1 Kgs 8:10-13). Its resultant effect on those

---

[27] See similarly, J. Faur, "The Biblical Idea of Idolatry," *JQR* 69 (1978) 1-15.

[28] See *ibid.*, 10-2 for a similar distinction. Faur, however, goes too far in suggesting an additional distinction between "pagan rites of inducement" used to animate an image and those rites used in ancient Israel that were based solely on YHWH's word or commandment.

enveloped in the cloud, such as Moses, underscores the lasting presence of numinous power. As such, it might point to an underlying
ritual complex and conceptual setting intimately related to the
animation of the deity's image (cf. Exod 34:29-35, but contrast
40:35). Whenever Moses exited from the cloud to proclaim YHWH's
word, his face glowed with a radiance (קרן אור) that tangibly confirmed the divine origin of his words. The narrator informs the
reader that the people could see this radiance on each occasion
when Moses approached the assembly. There was no mistake as to
its import. When Moses was not functioning in the capacity of
diviner, however, he would cover his face with a veil or mask
(מסוה). The wearing of the mask should not be interpreted as an
attempt to protect the people from the radiance of his face, since
they stand before it as he proclaims the deity's word.[29] More likely, it expresses his role as "private citizen" in contrast to his function as the deity's mediator, which he carries out when the mask is
removed.[30] Haran even suggests that while the mask might represent an attempt to conserve the divine light, the mask itself had no
cultic significance because Moses wears it only when he is not
engaged in divination.

While Haran's assessment of how the mask functions in the
narrative is on the mark, his dismissal of the use of the mask in the
cult hardly takes into account what might very well constitute the
underlying ideology of the passage.[31] In fact, Moberly might be
closer to the heart of the matter in his proposal that the resultant
shining face of Moses and the wearing of the veil when not engaged
in divination is a polemic against the use of a cultic mask to repre-

---

[29] Contra A. Jirku, "Die Gesichtsmaske des Mose," *ZDPV* 67 (1945) 43-5, who
also interpreted קרן as "sprouted horns." See also J. Sasson, "Bovine Symbolism in
the Exodus Narrative," *VT* 18 (1968) 385-7.
[30] So e.g., B. Childs, *The Book of Exodus* (OTL; Philadelphia: Westminster, 1974)
609-10, 617-9 and M. Haran, "The Shining of Moses' Face: A Case Study in Biblical and Ancient Near Eastern Iconography," in *In the Shelter of Elyon: Essays on
Ancient Palestinian Life and Literature in Honor of G.W. Ahlström* (ed. W.B. Barrick
and J.R. Spencer; JSOTSup 31; Sheffield: JSOT, 1984) 162-3.
[31] Haran, "The Shining of Moses' Face," 159-73. The facile dismissal of this and
similar proposals by J.I. Durham is unwarranted (*Exodus* [WBC 2; Waco,TX:
Word Books, 1987] 466, 468).

sent the deity.[32] This would explain the peripheral role of the mask in the narrative. It was deliberately marginalized. The narrator not only argues that the radiance was directly attached to Moses, but that this was a phenomenon that took place in the nation's distant past. Thus, for later generations, the deity's presence could not be accessed cultically via the mask that Moses had used to cover that radiance. A similar strategy of marginalization is applied to the bronze serpent or Nehushtan. While it functioned as Moses' divining rod in the wilderness, it later became an object of worship that, according to deuteronomistic tradition, had to be removed (2 Kgs 18:4). Whereas Nehushtan was tangibly expelled from the cult, the mask was simply portrayed as devoid of any cultic function it might have otherwise possessed.

The description of Moses' face, his use of the veil or mask, and the widespread use of cultic masks in the ancient Near East suggest that the mask, while of lesser import to the narrator in comparison to the light emanating from Moses' face, symbolized the deity's presence and so might have formerly functioned as a divine image in some circles of the Yahweh cult.[33] The reader should note that a portion of the deity's radiance was transmitted to Moses, making his face a measure of the shining face of YHWH (for which, see Num 6:25; Ps 80:4,8,20). In Num 27:20, that same radiance is trans-

---

[32]   R.W.L. Moberly, *At The Mountain of God: Story and Theology in Exodus 32-43* (JSOTSup 22; Sheffield: JSOT, 1983) 108, 179.

[33]   For the archaeological evidence documenting cultic masks, see the synthesis in Schroer, *In Israel gab es Bilder*, 146-54. The earlier article by G. Hoffmann and H. Gressmann remains very useful ("Teraphim, Masken, und Winkelorakel in Aegypten und Vorderasien," *ZAW* 40 [1922] 75-137). Whether or not these data are to be related to the biblical תרפים on the basis of biblical passages, as argued recently by Schroer (*In Israel gab es Bilder*, 136-46, and see 1 Sam 19:11-17), is irrelevant to the present argument. So, too is the use of cuneiform evidence to support the ancestor cult figurine interpretation of the תרפים, as recently advocated by H. Rouillard and J. Tropper, ("*TRPYM*, rituels de guérison et culte des ancêtres d'après 1 Samuel XIX 11-17 et les textes parallèles d'Assur et de Nuzi," *VT* 37 [1987] 340-61) and K. van der Toorn, ("The Nature of the Biblical Teraphim in the Light of the Cuneiform Evidence," *CBQ* 52 [1990] 203-22). Against the latter proposal, see my volume, *Israel's Beneficent Dead: Ancestor Cult and Necromancy in Ancient Israelite Religion and Tradition* (FAT 11; Tübingen: JCB Mohr [Paul Siebeck], 1994) 122-31.

ferred to Joshua.[34] Elsewhere, it is described as transferable to the king (Ps 21:6; Zech 6:13). Moreover, the veil or mask might have possessed the same residue of divine radiance as Moses' face, making it not only an object of fascination and awe, but perhaps a representation of the divine much like the images of Mesopotamian and Egytian gods.

Such an animated cultic mask would continue to maintain access to the divine presence in a form that could be animated by the enveloping cloud long after Moses had died or his radiance had paled. The total silence of biblical traditions about the duration of Moses' glow, the denial to Moses of any subsequent direct access to the cloud in the tradition in Exod 40:35, the later Jewish midrashic speculation on the diminishing splendor of Moses' shining face (e.g., Rashi) and the account of Moses' eventual death all lend support to the notion that in some circles of Israelite society there might have been a quest for perpetually maintaining the divine radiance long after it had departed from Moses. If what was once preferred was a lasting symbol of the divine presence that could be intimately associated with the theophanies at Sinai, the wilderness tabernacle, and the temple, then the tradition of Moses' mask could have readily fulfilled that requirement. The point to be underscored here is that traditions associated with the power abiding in the presence of a cloud, manifested in Moses' shining face, and preserved as a residue on his mask might presuppose the ancient observance of rituals of animation involving an enveloping vapor. While such rituals were in certain instances recognized as efficacious by the biblical writers, in instances where they were associated in older traditions with a competing image or symbol that had taken on central cultic importance such as Moses' mask, the ritual was partially suppressed, the object marginalized, and access to the animating power unmediated (clues suggesting otherwise notwithstanding).

Other traditions point to the possible role of incense in animating the cultic image. In Lev 16:2,13, the role of incense, or more

---

[34] The term הוד is used in Num 27:20, but see Hab 3:3-4, where it appears as YHWH's radiance alongside קרנים, "rays," and אור, "light". Haran attempts to distinguish between the meaning of הוד and כבוד ("The Shining of Moses' Face," 167). The former constitutes the light radiating from a figure while the latter is the thick covering that envelopes the divine image concealing it from outside.

specifically, the cloud or ענן that was created by the smoke of burning incense, is typically interpreted to have provided a screen to conceal the divine presence from the high priest who entered the הקדש or adytum.[35] However, it may also have served to compel the deity to take up residence not just in the adytum where the ark was located, but also in an image provided for that purpose. A passage like Num 16:17-20 underscores the central role of incense in the appearance of the deity (and, we would argue, the animation of the divine image). Only after the offering of incense "before YHWH" (לפני יהוה), albeit by the rebellious Korah and his cohorts, does YHWH himself appear, speak to Moses and Aaron, and, in the end, consume the rebels. The same setting perhaps underlies Ezek 8:3-11, only here the author explicitly portrays the incense as being offered in the temple by illegitimate officiants to an image other than that sanctioned by the author (see v.3: "the seat of the idol of jealousy" מושב סמל הקנאה). Be that as it may, v.4 mentions YHWH's resultant presence, suggesting that the incense ritual could nevertheless animate an illicit YHWH image![36] In other words, the biblical writers did not work on the assumption that all idols were wholly lifeless, nor were they entirely bound by issues of purification when it came to the power associated with images.

The biblical writers shared with their antagonists the belief in the efficacy of the animation ritual and it is this power, when associated with a deity other than YHWH or an image other than the one permissible in deuteronomistic and related circles, that functions as the object of their derision. Typically, the animation rituals of competing cults are portrayed as either powerless or defiling in contrast to YHWH's animating power. In fact, there are instances where the emphasis on YHWH's animating power even overrides the biblical concern for pollution. In the final analysis, both a legit-

---

[35] See J. Milgrom (*Leviticus 1-16*, 1013-5, 1028-31) for a detailed discussion of the traditional interpretive options regarding the role of incense vis-à-vis the divine presence in the cult as described in Leviticus 16.

[36] This animating power of incense might have its parallels in Mesopotamia and perhaps in Egypt. For the cultic use of incense in the ancient Near East, see the summaries in K. Nielsen, *Incense in Ancient Israel* (VTSup 38; Leiden: E.J. Brill, 1986) 3-33 and W. Zwickel, *Räucherkult und Räuchergeräte: exegetische und archäologische Studien zum Räucheropfer im Alten Testament* (OBO 97; Freiburg: Universitätsverlag and Göttingen: Vandenhoeck & Ruprecht, 1990).

imate image of YHWH and a distinctive set of animation rituals are presupposed in the biblical traditions. The biblical polemic against icons is not one constructed unequivocally or consistently along the lines of image vs. no image, coersion vs. revelation, popular religion vs. official religion or animation vs. no animation. Instead, it is often a matter of wrong vs. right image and the wrong animation ritual of coersion vs. the acceptable coercive act of animation.

Summary

Having offered a selective survey of biblical passages pertaining to the issue of aniconism, the conclusion to be drawn is that nowhere in the biblical traditions was the ban on images necessarily understood by its early readers/hearers as an unqualified prohibition against all concrete forms of the deity. Regardless whether YHWH or some other deity was in view, the legal texts prohibit only those man-made images that represent the creaturely worlds and the astral bodies as attested in their natural state. Although they undoubtedly served as images in the competing versions of Yahweh religion and in neighboring foreign religious traditions, concrete depictions of animals, humans, and the greater and lesser lights were eliminated as acceptable symbols and receptacles of YHWH by biblical writers. However, inanimate objects, floral forms, and part animal, part human composite images were not. So the question arises, is it possible to identify an acceptable image of YHWH underlying the biblical ban on competing images? While the archaeological record is most suggestive at this juncture, given the present limits of space, only one such potentially informing datum can be treated here. Since its discovery, the drawing and inscription on a pithos found in the bench room of the western structure at Iron Age Kuntillet 'Ajrud (see *Fig. 1* on page 105), has taken center stage in discussions regarding the early Israelite iconography of YHWH.

Archaeology: Yahweh and his Asherah

Ironically much of the secondary literature pertaining to the inscription and pictorial art of pithos A has sought to disassociate the inscription from the two figures in immediate proximity to and, in fact, overlapping with that inscription (hereafter figure L [left] and figure R [right]).[37] Although the relevent portion of the inscription reads, "... ברכת אתכם ליהוה שמרן ולאשרתה ..." I bless you by Yahweh of Samaria and his Asherah,"[38] the figures have been identified as two renditions of the Egyptian god Bes. Some have gone so far as to separate chronologically the inscription from the drawing, suggesting that the inscription was added subsequently to the drawings or that the drawing of figure R and the lyre player preceded that of figure L, which in turn was earlier than the inscription.[39] At the risk of rendering archaeology and art history the domain of formalist literary theory, I draw upon redaction criticism as an appropriate analogy when I suggest that for the "final redactor" of the scene on pithos A, the confluence of figures and inscription may have in fact conveyed a significant, unified field of meaning! Assuming that the parts comprising the final scene are to be related as a single unit (see below for further support), it is difficult to avoid the conclusion that by recording the inscription,

---

[37] For an extensive summary of previous scholarship, see J.M. Hadley, "Yahweh's Asherah in the Light of Recent Discovery" (Ph.D. dissertation, St. John's College, Cambridge University, 1989) and add S.A. Wiggins, *A Reassessment of "Asherah": A Study according to the Textual Sources of the First Two Millennia B.C.E.* (AOAT 235; Kevelaer: Butzon & Bercker and Neukirchen-Vluyn: Neukirchener, 1993) 171-81; J.M. Hadley, "Kuntillet 'Ajrud: Religious Centre or Desert Way Station?," *PEQ* 125 (1993) 116-24; R. North, "Yahweh's Asherah," in *To Touch the Text: Biblical and Related Studies in Honor of Joseph A. Fitzmeyer* (ed. M.P. Horgan and P.J. Kobelski; New York: Crossroad, 1989) 118-37; Mettinger, (*No graven Image*, 31 n.76) consciously avoids the study of Asherah in his work.

[38] I cannot fully enter into the debate over the significance of the suffixed ה- on אשרת except to reiterate the point that such suffixes occur on personal names in other Semitic languages (Akkadian, Ugaritic[?], Ethiopic, and Arabic), as noted years ago by G.R. Driver ("Reflections on Recent Articles," *JBL* 73 [1954] 125-36), and that the rather limited data of biblical Hebrew hardly suffices as an adequate base for dismissing the possibility that such might show up in preexilic epigraphic Hebrew. In any case, one should note the recent resurrection in the secondary literature of Wellhausen's intriguing reconstruction of just such an occurrence in Hos 14:9: "I am his Anat and his Asherah," אני ענתו ואשרתו. (YHWH here lays claim to the powers of fertility attributed to these deities).

[39] So P. Beck, "The Drawings from Horvat Teiman (Kuntillet 'Ajrud)," *Tel Aviv* 9 (1982) 3-68, esp. 36 and J.M. Hadley, "Some Drawings and Inscriptions on Two Pithoi from Kuntillet 'Ajrud," *VT* 37 (1987) 180-213, esp. 194-5.

someone consciously sought to interpret the drawings as a depiction
of Yahweh and his Asherah.[40]

The argument for successive stages of development typically in-
vokes the overlapping of the inscription with the drawing of figure
L. It suggests that the spatial boundaries of the drawings, having
been rather narrowly delimited by the first set of illustrations (the
lyre player and figure R), forced the later artist of figure L and then
the writer of the inscription to overlap their elements when they
added them. Such overlapping in the markings on pithos A could,
however, be interpreted as an intentional technique employed for
the deliberate association of figures L and R and the inscription,
since both the inscription and figure L as well as figures L and R
overlap. The Arslan Tash inscriptions likewise preserve the overlap
of icon and inscription.[41] Inscriptions superimposed over the skirt
of a royal figure are also attested in three-dimensional statuary, like
the Tell Fekheriye inscribed statue. Such a design makes explicit the
association of text and image. In the case of pithos A from Kuntillet
'Ajrud, the overlapping might also have served to create a three
dimensionality for an otherwise "one dimensional" surface drawing.

As others have pointed out, the positioning and graded size of
figures L and R reflect what has been interpreted as a typical means
of rendering joined figurines elsewhere in the Levant or the male
and female divine couple in Egyptian art.[42] Figure R is smaller and
set to the (left) side and *behind* figure L (an additional perspective
afforded only by the technique of overlapping). As for the gender

---

[40]   Whether they be passers-by or priests is, at the foundational level of religious
expression, unimportant. The dichotomies derived from biblical categories such as
official vs. popular religion or Israelite vs. Phoenician unfortunately still typify
much of the interpretive work on the data from Kuntillet 'Ajrud. In any case, did
priests not travel? Just who was capable of writing such inscriptions? Is script a
clear indicator of ethnicity for this region and time period as Hadley supposes
("Kuntillet 'Ajrud: Religious Centre," 116-7)?
[41]   Beck ("Drawings from Horvat Teiman," 46-7) cites examples where an inscription associated with a drawing (that do not necessarily overlap) do indeed coincide.
[42]   For Levantine joined figurines from the second millennium BCE, see O. Negbi,
Canaanite Gods in Metal (Tel Aviv: Institute of Archaeology, 1976) 4-7, pls. 2-5.
For the consort position in Egyptian art, see M. Gilula, "To Yahweh Shomron and
his Asherah," *Shnaton la-Miqra* 3 (1978-79) 129-37 (Hebrew; English summary xv-
xvi).

of the two figures, L would appear to have a phallus (in addition to a hanging tail?) between his legs.[43] Figure R has only what might appear to be a tail, although in the published photograph, the space between R's legs appears vacant.[44] Figure R also shows two clear breast markings. While male Bes figures appear with breast markings elsewhere, when two such figures are drawn together (or brought together) and only one possesses such markings, the distinction might be more than a matter of mere stylistic variation. In the light of the smaller size, consort positioning, and absence of a phallus on that figure over against the larger, dominant figure with a phallus, it would seem that a gender distinction was part of the deliberate design.

Nevertheless, what is most disturbing from a methodological perspective is the overly simplistic separation of the depictions and the accompanying inscriptional references by modern commentators solely on the basis of what has been deemed as the presence of Bes iconography. The argument goes something like this. The drawings are those of Bes figures; therefore, they cannot represent Yahweh and his Asherah. Firstly, this overlooks the fluidity that can typify the use of a given iconographic element or combination of elements for representing distinct deities. Egyptian and Mesopotamian tradition are quite clear on the matter that an image did not so much exclusively embody the physical appearance of a particular deity as it did symbolize aspects of the function and character of a god. This is borne out by the general similarity of form evident among divine images accompanied by the presence of particular accoutrements that permits the identification of a specific deity.

This state of affairs particularly applies in the case of Bes iconography. In a study published twenty years ago, Veronica Wilson began her lengthy study of "Bes" iconography (her quotes) by highlighting the caution that ought to attend the direct identification of

---

[43] Note that Bes figures appear with both phallus and tail; see V. Wilson, "The Iconography of Bes with Particular Reference to the Cypriot Evidence," *Levant* 7 (1975) 79 (Figs. 1.1, 1.2, 1.3.); V. Dasen, *Dwarfs in Ancient Egypt and Greece* (Oxford: Clarendon, 1993) 79 (Fig. 6.1).

[44] So also M. Coogan, "Canaanite Origins and Lineage: Reflections on the Religion of Ancient Israel," in *Ancient Israelite Religion: Essays in Honor of Frank Moore Cross* (ed. P.D. Miller, Jr., P.D. Hanson, and S.D. McBride; Philadelphia: Fortress, 1987) 115-24, esp. 123 n. 24.

Egyptian dwarf-god imagery and the god Bes. The sheer number of
dwarf gods in Egypt and elsewhere in the ancient Near East pre-
cludes any certainty in the matter. In those regions outside of Egypt
where dwarf-god iconography has been identified, the absence of
inscriptional correlation only serves to underscore further the need
for circumspection. She also demonstrated, through a detailed
chronological analysis of the so-called Bes imagery outside Egypt,
the high degree of fluidity and interchange of elements that characterized the development of dwarf-god iconography. She cited several
examples of the intermixing of dwarf-god iconography with that
characteristic of gods, demons, and heroes from indigenous regional
cultures. In a handful of instances, the (con)fusion or transformation
involving Bes iconography and the iconography of non-Egyptian
gods, demons, and heroes was so extensive that Wilson concluded
that Bes could (and did) assimilate the iconography of a west Asiatic
god like Baal or that of a Mesopotamian god like Humbaba![45]

With these qualification set forth, one must appoach the drawings on pithos A from Kuntillet 'Ajrud with vigilance. Elements
that can be considered characteristic of "Bes" iconography are
indeed present in the drawings: grotesque features, a frontal view,
bandy legs, exposed nipples (only in one case), the feathered crown
(only in the other case), the skirt(?), the tail (of a lion or leopard
skin?) hanging between the legs, musical associations (assuming that
a lyre player sits in the background) and perhaps "Bes" animal
mastery. However, other "Bes" elements such as the square-cut
beard, the hands resting on the thighs, the shaggy-haired mane,
dwarflike dimensions (e.g., short neck, broad body, splayed belly
and short legs), squatting position, and lion or leopard skin are
missing. In fact, several interpreters see in these drawings a strong
tendency toward bovine rather than leonine imagery.[46] Moreover,

---

[45] Wilson, "Iconography of Bes," 77-103. For many of these same qualifications,
see J. Romano, ("The Bes-image in Pharaonic Egypt." [2 vols.; Ph.D. dissertation,
New York University, 1989] 212-21) and Dasen (*Dwarfs*, 55-83).

[46] So, e.g., P.K. McCarter, Jr. ("Aspects of the Religion of the Israelite Monarchy:
Biblical and Epigraphic Data," in *Ancient Israelite Religion: Essays in Honor of
Frank Moore Cross* [ed. P.D. Miller, Jr., P.D. Hanson, and S.D. McBride; Philadelphia: Fortress, 1987] 146-9), who sees in the taller figure a human torso, a bovine
face with large horns, bovine hooves and a tail hanging behind a short skirt. He
concludes, "The god is probably Yahweh, depicted with some of the features of a

several innovations typical of "Bes" iconography in Phoenician and Syrian settings are lacking. The figures in question are not fully clothed,[47] and the human guise, the four wings, the snake breathing, and the crossing of the arms over the chest that are so characteristic of eastern "Bes" imagery are nowhere portrayed at Kuntillet 'Ajrud. These factors led Pirhiya Beck, the leading advocate of the Bes identity of the two figures, to admit in the end that these figures were "unlike anything known so far in the Levant."[48]

In an article published in 1976, William Culican anticipated the present debate over the presence and significance of Bes imagery at Kuntillet 'Ajrud. He argued that the Phoenicians had a demonic imagery of their own that predated the widespread adoption of Bes imagery in the Levant during the Achaemenid period. He also noted on the basis of later Hellenized forms that what he identified as a Phoenician horned demon could fuse with Bes imagery.[49] This demon has a coarse wrinkled face or beard, a broad nose, oblique eyes, a wide mouth and animal ears and horns and is well-attested in the Levant during the Iron Age. Each of these elements has its corresponding counterpart in the drawings from Kuntillet 'Ajrud. In the light of Culican's iconographic evidence for Phoenician influence in Judah during the 7th century BCE, perhaps it was the Phoenician horned demon that dramatically informed the drawing

---

bull; he is, therefore, the 'young bull of Samaria' (עגל שמרון) of Hos 8:6. The goddess, then, is Yahweh's consort" (147). The overlapping of figure L with the cow as illustrated in the drawing might constitute further evidence for the bovine connection of the two figures R and L.

[47] On the Megiddo ivories, Bes is fully clothed, with only one exception (fig. 2.3 in Wilson, "Iconography of Bes," 84).

[48] Beck, "Drawings from Horvat Teiman," 30. She also recognized the strong likelihood that the artists at Kuntillet 'Ajrud were familiar with the iconography of Phoenicia, north Syria and Arabia. The attempt by J. Hadley to strengthen Beck's iconographic analysis in favor of Bes figures by arguing for a crude dwarfism, by attributing a leonine appearance to the nose and ears, and by aligning the non-feathered crown of figure L with those of Bes figures from much later periods is unconvincing ("Some Drawings and Inscriptions," 180-209, esp. 190-1).

[49] W. Culican, "Phoenician Demons," JNES 35 (1976) 21-4.

of YHWH preserved at Kuntillet 'Ajrud rather than Egyption "Bes"
or dwarf-god imagery.[50]

Conclusion

This exploration into the world of ancient Israelite aniconism has
sought to illustrate the range of issues that remain to be addressed
in future treatments. The aniconism of the biblical traditions is no
iconoclastic cult at all because it leaves open the question of the
acceptable image of YHWH. Certain traditions might, in fact, hint at
the character of that image. While inanimate objects, floral or veg-
etal images or composite forms are the most likely candidates for
the acceptable YHWH image of biblical traditions, I have been able
to explore only one avenue here, the drawing of Yahweh and his
Asherah on pithos A from Kuntillet 'Ajrud.

The iconographic tradition attested at 7th-century Kuntillet
'Ajrud might be representative of what was deemed appropriate
imaging of YHWH in certain Israelite sectors of society with its
analogies in biblical traditions: namely, a composite form consisting
of human and animal elements, a so-called *Mischwesen*. This stands
in spite of the efforts to dismiss the potential importance of the
Kuntillet 'Ajrud drawings by labelling the accompanying inscriptions as graffiti or the drawings as crude. Unlike modern graffiti,
that of ancient times might be representative of the wider religious
Zeitgeist. In any case, the composite character of the biblical YHWH
image might find confirmation in the similar nature of the
cherubim. They were viewed as legitimate forms of religious
iconography and are depicted in the narrative traditions as integral
elements in the architecture of the tabernacle and its successor, the
temple.

---

[50] For evidence of Phoenician influence on Judahite iconographic traditions of the
preexilic period, see the contributions in *Studies in the Iconography of Northwest
Semitic Inscribed Seals* (ed. B. Sass and C. Uehlinger; OBO 125; Freiburg: Univer-
sitäts-Verlag and Göttingen: Vandenhoeck & Ruprecht, 1993). Of course, what is
specifically Phoenician in Phoenician iconography also remains a crux, as recently
acknowledged by Uehlinger ("Northwest Semitic Inscribed Seals, Iconography and
Syro-Palestinian Religions of Iron Age II: Some Afterthoughts and Conclusions,"
ibid., 267).

Conceptually speaking, composite forms communicate something
of the complex nature of a deity in a way that is not possible for
unmixed forms. While the animal attributes conveyed the otherness
of the god, its anthropomorphic aspects expressed the sameness of
the god. When combined, however, they gave the impression that
the god was of a wholly different order than humanity. Nevertheless, male high gods were typically portrayed in Levantine tradition
in one of three ways: as a seated old man with a beard, as a standing young man with a club in his raised hand, or as a bull. The
composite image often represented numina of the lower stations,
such as demons or monsters.[51] When applied to the specific case of
the drawings from Kuntillet 'Ajrud, the composite image might
point to Yahweh's former status as a lesser numen, a monster
whose imagery was preserved long after he rose to higher rank.[52]
His monster status might also highlight his "outsider" origins viv-à-
vis the local Levantine high gods as well as his propensity to inter-
vene supernaturally in human affairs, that is, if the broader
Mesopotamian monster traditions have any contribution to make
on this point.

While some interpreters have acknowledged that the biblical
writers recognized a legitimate iconography associated with YHWH,
such as the cherubim or the ark, the throne or footstool of the
deity, no one to my knowledge has suggested that the biblical
writers recognized and embraced a cultic image of YHWH that was
a *Mischwesen* or a composite made up of anthropomorphic and
theriomorphic elements along the lines of the figures attested at
Kuntillet 'Ajrud. Instead, interpreters usually view the "official cult"
as aniconic and the use of such images as a popular practice and cite
the traditions that portray the use of the cherubim as mere votive
images serving as supplicants before YHWH. Why then the avoidance, if not total silence in biblical tradition, as to the details of
YHWH's cultic image?

---

[51] For a detailed treatment of the use of the composite image in Mesopotamian
tradition for depicting monsters, see F.A.M. Wiggerman, *Mesopotamian Protective
Spirits* (Groningen: Styx & PP, 1992) 143-64 and the earlier article by A. Green,
"Beneficent Spirits and Malevolent Demons," *Visible Religion* 3 (1984) 80-105.
[52] See Dasen, *Dwarfs* 59, 63-7, for a similar monstrous or demonic origin for Bes
as suggested in part by Bes' composite form.

With the capture of the animated image by the invading Babylonians and the departure of the deity, the image "experienced" a loss of power.[53] Over the course of time, a full account of the cultic image had been lost to memory or suppressed in reaction to the dramatic appearance of alternative YHWH forms such as theriomorphic (e.g., ophidian) and physiomorphic forms (i.e., the astral bodies). This is not an aniconism or iconoclasm in the full sense of the term as it more closely approximates the diviner's practice of holding fast the words and formulae of incantations in order to maintain sole proprietorship over access to the divine. Just as the proper rituals and incantations were crucial for unmitigated access to a deity (cf. again Num 16:17-20, Ezek 8:3-11), so it was in the case of the knowledge of the deity's concrete form. The full details of the divine image became the exclusive prerogative of the deuteronomistic priesty classes. As I have attempted to demonstrate, many of these developments are only hinted at in the traditions. Owing to their allusive character, these traditions generated a great deal of speculation among later Jewish and Christian writers as well as among the wider Greek and Roman authorities.[54] In fact, the

---

[53] For a similar series of developments surrounding the capture of divine statues in contemporary Babylonia itself, see the summary by Hallo ("Cult Statue," 12-4). In one instance, a statue of Shamash was captured by Sutians, and the sun-disk was substituted in its place. However, when a facsimile of the statue was constructed much later based on a model of the original that was rediscovered, the sun-disk was replaced and a clear preference for the original statue was given expression.

[54] Needless to say, the attempt to make the biblical ban and tendencies, which supposedly were observed by those who produced the Judahite glyptic of the 7th and 6th centuries BCE, convergent with the rise of the name theology must be reassessed. Uehlinger's nonreligious explanations for the rise of aniconic glyptic seem cogent and eliminate the need to offer a "synergy" of religious and nonreligious motivations. The rise of name theology does not necessitate the prior development of aniconism in ancient Israel, or more specifically, in biblical traditions, contra Uehlinger ("Northwest Semitic Seals: Afterthoughts," 257-88). Moreover, the conclusion of Keel and Uehlinger that there existed no intrinsic Yahweh iconography in Israel and Judah is premature (*Göttinnen, Götter und Gottessymbole: neue Erkentnisse zur Religionsgeschichte Kanaans und Israels aufgrund bislang unerschlossener ikonographischer Quellen* [QD 134; Freiburg: Herder, 1992] 472). It is worth noting, however, that on the basis of iconography, they do conclude that other gods were symbolized (and worshipped) in preexilic Israel and Judah. This contradicts the conclusion often reached by others on the basis of analyses of theophoric names that other gods were not symbolized or worshipped in these regions.

place one should look for the "origins of biblical iconoclasm" is in these postand extrabiblical contexts!

Fig. 1   Inscription and Drawing from Pithos A, Kuntillet ʿAjrud (after P. Beck, *Tel Aviv* 9 [1992] 28).

The Intellectual Matrix of Early Biblical Narrative
Inclusive Monotheism in Persian Period Palestine
Thomas L. Thompson

In John Van Seters' 1992 publication, *Prologue to History*, he continues his reevaluation of Wellhausen's documentary hypothesis by attempting to define the work of J as a blend of historiographical and antiquarian interests that derives from Greek historiography in a context in the Jewish diaspora in Babylon during the exilic period.[1] Van Seters resolutely and convincingly establishes the thesis that the Yahwistic tradition is a product of the reemergence of Israel rather than of its "Golden Age."[2] The completion of this huge project and Van Seters' rejection of any possible context for the pentateuchal tradition within the time periods reflected in Genesis–II Kings is unequivocally a major achievement.

The circularity of argument, however, is not entirely broken. On internal grounds alone, this core of the Pentateuch postdates any biblical view of history the literature projects. Van Seters presents an argument for the dating of J and the Pentateuch that rests finally on his assumption that there is a historical exilic period to which he assigns the tradition, but such a period is unknown apart from the tradition. Van Seters' approach begins from within the literature, and, assuming the rationalistic paraphrase of Israel's history that our field has created for him, asks only after the earliest appropriate date for the tradition within that paraphrase that has been known as the history of Israel. The appropriateness of the date is then seen to be confirmed by the citation of analogous Greek and

---

[1] J. Van Seters, *Prologue to History: The Yahwist as Historian* (Louisville: Westminster and John Knox, 1992).
[2] *Contra* T.L. Thompson, "A New Attempt to Date the Patriarchal Narratives," *JAOS* 98 (1978) 76-84.

Babylonian texts drawn from literature that is ideologically and formally comparable.

Similar arguments might be made to epitomize the earliest possible intellectual world appropriate for the tradition to identify as historical context. So might be seen the Persian period, with a construction of a temple in Jerusalem and the consolidation of a self-conscious formation of a people understanding themselves as the remnant of Israel that that construction would have initiated.[3] Such arguments, however, do not establish an independent historical context for the literature so much as they point to literary and intellectual worldviews, which are not adequate for dating the traditions historically. At most they provide earliest possible dates. Both the exilic period and the construction of the second temple under Ezra and Nehemiah are not periods or events known from independent evidence. They are known as tradition, not history, and as such are not entirely viable as historical contexts. It is very important to allow evidence to dominate discussions over against the rational coherence of an imaginary past.

In this question there is no luxury of the higher road of biblical criticism. We are compelled to begin, not from theory, but from the foundation of what is known historically about the tradition; that is, from the contexts in which the traditions have been handed down. Only from such secure later contexts can the earlier periods that are implicitly more speculative be tolerably entered. Arguments based on literary and intellectual contexts are not destroyed by this discussion. It is only the historical anchors and the security of what is only seemingly known that are cut loose. As N.P. Lemche argued so well in a recent programmatic article, it is only the perception of a postexilic world that is gained from the literary world of the Bible that marks both this and the "exile" as distinctive periods in which

---

[3] T.L. Thompson, *Early History of the Israelite People: From the Written and Archaeological Sources* (Leiden: Brill, 1992) 415–23.

to find a home for the Old Testament.[4] Such perceptions do not render historical context.

The LXX version of the Old Testament, which can be reasonably dated to the 2nd century BC or later, can only to a limited extent be described as a translation of the Hebrew Bible. Many of its traditions are wholly independent of the Hebrew Bible; many originated in Greek and yet others might be plausibly described as variant traditions of the extant Hebrew tradition, which itself betrays many characteristics of the Hellenistic period.

In the LXX text of 2 Mac 2:14, there is an interesting reference to a collection of writings, understood as traditional, that the writer of 2 Maccabees describes as texts that had survived the Maccabean wars. Whether this is a plausible and accurate depiction of a known library or is ideologically oriented rhetoric attempting to present the collection as surviving remnants of very ancient tradition is uncertain. The offer to lend books from the collection, while conceivably a fictitious claim of historicity, nevertheless asserts the significance of "library" as meaningful and essential to the ideology fundamental to tradition collection. The additional reference in 2 Maccabees to the library of Nehemiah that was lost in the distant past is a much more potent ideological concept. While perhaps only a reference to a legend, it suggests that the author knows of no earlier collection of written tradition that survived the Maccabean wars but still sees Nehemiah as meaningful in the formation of national tradition. In 2 Maccabees 4, which is dedicated to a recounting of the survival of past tradition, neither the traditions of Ezra's lawgiving nor that of Nehemiah's library are accessible to the writer of 2 Mac 2:14; only, it is claimed, the efforts by Judas Maccabeus to preserve a past that is now fragmented. In itself, this text offers a serious argument against understanding the final redaction of the Hebrew Bible as a whole significantly prior to the second half of the 2nd century BC.

---

[4]   N.P. Lemche, "Det Gamle Testamente som en hellenistisk bog," *DTT* 55 (1992) 81–101; updated English revision in "The Old Testament — A Hellenistic Book?," *SJOT* 7 (1993) 163–93. This article underscores what is known about the textual evidence of the Old Testament and particularly, its character as a product of the Hellenistic period.

Moreover, the Hebrew Bible underwent a considerable and integral redaction some time after the so-called rededication of the Jerusalem temple in 164 BC. This orientation of the Massoretic text to the late temple has been known for more than a century and needs no further discussion here,[5] except to point out that this revision of tradition substantially affects access to earlier strata of the tradition.

The legends of Ezra and Nehemiah are centered in the national ideology of the temple in Jerusalem, a theology that has its first and most clearly secure context in the events surrounding the efforts by Antiochus IV to drive a wedge between the potentially pro-Ptolemaic Jews of Jerusalem and the Jews of Alexandria. His conflict with the Ptolemies for the control of Palestine cast him in the role of enemy particularly among the most hellenized portion of the population of Jerusalem and Yehud. The conflict led him increasingly into more insistent demands that the Jewish form of Hellenism in Jerusalem now be led from Antioch, the new seat of political power, rather than from Alexandria, as it had been. In doing this, he was seen as attacking not only Jerusalem's religious and intellectual leadership but some of Jerusalem's most cherished customs as well. The highly charged intellectual movement of nationalism that ensued supported and substantially altered the character of the originally reactionary, pro-Ptolemaic Maccabean revolt. The intellectual and cultural character of this nationalism was institutionalized in the rededication of the temple, the event that structures internal Massoretic chronology. This renders an *a quo*, not an *ad quem* dating for the extant tradition. It is in the historical context of the Maccabean state that Palestine clearly possesses for the first time both the independent state structures and the national consciousness necessary for the development of a library and of a coherent collection of tradition so marked by self-conscious ethnicity.[6] Unlike

---

[5]   See T. L. Thompson, *The Historicity of the Patriarchal Narratives: The Quest for the Historical Abraham* (BZAW 133; Berlin: Walter de Gruyter, 1974) 4-15.

[6]   This is not a situation involving government administrative archives that might have been expected to exist in Jerusalem under the Persian empire or under any earlier political state, but specifically a collection of national tradition. See further on this E. Posner, *Archives in the Ancient World* (Cambridge: Harvard University, 1972) and more recently, K.A.D. Smelik, *Converting the Past: Studies in Ancient Israelite and Moabite Historiography* (OTS 28; Leiden: Brill, 1992).

earlier periods in Palestine, there is every reason to believe that the Hellenistic period was immensely creative and literate. The development of tradition, an aspect of intellectual history, requires no broad chronological spectrum. It is both synchronic and diachronic.

When the traditions are examined for an understanding of the formation of tradition, the earliest possible context for the onset of the process of collection must be placed with the formation of the Jewish people and their identification of themselves as "Israel." Van Seters' discussion has clearly shown that the issue of Greek influence in the collective tradition need not necessarily lock in a date in the Hellenistic period. But it also does not spring the collection from it. The understanding of such perceptions as "Greek" reflects more a comparison of Greek literature with an ancient Near Eastern worldview that has only been assumed of the tradition in the past than a comparison with any large body of contemporary literature. Arguments of derivation are fragile and tendentious. *Palestine*, on the Mediterranean fringe of the Persian world, comes into contact with the Aegean world at least from the onset of hostilities between the Greek city states and *Persia*. What is typically defined as Greek thought might far better be understood as a specific regionalization of intellectual understanding that reflected increasingly shared perceptions of reality across the entire ancient world, with each area developing its own literature that was geographically and linguistically particular: in far-off India as in Egypt, in Babylon as in Syria-Palestine, in Old Persia and in Anatolia. The Hebrew expressions are not themselves intrinsically Greek. They reflect only a comparable or shared worldview.

For purposes of clarity, I would recommend that the discussion be cast in terms of three discrete categories: 1) traditions and fragments of traditions that reflect a viable intellectual context independent of and logically prior to the process of tradition collection, and which can verifiably be traced to earlier periods or which reflect an origin in collected tradition; 2) traditions and the composites of collected traditions that either reflect an originating worldview expressive of an emerging form of universalist and inclusive monotheism or which recast the traditions collected in terms of such a pluralistic worldview; and 3) those traditions and aspects of the tradition that, in reaction to syncretism, reject tolerance of alternative religious expressions in favor of a universalist but exclusive monotheism.

Thus, to understand the chronological spectrum of the texts an analysis of received tradition should be followed that highlights what might be recognized as specific paradigmatic transvaluations: definable impulses to tradition building, which might then be associated as definable intellectual points of departure. Axiomatic to this approach is the assumption that the tradition had been formed into a coherent literary whole that created Israel's self-identity under the influence of a fluid and changing *Zeitgeist* and through the efforts of teachers and their associates. Those responsible for the tradition are called philosophers by the Greeks and Josephus and צדיקים by the Jews.

The three categories:

1) *Surviving fragments from the past:* Some of the collected materials can be shown to preserve or reflect original contexts that can be understood only in terms of very early periods, even as early as the Assyrian period. Some of the best candidates preserving such early references are parts of the Ishmael traditions, the Shem and Ham genealogies, the Bileam legend and the Israelite dynastic lists from Omri on, as well as aspects of the destruction accounts of Samaria and Jerusalem. There are many more, and we need to be open to even earlier possibilities, however unlikely this may seem. Such confirmable elements of historicity in the traditions clearly support the understanding that they reflect a representation of the past that is not wholly fictive. The use of such materials and remnants of the past, however, must proceed with great caution. Both their fragmentary character and their displacement from their original contexts prevent a reconstruction of their original significance and an identification of their original contexts with their later contexts, where they become part of meaningful tradition.

2) *The world view of inclusive monotheism:* Concepts and literary works commonly thought to be exilic and postexilic have referents recognized as adhering to the defining ideology of Exile — whatever the exile's actual historicity. In such literature, the exile is presented first of all as an event of the mind within the intellectual world of early Judaism and functions as a literary matrix for large portions of the Bible. This is true whatever events, if any, actually occurred that might be regarded as a "return." What are commonly designated as exilic and postexilic texts, as well as some of the larger composite collections of the Old Testament, whether the Septuagint

or the later Massoretic collection called the Hebrew Bible, all flow from this intellectual matrix and must, therefore, be chronologically subsequent. The relationship between purported event and perceived event is fragile and complex. So-called exilic and postexilic texts are datable only in terms of a relative chronology. They were created no earlier than the onset of the ideology of exile. This central concept, "exile," is quite distinct from historical context and is rather a multifaceted and very comprehensive interpretation of tradition, both living and shattered.

The specific body of literature that is known as wisdom literature relates to the collections of Torah and Prophets as hermeneutics does to tradition. That is, specific collections of writings such as Proverbs, Qohelet and Job provide an entry into the intellectual visions that have cast the collections that come as Torah and Prophets. In their explicitly self-conscious understandings as works of the intelligentsia about tradition, their visions reflect the intellectual transvaluation that the concept of exile brings to the traditions. It is through the inclusive monotheistic and universalistic lenses of such a text as 2 Isaiah that the immediate and inescapable corollary is drawn that 2 Isaiah and comparable texts are logically prior to the perception and inclusion of such a text as 1 Isaiah within the tradition. This is because they provide meaning for the composite tradition. It needs to be argued that in such literary productions as Job, Qohelet and 2 Isaiah an intellectual ferment is reflected that is fully analogous to what occurred in the Aegean in the writings of a Plato or a Sophocles. This is glimpsed only piecemeal and incompletely in cuneiform literature: for example, in the dedications in the temple of Sin in Harran and in the kind of Persian propaganda reflected in the Cyrus cylinder; in Aramaic texts, from those containing early references to בעל שמם to the Elephantine letters; and in Hebrew citations from real or imagined Persian documents in 2 Chronicles, Ezra and Nehemiah. All of these texts seem marked by a philosophical and theological perception that is substantially more than the commonplace understanding of much ancient Near Eastern literature that might legitimately be understood as particularized and polytheistic. From at least the twilight of the Assyrian empire, the intellectual perception of reality had been forced into a defining crisis, created by the growing awareness of the growing irrelevance of past tradition. This crisis was eventually resolved in the course of the late Persian and early Hellenistic periods in a variety of very specific and unique ways across the immense geographical spectrum of the ancient world. In the Aegean, the intelligentsia rejected the gods and the cosmology of Homer and Hesiod as no longer viable — so clearly reflected in the distinctions by the early historians that separated legend from research, in Plato's portrayal of the ideal philosopher as a servant of reflection, and even in the hermeneutics of mockery found among the Greek playwrights. This awareness of the twilight of the gods of tradition is already apparent in forms of religious syncretism in the Assyrian period.

Not just the Greeks, but the East also had to deal with gods of clay feet. In Asia, this intellectual crisis was resolved in the clear distinction between the reality of spirit, the true abode of the divine, and the realities of the human world, including the gods of human making, which are intrinsically partial and increasingly understood as fallacious, reflective of the real world of spirit through misdirection. In the Semitic world, the crisis of tradition was resolved in a contrast between the perceived and contingent, limited human perceptions of reality, over against those unperceivable and ineffable qualities of spirit that were divine reality. Traditional understanding and religion were not so much false as human. Traditions needed not to be rejected, only reinterpreted. Older traditions of the gods that were interpretable as transcendent, both those reflecting transregional manifestations and images of the heavenly court and those that portrayed the divine realm as far removed from humanity and its religious preoccupations, were thrown into a polarized contrast to what was perceived as the limitations of human activity with its prolific manufacturing of gods. The latter approach is now understood as fragile and the result of incomplete efforts to express a reality that was intrinsically transitory in humans: the reality of spirit and of life.

Such ideas were still very much alive in the middle of the Hellenistic period and they did not run their course for many additional centuries. In Palestine they already had a potentially long history beginning at least from the efforts of the imperial Persian administration to expand centralized rule in forms of indigenous home rule. The military and administrative conception of the emperor as king of kings corresponded with Persian religious ideology of the transcendent god of spirit, Ahura Mazda.[7] In addition, this concept corresponded with the perceptions of the ultimately divine as understood among conquered peoples in the distinct regions of the empire, whether as Marduk of Babylon, Sin of Harran, Baal Shamem of Syria, or their counterparts, the elohe shamayim of Palestine or the Yahu/Elohaya of Elephantine. The intellectual associations involved in the identification of these linguistic referents to the divine as spiritual reality are fundamental issues of translation. Intrinsic to the evocation of such a perception of the divine is lack of specificity. The divine is no longer perceived equivocally in terms of gods needing names — it is only the human world that needs the defining quality of names. Rather, the existence of expressions that located the divine in heavenly, life-giving spirit in terms of specific, regionally-defined names confirms the validity of provincial traditions and gives them viability as specifically human expressions about the ultimately one and true divine spirit. The use of Elohaya Shamayim by the Persian administration to designate the overlord of the empire when addressing its subjects in Elephantine is not simply a manipulative move. Nor does it arise from a difference in the perception of reality. Rather, it reflects a world view that distinguishes relative perceptions that are contingent geographically and religiously from an assertion of ultimate reality that is beyond human expression, perception and understanding.[8] The divine title reflects a perception that is grounded in the religious traditions of a specific past.

This solution of the crisis of past tradition is resolved in Asia within a conceptual framework that can be epitomized in the term "inclusive monotheism." Its initial development can be observed already during the Persian empire. In contrast to the Greek histor-

---

[7]   M. Boyce, "Persian Religion in the Achaemenid Age," *The Cambridge History of Judaism* (ed. W.D. Davies and L. Finkelstein; 3 volumes; Cambridge: Cambridge University, 1985) 1.279-307; also see M. Smith, "Jewish Religious Life in the Persian Period," *The Cambridge History of Judaism*, 1.219–78. The Persian religious ideology moved in a dualistic direction (see below, note 17) while much of the Semitic world eventually subordinated the different powers of evil in the interests of an increasingly exclusive monotheism (in both Judaism and Islam).

[8]   For this discussion and for many issues of this paper I am indebted to the insight and observations of my former student, T. Bolin, who completinged his doctoral dissertation at Marquette University in 1995 (esp. below, note 15).

ians, philosophers and playwrights, the intellectuals of Asia chose not to reject but to affirm the traditions of the past as expressions of true reality that previously had only been perceived darkly in limited human terms. This defining concept of inclusive monotheism is one that finds its home in efforts to maintain polytheistic and henotheistic conceptions in universalistic terms. Inclusive monotheism is not primarily antagonistic toward polytheism; instead, it interprets and restructures it.

In biblical tradition such a perception is particularly clear in what most scholars would recognize as late, i.e. Hellenistic texts. In the citation of the Cyrus decree in Ezra 1:1-3, in contrast to the less nuanced citation in 2 Chronicles, אלהי השמים, identified with יהוה, the ancient god of the state of Israel, charges Cyrus to reestablish his people by building a temple dedicated to יהוה of Israel, who is God in Jerusalem of Judah.[9] In this text, the author of Ezra 1 expresses an understanding of the people of the province of יהד not only as the legitimate successors of the neglected or forgotten Yahweh traditions of ancient Israel (that is, Samaria) but also identifies those traditions as traditions about God; that is, אלהי השמים.

Similarly, at the core of the origin traditions of the Pentateuch lies an editorial hand that not only collects but recasts old traditions and reinterprets them as a whole: Exodus 3 and Exodus 6.[10] These

---

[9]   Contra P. Davies (*In Search of 'Ancient Israel'* [JSOTSup 148; Sheffield: JSOT Press, 1992]), Yahweh God of Israel is transposed to Judah and Jerusalem by the Persians! This is against Davies' statement, "And given the centrality of Judah in the biblical literature, there can hardly be any doubt that this is where we need to look for the origin of the literary Israel. That may be one of the few uncontroversial conclusions of this book" (78). However, Davies' statement reflects a thesis that presupposes the historicity of the divided monarchy, as indicated by his reference to the choice between Israel and Judah. The best place to look for the origin of the literary Israel is in the *decision* to build a temple to Yahweh, the God of Israel in Jerusalem, and this decision was made in the context of the Persian administration, (not that of a post-temple period in Jerusalem,) which developed the literary Israel.

[10]   I am uncertain whether the prophetic foreshadowing of the prophets of doom in Exod 23:20-25 is intrinsic to or subsequent to the revisions of Exodus 3 and 6. It unquestionably recasts the future, whether of the wilderness wanderings or of Israel in the land, in terms familiar from the prophetic collections. As meaningful traditions, prophecies of doom logically presuppose the theology of repentance and forgiveness of a saved remnant.

two passages of Exodus present variant theophanies. In terms of story and plot they perform comparable functions: identifying the deity and linking the Moses of the theophany with the Moses of the Exodus. In terms of tradition collection, however, these very distinct episodes perform not only similar but complimentary tasks, to be alienated from each other only by presuppositions of a documentary sort,[11] where issues of theology and ideology play a more dominant role than those of an intellectual coherence that is endemic to tradition building. In Exodus 3, Moses goes to the mountain of Elohim. There he experiences a theophany, expressive of divine ineffability: a bush burning but not burning up. As a narrative, the story encounters great difficulties because it has a messenger of יהוה appearing to Moses as well as יהוה speaking to him directly. The narrative as such loses meaningful plot coherence, unless in this composite theophany of tradition the three numina, אלהים, מלאך יהוה and יהוה are understood to be identical:[12] the one god

---

[11]   The central objection that I have to the documentary hypothesis is that it has encouraged the avoidance of a coherent reading by marking the text as a whole as an unintended accident of the history of composition. Ultimately, it excuses the dissonance and incoherence of the text by asserting that the various sources of the tradition had already been accepted as revered sacred traditions by the time they were brought together and hence, were unchangeable by the pedantic redactors. Originality belonged to the source compositions, not to the creators and transmitters of the tradition qua tradition. Unfortunately, this ignores the significance of the hundreds of known and observable changes that were made deliberately in the narratives in order to create links of transition from Genesis 1 to the closure of Deuteronomy.

[12]   This is not a compositional observation. The documentary hypothesis begins with the reasonable and correct observation that the differences in divine names and titles — for example, יהוה אלהים, אלהים, אל שדי, אל קנא, אל עולם, יהוה, אלהים האבות, יהוה אלהי ישראל, אל אלהי ישראל, and many others make it extremely difficult to read these narratives as cut from the same cloth. They rather imply originating contexts that are radically distinct. Even in terms of plot, the יהוה stories of Genesis can hardly be understood as consonant with the narrative of Exodus 6 where it is said that יהוה first revealed his name; he had already done so to Moses in the wilderness. Nevertheless, the division of the tradition into sources — those that have יהוה as their God and those that have אלהים — does not really resolve the problems of the text, but only puts them off to a later stage of the tradition. Whether at an early or later stage of the tradition's formation into a coherent whole, it still needs to be asked how it came about that יהוה could be understood — at the level of the texts themselves — as אלהים and the other Els,

of Israel. And indeed, this is the very function of the episode as meaningful tradition. The deity identifies himself: "I am the אלהים of your father, the אלהים of Abraham, the אלהים of Isaac, and the אלהים of Jacob." Notice in this narration, that however the name יהוה is used, the referent is Elohim, and יהוה is his name, now identified with the ancestral deities of the patriarchs. However philosophically the pun on Exod 3:14 is understood — a pun whose degree of sophistication is not foreign to the Hellenistic period — אלהים is identified with the name of the traditional deity of Palestine, יהוה, who in turn is identified with the ancestral gods of the patriarchs. Not only does this identification establish Exodus as the interpretive matrix of Genesis, but it establishes Elohim as the ultimate referent of the Exodus tradition. In this matrix, the mountain of אלהים becomes the geographical interpretive center, regardless of the range of names for the divine mountain in various collected traditions, i.e. Horeb, Sinai or Kadesh. The Pentateuch becomes a narrative kaleidoscope, reflecting ultimate reality in the variability of tradition, understood in the intrinsically variable human contingency of the past. While Exodus 3 concentrates on identifying the ancestral deities of the patriarchs with the transcendent, recreated with its play on the name יהוה, Exodus 6 reflects a greater ambition. It expands the philosophical implications of Exodus 3. Not only is it implicit that יהוה is אלהים, who is to be equated with the gods of the patriarchs, but these gods, even when not known as יהוה, but for example as אל שדי, are henceforth to be understood as really, in truth, referring to the one God of spirit

---

and how אלהים could be understood as יהוה; for it is only through such an implicit identification that the stories can be understood to cohere and form part a common tradition. Who is יהוה? Is יהוה or is אלהים the God of the Old Testament? There is a substantial difference. Yahweh is identified with the אלהים of Israel, but always? Everywhere? And is that the same as what the tradition understands as GOD? Is it the same as the concept of the divine implicit in the tradition as a whole? Or is this concept only a later addition and intrusion brought to the tradition at a very secondary stage? And what is this clearly plural word אלהים that performs such a recurrent function, conceptualizing the divine world not so much in its plurality, but in its totality and transcendence? Such signification is found not only in individual tales but in the redactive structures of the Old Testament tradition as a whole. There are very difficult grammatical and semantic problems involved here.

whose name in the tradition is יהוה.[13] The complete and whole tradition reflects the providence of אלהים, who previously had been previously known in the forgotten traditions of the past by the

---

[13] It is a mistake to identify early west Semitic adherence to the God יהוה exclusively with Israel or Judah/Judaea. Religions centered in Yahweh had a much larger geographical spread. For example, textual evidence regarding the *Shasu* of Yahweh is not directly relevant to the origins of Yahwism in Israel and Judah. References in Assyrian texts to a prince of Hama with the name Ilu-/Iau-bidi are not necessarily evidence of Israelite or Judahite dispersion and the existence of Yau and Yahu names in Babylonia are not a direct measure of the existence and status of Israelite and Jewish exiles there. While such names may suggest religious and even linguistic associations of these people with greater Palestine, they do not indicate ethnicity. (See, e.g., Smith, "Jewish Religious Life.") Nevertheless, the identification of יהוה with Israel and Judah drives all scholarly analysis of Judahite, Judaean or Israelite ethnicity. However, an analysis that is historically sensitive and which focuses on the deity in biblical tradition dating to the Persian period, particularly on the deity's function as an ethnic marker, neither centers itself in יהוה, nor does it focus on any of its other originative components. The God of Israel as exemplified in the composite of biblical tradition is not יהוה — though it is explicitly identified with יהוה. Yahweh was once the most important deity of the now dispersed and defunct state of Israel and also of much of the disoriented and substantially dislocated population of the Judaean hills. He is still a significant deity elsewhere in Palestine, such as at Ekron and among some religiously associated groups abroad, such as the Persian military colony at Elephantine. He is also one of the central deities of most of the stories, songs and oracles collected and redacted by the traditionists. Nevertheless, that deity is not to be identified simplistically with the "God of Israel" around which the traditionists create the concept of an ethnic unity that can be understood as the Bible. In the received tradition, Yahweh is rather the name — and increasingly the ineffable name — of a deity that transcends both the particularistic Yahweh and the traditions attached to that name. For the creators of the tradition, the divine is expressed by the non-specific inclusive literary concept אלהים, which is by definition not a God of any cult, story or oracle. This is emphatically clear in the form used by 2 Chronicles and Ezra: אלהי הומים.

Yahweh is a very specific deity, probably originating in the *Shasu* regions of Seir or Edom. Certainly Judah of the 8th-6th centuries and Samaria of the 9th-7th centuries maintained Yahweh among their dominant deities, along with El, Baal, Anat, Asherah, and others. However, there were many Yahwehs. In tradition, he had been understood as a god that had originated from Seir and Sinai; the inscription from *Kuntillet 'Ajrud* identifies him with Teman and Samaria. In the name of a Syrian prince from Hama he is identified with El/Ilu.

That some in Judah saw his consort as Asherah is hardly any longer debatable, but that he was the sole god of Jerusalem or of the state of Judah seems unlikely. One should no more identify the many Yahwehs than the various Baals (with whom Yahweh is identified) or Els (of which the biblical tradition is replete).

name יהוה.[14] In this, the antiquarian efforts of tradition-collection and tradition-building recreate a meaningful tradition from what was no longer a viable past, whether real or perceived.[15]

This transvaluation of Palestine's ancient traditions can be seen full-blown in the long-recognized critical recasting of historiographical poems found in the prophetic books: Hosea 2, Amos 5 and 9, Micah 4–5, and especially 6:2–7:7, and nowhere more clearly than in Isa 44:28–45:13, read in context with 1:1–2:5 and Isaiah 6. The collectors cast these poems into the hoary antiquity of the Assyrian period, using a tradition-building technique technique of story-writing that is far better understood in the commentaries of Ruth, Jonah and Esther and which is dominant in the collected traditions of Genesis–2 Kings. They not only recast Yahweh as the universal God of heaven, but they recreate Palestine's past as meaningful tradition, identifying the new Jerusalem of the future as the remnant of Israel saved. The underlying doctrine of transcendence is that God is the author of the world, both evil and good, and that he had created it for his own purposes, not those of humanity. History; i.e., tradition, reflects his glory. Israel, having committed unforgivable crimes, is forgiven. How else describe the wonder of the God of mercy? The task of the prophetic audience is not to

---

[14] *Contra* A. Alt, *Der Gott der Väter* (BWANT 12; Stuttgart: W. Kohlhammer, 1929).

[15] The multi-faceted biblical sources identify Yahweh with Baal and with El. He is El Qanah and El Emounah; he used to be El Shaddai. In story he may be El Ro'i; in essence he is to be described as El Qone 'arṣ, but all of the later redactions identify him with Elohim, an inclusive concept with generic and universalistic implications. In the Hebrew Bible, אל is used as a personal name or as a name followed by an epithet. אלים is used as a grammatical plural signifying "gods." אלוה, on the other hand, is a common noun signifying "god" as in יהוה אלוה ישראל; אלהים, however, is not used as a personal name in biblical tradition and only rarely is it used as a common noun in the sense of *a god*. It is seldom used outside of a context that may understand it as an inclusive theologumenon, such as "the divine," or the like. In the context of the Persian period and later, such an inclusive monotheistic concept as אלהים is necessary if Yahweh is to survive. The origins of the God of Israel, however, are transposed and given new signification. Neither El nor Yahweh, as the ancient Gods of Palestine, are any longer viable in themselves. Yahweh survives specifically as the ultimately unnamed and unnamable deity of tradition, and as such is comparable to Ahura Mazda of Persian tradition.

hope, but to reflect on the tradition and to understand the task of philosophy.

In Genesis 2 and 6:1-4 life is characterized as a divine element: the breath of יהוה אלהים, which resides only fleetingly[16] in the physically delineated multiplicity of creatures. In this mortal world, the divine spirit is transient; this defines the human. It is only a quite late development in Hellenistic thought that allows Plato's world/spirit dichotomy to be read through the lenses of matter/form polarity, allowing the collusion of individuation and immortality.[17] The Semitic difficulty in understanding personal immortality need not be taken to express a lack in their philosophical

---

[16] In this respect, הבל of Gen 4:2-4 should be considered, along with the contrasting of רוה/הבל in Qohelet.

[17] The Yahweh of tradition is not directly identified with the divine but only indirectly identified; that is, the traditions about Yahweh can be understood and interpreted as reflective of what is understood as truly divine through explicit and implicit associations with Elohim — a concept that implicitly embodies the אלהי השמים who is now associated in tradition with the name of the ancient god of Palestine's former traditions: Yahweh. This enabled the tradition builders to express through the tradition as a whole their own understanding of a universal world order under the single coherent concept of the universal and transcendent deity Elohim. At the same time, they could preserve the *personal* aspect of the divine that is endemic to the traditional folklore of Palestine, expressed in the characters of the myths and stories of the populace. In terms of intellectual history, the world view of the collectors of tradition is solidified through the integration of a coherent concept of a transcendent universal expression of ultimate reality (Elohim) with the personal aspects of the divine that are characteristic of the long-established popular, regional and traditional religious language. This might be described as a middle ground between the idealism of Plato, which eliminates the world of the gods, and hellenistic synchronism, which rationalizes that world. It expands the understanding of the divine to include both the personal and the universal. This enabled the tradition collectors to pursue their primary goal of preserving the shattered and fragmented traditions of the past through a reunderstanding of these past traditions in a manner consonant with their own world view. In this process, they also transformed that world view. The interpretive matrix for this understanding of tradition can be found expressed in the phrase, Yahweh Elohim, "The Divine Yahweh," which is grammatically impenetrable but not redundant. It identifies Yahweh as Yahweh Elohe Shamayim and as Yahweh Elohe Yisrael whose temple was/is to be rebuilt in Jerusalem, there to form the core of a redeemed Israel through the self-identification as a reconstructed nation whose origin and identity is that of a remnant saved from exile, returning to both its tradition and its God.

world view nor be taken as an indication that this group resided at a lower level of intellectual evolution. It would be more historically sensitive to understand these metaphors to reflect an integral part of their world view that presents itself as substantially other than school platonism, not emphasizing an understanding of the individuality of the human spirit, but rather one that contrasts the divine world of spirit (a metaphor derived from the experience of life, understood as ineffable and transcendent) with that of this world, understood as transient, tragic and whimsical. Reflection on this דרך צדקה (i.e., philosophy) not only promotes a salient humility regarding the divine, as is clear in the hermeneutical rendition of Job and Qohelet, but reflects a substantial and abiding awe and respect for life, both human and animal, as well as an ultimate disrespect for the assured dogmatism of religion's answers to humanity's impenetrable tragedies. The answer to Job's dilemma and challenge to the divine as justice is clear and succinct, explicit in prophets such as Hosea, Isaiah and Micah and pervasive in much of the earliest writings of the Old Testament: the Divine creates and is responsible for both good and evil, but his mercy is without end. This perception of reality is neither paternalistic nor indifferent to suffering, but a realistic reflection on experience. It does not so much fail to answer the hypothetical problems of suffering and justice as it refuses to assert an answer in ignorance, as human values and hopes collide with human experience.

3) *The world view of exclusive monotheism:* A discriminating ideology is apparent in ancient texts from as early as the efforts by Xerxes to consolidate and centralize the government's control over religious ideology by banning indigenous religious associations that were perceived to pose a threat to the centralizing thrust of imperially supported dogma.[18] The concept of the spirituality of the hu-

---

[18] Efforts by M. Boyce to interpret Persian texts from the perspective of a Zoroastrianism current in the Hellenistic period share many of the weaknesses of biblically oriented tradition histories ("Persian Religion in the Achemenid Age," 293). Both yield a recreation of the past based on ideology that is mistakenly thought to reflect history. Nevertheless, her comparison between Xerxes' intolerance of certain cults with Isa 45:7 is both pertinent and illuminating. Such exclusivistic religious campaigns, whether they are found within a polytheistic or a monotheistic perception of the divine world, are functionally equivalent tendencies of the universalist world view shared in common. It does not matter whether they

man person, which may have originally been a Greek idea, ultimately developed its intrinsic claim to immortality. This concept
found a platform in Asia where the path had long been laid
through these traditions of language that had individualized competing perceptions of the divine. In the western province of Yehud, a
refraction of this movement that was discriminating (but potentially
intransient and intolerantly repressive) might be inferred from some
biblical traditions, especially parts of Ezra, which have been
described quite accurately to reflect a world view of exclusive monotheism. This worldview is epitomized in the totality of the metaphor of goodness and power at war with false gods who ride this
slippery slope of metaphor towards a personification of both good
and evil.[19]

The deep-rooted merchant's penchant for syncretism in the
world of the Seleucids, with its inevitable tendency to see a plurality of religious expression as essentially a problem of commerce,
met a bitter and reactionary resistance in Palestine. There, in contrast to the more dominant, international and inclusive religious perceptions, the exclusivity of an alternative traditional and regional
deity of Yahweh represented for many the sole signification of the
heavenly spirit. In contrast to their perception of what had been
understood as the support of the Jews' אלהי השמים by the Persian
and Ptolemaic empire, Antiochus IV's insouciant indifference and
lack of discrimination to the originative location of true and false
and good and evil in the world of divine metaphor allowed what
was perceived as a foreign danger of syncretism eventually to become a rallying cry of both traditionalists and nationalists against
the dominant greater world of the Hellenistic empire. The world represented an all-pervasive power that (with the Seleucid takeover)
was seen to threaten their very existence: their language, their tradition and their God. The ideology of this conflict not only found

---

are presented as a struggle between Ahura Mazda and Daiva or, as in 2 Kings, as
a struggle between Yahweh and Baal. Nevertheless, this commonality does not
support Boyce's claim that 2 Isaiah is directly dependent on Zoroastrianism.
Rather, it marks these traditions as parallel, regionally-specific intellectual developments.
[19] Inclusive and exclusive monotheism are at most older and younger contempor-
aries of the Persian and Hellenistic worlds.

success in, but was forged by the resistance and revolt that led to independence behind the armies of the Maccabean insurrection, the success of which marked Palestinian Judaism with a sharply distinctive national consciousness.

Exclusive monotheism, logically a secondary and reactionary development in the intellectual history of ideas, nevertheless comes into being close to the time of the formation of our traditions: not subsequently, but contemporaneously. The need to reject syncretism and the dominance of Greek culture in *exclusive* monotheistic terms created a need to affirm the indigenous tradition of *inclusive* monotheism in *exclusivistic anti-hellenistic* terms. This created a large spectrum of political, religious and philosophical divisions, relating to both syncretism and hellenization among Jews, which was not to be fully played out for some four centuries.

The Temple of יהו at Elephantine and Persian Religious Policy

Thomas M. Bolin

With the renewed focus on the Persian period[1] the papyri from the Jewish garrison of Elephantine[2] merit reconsideration, specifically surrounding issues of religious practice.[3] Of particular interest is the identification by the Jews of Elephantine of יהו as אלהא שמיא in their letter to the Persian governor Bagohi (A.P. 30) requesting permission to rebuild their temple to יהו. This identification by the Elephantine Jews of יהו as the god of heaven can and has been viewed as evidence of the Israelite deity absorbing elements of other gods,[4] as a revival of an ancient biblical/Syro–Palestinian title,[5] as

---

[1]   See most recently T.L. Thompson (*Eary History of the Israelite People: From the Written and Archaeological Sources* [SHANE 4; Leiden: Brill, 1992]) and P.R. Davies (*In Search of 'Ancient Israel'* [JSOTSup 148; Sheffield: JSOT 1992]) for the Persian period as the provenance for the biblical traditions. This is a complete reversal of earlier views, e.g. A. Vincent, (*La religion des judéo-araméens d'Éléphantine* (Paris: Geuthner, 1937), who sees some Persian era biblical traditions as "un souvenir des plus anciennes traditions d'Israël, mais ravivé ... à cette date ... sous l'influence des Perses" (109).

[2]   For the most recent treatment of the papyri, see B. Porten, "Elephantine Papyri," in *Anchor Bible Dictionary* (ed. D.N. Freedman; 6 vols.; New York: Doubleday, 1992) 2.445–55. The most recent text and translations of A.P. 30, 31 is that by J. Lindenberger, *Ancient Aramaic and Hebrew Letters* (SBL Writings from the Ancient World 4; Atlanta: Scholars, 1994) 63-8.

[3]   Indeed, if HB traditions can be placed in the Persian period, then one need not puzzle over the apparent laxity of the Elephantine Jews regarding the so-called Josianic reform, or even wonder why they apparently possessed no copies of biblical texts. See the incisive remark of A.E. Cowley: "So far as we learn from these texts Moses might have never have existed, there might have been no bondage in Egypt, no exodus, no monarchy, no prophets" (*Aramaic Papyri of the Fifth Century B.C.* [Oxford: Clarendon, 1923] xxiii).

[4]   Thus E.G.H. Kraeling sees it "reflecting Yahweh's absorption of the title of the god Baalshamim" (*The Brooklyn Museum of Aramaic Papyri* [New Haven: Yale University, 1953] 84).

indication of a shift in Israelite theology from polytheism and/or henotheism to universalism,[6] or as the Jewish garrison's attempt to equate their god with the Persian *Ahura Mazda* in an effort to have their request more favorably received. This article argues for the last option and sees the equation as necessary, since official Persian religious policy during this time was inclined towards an inclusive monotheism (belief in a single god of spirit, with regional refractions)[7] centered on *Ahura Mazda*. Thus, in this text and in the Aramaic portions of Ezra and Nehemiah, the equation of יהוה/יהו with the god of heaven is neither evidence of the Israelite deity absorbing elements of other gods, nor of a new Israelite worldview driven by an inclusive monotheism, but rather of the attempts by the Jews to have their regional god identified by the Persians as the one true god *Ahura Mazda*. The equation cannot be attributed to an insight generated by theological reflection but, like Persian religious policy itself, is to be attributed to matters of political expediency.

---

[5]   A. Vincent sees Genesis 24 as the most ancient usage of the ephitet for Yahweh and its appearance at Elephantine represents it redivivus (*Religion d'Élephantine*, 110–4). For H. Niehr, the title's origins lie in a "syrisch-kanaanäischer Provenienz," and is drawn upon by the Jews of Elephantine due to their ethnic background (*Der höchste Gott: alttestamentlicher JWHW-Glaube in Kontext syrisch-kanaanäischer Religion des 1. Jahrtausend v. Chr.* [BZAW 190; Berlin and New York: Walter de Gruyter, 1990] 460; see also O. Eissfeldt, "Ba'alshamem und Yahweh," *ZAW* 16 (1939) 1–31.

[6]   So B. Porten, for whom the equation in A.P. 30 represents "the immanence-transcendence theology of ancient Israel" ("The Jews in Egypt," in *The Cambridge History of Judaism* [2 vols.; ed. W.D. Davies and L. Finkelstein; Cambridge: Cambridge University, 1984] 1.385–6); D.K. Andrews, "The God of the Heavens," in *The Seed of Wisdom: Essays in Honor of T.J. Meek* (ed. W.S. McCullough; Toronto: University of Toronto, 1964) 53–5 and T.L. Thompson, "The Intellectual Matrix of Early Biblical Narrative: Inclusive Monotheism in Persian Period Palestine" in this volume.

[7]   So Thompson, *Early History*, 383–99; 415–23.

1. *The Jewish Request*[8]

A.P. 30 exhibits many features common to Aramaic epistolography: the use of the preposition אל (line 1) that is rare in most all written Aramaic but common in formulaic addresses of official documents; the use of כען as a transitional marker to pass from one subject to another (lines 4,22); the placement of the subject of the letter at the beginning of sentences, in spite of grammatical awkwardness (lines 9–10 *inter alii*); and the inclusion of a date at the end (line 30),[9] as in almost all Aramaic letters. Due to additions and erasures (lines 5,11, 20,24,29,30; A.P. 31:6) in the two surviving copies found at Elephantine, it is clear that they are drafts and that a presentable copy was sent to Bagohi, the Persian governor of Yehud,[10] possibly by Persian imperial messenger.[11]

---

[8]   A.P. 30; text, translation and comments in A. Cowley, *Aramaic Papyri*, 108–19; plates in E. Sachau, *Aramäische Papyrus und Ostraka aus einer jüdischen Militärkolonie zu Elephantine: Altorientalische Sprachdenkmäler des 5. Jahrhunderts vor Christus* (2 vols.; Leipzig: Heinrichs, 1911) 1.2; complete bibliography in *An Aramaic Bibliography. Part I: Old, Official and Biblical Aramaic* (eds. J.A. Fitzmyer and S.A. Kaufman; Baltimore: Johns Hopkins, 1992) 64; translations in *ANET*, 492 and *Documents from Old Testament Times* (ed. D.W. Thomas; London: T. Nelson, 1958) 262–5.

[9]   Cf. F. Rosenthal, *A Grammar of Biblical Aramaic* (Weisbaden: O. Harrassowitz, 1963) 35–6; P.S. Alexander, "Remarks on Aramaic Epistolography in the Persian Period," *JSS* 23 (1978) 155–70, esp. 164; P.E. Dion "La lettre araméenne passe-partout et ses sous espèces," *RB* 89 (1982) 528–75, esp. 547–54, tables 573–5, and B. Porten, "Aramaic Letters: A Study in Papyrological Reconstruction," *JARCE* 17 (1980) 39–75, esp. 41–3.

[10]   His title is פחת יהוד in A.P. 30:1 and in Josephus Βαγώας στατηγος τοῦ ᾽Αρταξέρξου (Ant 11.7); see K. Galling, *Studien zur Geschichte Israels im persischen Zeitalter* (Tübingen: JCB Mohr, 1964) 161–5. It is worthy of note that Josephus relates an incident involving Bagohi and the officials of the Jerusalem temple. When the governor's candidate for high priest was murdered and replaced by his brother, Bagohi imposed as punishment a tribute of fifty drachmas on every lamb offered in the Temple.

[11]   Cf. P. Alexander (*Aramaic Papyri* 158–59) and Xenophon (Cyro 8.6.18) for a description of the Persian mounted post established by Cyrus. Note especially Xenophon's observation of their speed ἀλλ᾽ ὅτι γε ἀνθρωπίνον πεζῃπορειων αὑτη τάχιστα.

Yedoniah's[12] letter to Bagohi yields the following information:

1) In 411 BCE, while the Persian satrap of Egypt, Arsames, was away at the court of Darius II, the priests of the temple of Khnum[13] in Elephantine plotted with Widranag,[14] then the regional governor, and his son the current garrison commander. Together they destroyed the temple of יהו, plundered its goods and burned it to the ground.

2) This temple had existed in Elephantine before the Persian conquest by Cambyses, and he had allowed it to stand in spite of his destruction of other temples in Egypt.[15]

---

[12]   There are two men by the name of ידניה in the Elephantine texts. The first is dated to the second quarter of the 5th century; the latter, with whom we are concerned, was possibly the grandson of the former (pappynomy was common in Elephantine). That the younger Yedoniah was clearly a leader of the Jewish community at Elephantine is further evidenced by letters addressing him as מרא, the same title Yedoniah himself uses in his letter to Bagohi (cf. A.P. 21–22,25,37–38).

[13]   The letter distinguishes a Jewish priest as כהן (30:1) from the Egyptian priests as כמר (30:5). This same terminological distinction is found in the HB regarding priests of Yahweh and those of other gods (cf. 2 Kg 23:5; Zeph 1:4); see M.L. Margolis, "The Elephantine Documents," *JQR* 2 (1911–12) 419–43, esp. 428; and B. Porten, "The Jews in Egypt," 1.386.

[14]   A.P. 30:4–13; וידרנג appears in several Elephantine texts. From 420–416 he was garrison commander (רב חילא), being appointed to governor (פרתרך) sometime between 416 and 410, although see J.W. Epstein ("Weitere Glossen zu den 'aramaische Papyrus und Ostraka,'" *ZAW* 33 [1913] 138–50, esp. 138), who translates the term as "servant" or "official." Widranag's fate remains uncertain. The letter mentions that the Jews achieved revenge on those who had destroyed the temple, mentioning Widranag by name: "All the riches he had gained were destroyed and all the men who had sought to do evil to that temple were killed" (A.P. 30:16–17). However, Widranag appears in a papyrus dated 399, although noticeably without any title; contra B. Porten ("Jews of Egypt," 1.390), who thinks Widranag was punished by death. See also E.G. Kraeling (*Brooklyn Museum of Aramaic Papyri*, 83) and A.P. 27, dated 410, where Widranag and the priests of Khnum are accused of destroying storehouses of the king.

[15]   "When Cambyses came into Egypt ... the temples of the gods of Egypt all of them they overthrew" (A.P. 30:13–14). This appears to be a rhetorical flourish on the part of Yedoniah to advance his case. Archaeological evidence does not bear out the widespread destruction of Egyptian temples by Cambyses, who did, however, limit their revenues. This could be a piece of negative propaganda originated and/or fostered by Cambyses' usurper Darius I on which Yedoniah either is drawing or which he unconsciously is accepting as the truth; so M. Boyce, "Persian Religion in the Achemenid Age," in *The Cambridge History of Judaism* (2 vols.; ed.

3) Yedoniah has also written about this matter to the High Priest Johanan in Jerusalem and to Ostanes the brother of Anani, one of the Jewish nobles[16] and gotten no response.[17]

4) Since the destruction there has been no meal offering (מנחא), incense (לבונה) or sacrifice (עלוה) performed by the Jewish garrison.

5) Yedoniah is seeking Bagohi's permission because he has been forbidden to rebuild the temple by unknown officials.[18] If Bagohi complies, meal offerings, incense and sacrifices will be offered to יהו on his behalf.

6) In addition to the offerings, Yedoniah and his colleagues have also issued instructions about sending gold to the governor.[19] Most commentators see this as a bribe.[20] However, M. Vogelstein reads ועל זהב as a dittography caused by a scribe making the natural equation between זהב and כסף which occurs three words earlier on line 28. Vogelstein sees no need for a bribe to be so vague, since Yedoniah and his colleagues later explicitly offer a bribe to an unknown official in connection with the rebuilding of the temple (A.P. 33:13).[21] However, this evidence in A.P. 33 corroborates the position that A.P. 30 offers a bribe to the Persian governor in return for his favorable judgement. Since all known economic affairs at Elephantine involved either silver or goods, any offer of gold

---

W.D. Davies and L. Finkelstein; Cambridge: Cambridge University, 1984) 1.279-307, esp. 288. See Herodotus 3.27-30 regarding Cambyses' fanatical rage in his destruction of Egyptian temples.

[16] A.P. 30:18-19; cf. Neh 12:22-23 and Josephus, (Ant 11.7) for יוחנן/'Ιωάννης as high priest. In Josephus this high priest is a contemporary of Bagohi.

[17] A. Vincent represents the position of most commentators concerning the letter to the Jerusalem high priest. It "démontre d'un côté la bonne foi des Judéo-Araméens d'Éléphantine et de l'autre l'observation à Jérusalem de la loi sur l'unité du sanctuaire" (Religion d'Éléphantine, 336). D.H. Müller perhaps rightly characterizes the silence of the Jerusalem high priest: "Keine Antwort ist auch eine Antwort!" ("Die Korrespondenz zwischen der Gemeinde von Elephantine und den Söhnen Sanbalats," Wiener Zeitschrift für die Kund des Morgenlandes 21 [1907] 416-9, esp. 416).

[18] לא שבקן לן למבניה (30:23); the reference to "they" is unclear.

[19] ועל זהב על זנה שלחן הודען (30:28-29).

[20] So A. Cowley, Aramaic Papyri, 118. J.W. Epstein translates על as a specific sum, noting the term עליתא in the Mishnah ("Glossen zu den 'aramaische Papyrus und Ostraka,'" ZAW 32 (1912) 128-38, esp. 128).

[21] "Bakshish for Bagoas?," JQR 33 (1942) 89-92.

would have been extravagant, and such a phrase as is found in Yedoniah's letter would not be written in jest and certainly not as an
error.[22] Vogelstein's argument for dittography rests on the assumption that כסף and זהב naturally go together, even in a community
where gold was not a normal medium of exchange.

7) Yedoniah has also written to Delaiah and Shemaliah, the sons
of Sanballat the governor of Samaria. In addition, and indeed almost
as an afterthought, Yedoniah makes it clear to Bagohi that Arsames
knew nothing of the matter. Although it is not explicitly mentioned that Arsames is a subordinate of Bagohi and there is no information regarding any heirarchy among the Persian satrapies, it can be
surmised from this letter and from A.P. 32, where Bagohi and Delaiah direct Arsames to rebuild the temple, that the Egyptian governor was in some way answerable to the governors of Yehud and
Samaria.[23] Such an answerability need not have been formal, as
sources are clear that espionage among satraps vying for the king's
favor was commonplace. Yedoniah may not so much have been
going over Arsames' head as he was attempting to make the situation known among the governor's potential rivals who were each
eager for the goodwill of Darius. To say that Arsames knew nothing of the destruction of the temple can be an attempt either to dis-
tance him from a potentially politically harmful incident or draw
attention to his lack of knowledge and control over acts of violence
in his territory.

2. *The Governor's Response*[24]

Compared to the official correspondence sent by Yedoniah, the directive sent from Bagohi and Delaiah to Arsames fittingly deserves
the name of memorandum. The copy at Elephantine is riddled with

---

[22] See B. Porten (*Archives from Elephantine: The Life of an Ancient Military Colony*
[Berkeley: University of California, 1968] 62–102) for the rarity of gold in commerce at Elephantine and general economic conditions.
[23] So Cowley, *Aramaic Papyri*, 110–1; contra A.T. Olmstead, *History of the Persian Empire* (Chicago: University of Chicago, 1948) 230–1, 239-48; and J.M. Cook,
The Persian Empire (New York: Schocken, 1983) 77–90.
[24] A.P. 32; text, translation and comments in Cowley, *Aramaic Papyri*, 122–4;
plates in Sachau, *Aramäische Papyri*, 1.4; complete bibliography in Fitzmeyer,
Aramaic Bibliography, 65; translation in *ANET*, 492 and Thomas, *Documents*,
265–6.

sloppiness. There are erasures in lines 2 and 8, an added line between lines 1 and 2 and an added word in line 2. The document is
addressed to no one; that the instructions are to be relayed to Arsames is added. It tersely begins: "Memorandum from Bagohi and Delaiah, they said to me ..." There is a hole in the papyrus that was
apparently there before it was used, since the scribe has written
around it.[25] It agrees with the details of Yedoniah's letter on every
point but three:

1) It calls for the rebuilding of a house of offering; בית מדבחא,
and *not* a temple; אגורא (cf. A.P. 30:6,7,24 and A.P. 32:3).[26]

2) The building is to be dedicated to the god of heaven;
אלהא שמיא, and *not to* יהו, who is not even named in the memorandum. K. Galling notes that this absence "ist schwerlich Zufall,"
while A. Vincent surmises, although without any supporting evidence, that Bagohi was a Jew, and therefore, that Yedoniah wrote
to him using the proper name of the deity both men worshipped,
while in his response Bagohi, acting as a representative of the Persian empire, employed the generic term.[27] In fact, the omission of
the proper name יהו in A.P. 32 bears significance only in light of
the *equation* of the name with the title אלהא שמוא in A.P. 30.

3) The new building will be for meal offering and incense but
not for sacrifices. This absence is made all the more intriguing by
the fact that an erasure has occurred on line 8 precisely where the
permission for sacrifices would have occurred. Yedoniah's letter
twice speaks of meal offerings, incense and sacrifice in the same
order (30:21,25). The memorandum speaks of meal offering and incense in the same order, but omits sacrifice. B. Porten posits the
erased word to have been ועלותא,[28] but the papyrus is too difficult
to decipher with certainty. However, apart from the erasure, it is
clear that the memorandum does not allow sacrifices. This prohibition is reinforced by A.P. 33, wherein Yedoniah and his colleagues
offer a large bribe to an unknown official for rebuilding the temple
and promise that "sheep, oxen and goats are not offered as burnt

---

[25] See Cowley, *Aramaic Papyri*, 122 and B. Porten, "Aramaic Papyri and Parchments: A New Look," *BA* 42 (1979) 74–104, esp. 98–9.

[26] So Epstein, "Glossen," 139 and Vincent, *Religion d'Éléphantine*, 315–26.

[27] Epstein, "Glossen," 103 and Galling, *Studien*, 70.

[28] "Aramaic Papyri and Parchments," 98.

sacrifice there, but incense, meal offering and drink offering only."[29]

It is unclear why Bagohi would have forbidden burnt offering (cf. Ezra 7:17 where the Persians appear to allow animal sacrifice at the Jerusalem temple). Some have posited that the Egyptian priests of Khnum, who is represented as a ram, were scandalized and that this was the cause of the temple's destruction. Indeed, K. Galling traces the destruction to the so-called "Passover Papyrus," (A.P. 21), dated 419, which directs the Jews of Elephantine to observe the feast. For Galling, the Jewish garrison's obedience to the Passover Papyrus is the origin of ram sacrifice there.[30] Others feel that Bagohi, by virtue of being Persian, was a Zoroastrian and thus, would not want fire defiled by animal remains. However, M. Boyce sees Bagohi's assumed "Zoroastrian observance of animal sacrifice" as signifying that he "had no religious scruples about aiding those of other faiths to make similar offerings."[31] It should be remembered that, according to Josephus, Bagohi continued to allow animal sacrifice in the Jerusalem temple after the murder of his candidate for high priest but that he imposed a tribute for every lamb offered.[32] Since Yedoniah's request, tendered with a bribe, is granted, the possibility that Bagohi had no religious scruples whatsoever should not be ruled out. Others see the destruction of the temple as entirely political and tied to the continued loyalty of the Jews to Persia in the face of the Egyptian unrest that led to the revolt of 404. The Jews suffer because they are soldiers in the service of Persia, not because they are Jews.[33] There are a myriad of reasons, both political and religious, for Widranag and the Egyptian priests to have destroyed the temple: they may have been outraged by the sacrifice of rams, they may have been part of the Egyptian unrest with Persian rule that was to lead to full–scale rebellion, or they may

---

[29] ‏וקן תור ענז מקלו לא יתעבד תמה להן לבונה מנחה‎ (33:10–11).

[30] *Studien*, 152–4.

[31] "Persian Religion," 1.292.

[32] See note 12 above.

[33] So Porten, "Aramaic Papyri and Parchments," 99; *idem, Archives from Elephantine*, 291; Cowley, *Aramaic Papyri*, 124; contra S.A. Cook, "The Significance of the Elephantine Papyri for the History of Hebrew Religion," *AJT* 19 (1915) 346–82, esp. 377–8 and Vincent, *Religion d'Éléphantine*, 378–9, for whom the destruction is motivated entirely by political factors.

have been envious of the temple's economic influence.[34] That it was rebuilt is made clear by Brooklyn papyrus 12, dated 402, which makes reference to the אנורא זי יהו.[35]

3. יהו as אלהא שמיא

In A.P. 30 there is a curious progression of *nomina divina* demonstrating Yedoniah's attempt to have Bagohi equate יהו with the god of heaven.

1) Bagohi's health is commended to אלה שמיא (line 1)[36]
2) יהו is the god who is in Yeb (line 4)
3) The Jews pray to יהו מרא שמיא for revenge upon Widranag (line 15)
4) יהו is a god worshipped in Yeb (lines 24–25)
5) If Bagohi complies he will merit much before יהו אלה שמיא (lines 27–28)

A subtle shift is apparent. After commending Bagohi to the generic god of heaven (i.e. *Ahura Mazda*), Yedoniah next treats circumstances surrounding the temple of the local deity יהו. The letter ends with a promise of Bagohi's being blessed by the same god of heaven to whom he was commended at the beginning of the letter, except this time the god is equated with the local god of the Jews, יהו.[37] Although the role of the offered gold (see above) cannot be

---

[34] See A.P. 22, wherein the temple collects the large sum of 318 silver shekels in donations.

[35] In Kraeling, *Brooklyn Museum of Aramaic Papyri*, 268–80.

[36] Contra Vincent (*Religion d'Éléphantine*, 96) and Niehr (*Höchste(r) Gott*, 48), who see salutations as useless for making conclusions regarding *nomina divina*. Niehr's conclusion can be valid regarding the religious practices of the Elephantine Jews, but *nomina divina* in salutations are terribly important in determining how the sender wished the message to be perceived by the recipient. This is all the more important when the sender is an inferior writing to a superior in search of a favor, as is A.P. 30. Yedoniah could have commended Bagohi to "all the gods" as is done in other Elephantine documents such as A.P. 17:12, which possibly is addressed to Arsames (so Porten, "Aramaic Letters," 46), A.P. 21:2, which is from Yedoniah to אחי, and A.P. 37:1.

[37] In addition to the citations in notes 4–7 above, see also M. Smith, "Jewish Religious Life in the Persian Period," in *The Cambridge History of Judaism* (2 vols.; ed. W.D. Davies and L. Finkelstein; Cambridge: Cambridge University, 1984) 1.219–78, esp. 228, and Cook ("Significance of Elephantine Papyri," 374), who sees the title as merely "suggestive of Persian use." Andrews ("God of the Heavens,"

underestimated, Yedoniah's success in convincing Bagohi is evidenced by the fact that Bagohi grants permission for an offering house to be built to the god of heaven. This equation makes the granting of permission easier by the Persian administrative official as it then is consonant with imperial policy at that time.[38] This explanation makes better sense than others heretofore offered, since it does not require the traversing of many miles and centuries to the origin of the term "god of heaven" (so Niehr, Vincent, *inter alios*).[39] Nor does it require one to posit a new level of theological speculation on the part of the Elephantine Jews (so Porten, Thompson, *inter alios*).[40] There is confusion among the authors cited above regarding the *origins* of the term "god of heaven," its *significatiion* to the Elephantine Jews and the Persians (for these are two different things) and its *specific meaning* in A.P. 30. While the term's origins may lie in Bronze Age Syria–Palestine, its meaning for a Jewish community in their correspondence with the Persian adminstration a millenium later is another issue.

4. *Persian Religious Policy: Cyrus to Artaxerxes II*

In the Cyrus cylinder and the two texts of the Cyrus decree in Ezra 1 and 2 Chronicles 36 we see a policy wherein the emperor is portrayed as the chosen agent of the high god from the particular conquered region. Consequent to this is the implicit identification of the high god with the Persian *Ahura Mazda*. Thus, Cyrus "publicly appears as the devotee and servant of the religion of the (newly-

---

52-5) also acknowledges that the title "represents a definition by which the Persian authorities tested the claims of the Jewish religion and determined its legitimacy," but in addition, sees Jewish use of the title signifying their acknowledgement of knowledge of Yahweh by Gentile groups.

[38] This is borne out as well by the occurrences of the term. Of the ten occurrences of אלה שמיא in the Elephantine corpus, six are in A.P. 30 and 32. Similarly, אלהי השמים occurs in the HB only in the Cyrus decrees and when Jews are speaking to foreigners, except for the intriguing אלהיא די שמיא in Jer 10:11. The only possible exception to this could be Gen 24:3,7; however, here אלהי השמים is not the actual title but is only part of a larger title אלהי השמים ואלהי הארץ, which is seen by Vincent as the ancient source of the term (see note 5). See Andrews, "God of the Heavens," 45,48.

[39] See note 5 above.

[40] See notes 4, 6–7, 33 above.

won) country."[41] It must be stressed that this identification is as much a matter of political expediency as theological reflection; any distinction between the two regarding Persian religious policy would be false. Thus, when D.K. Andrews observes that "unless the use of the names Marduk and Yahweh by Cyrus is to be discounted as nothing but political propaganda, it must represent an identification of the various gods as local manifestations of one divine being or of a coherent pantheon," he fails to take into account that such an identification *is* political propaganda.[42] On the whole, Persian religious policy from Cyrus to Xerxes I is characterized as inclusively monotheistic.[43] Cambyses is said to have destroyed all of the temples of Egypt (cf. A.P. 30:13–14), and Herodotus reports that Cambyses killed the Egyptian calf–god Apis, which precipitated a massacre as well as the emperor's madness.[44] However, archaeological evidence does not support the widespread destruction of temples by Cambyses.[45] Darius I appears to be, or makes himself to appear to be, tolerant of Egyptian religion, repairing those temples destroyed by Cambyses and building new temples. In an inscription from Saïs, Darius is said to "uphold the name of all the gods, their temples, their revenues and the ordinances of their feasts forever," and in another his Egyptian architect calls him "the friend of all the gods."[46] However, in spite of Darius' generosity regarding temple construction in Egypt, he still reserved the right to ratify

---

[41] So G.B. Gray, "The Foundation and Extension of the Persian Empire," in *The Cambridge Ancient History* (12 vols.; ed. J.B. Bury, S.A. Cook *et al.*; Cambridge: Cambridge University, 1924-39) 4.1–25, esp. 15; and most recently Thompson, *Early History*, 348–51.

[42] "God of the Heavens," 57.

[43] See Cook's discussion of Persian religious policies (*Persian Empire*, 147–57, esp. 148–9) as well as his observation that the Persians were reluctant to involve themselves in the religious matters of their subject peoples. Evidence does not bear out this second assertion; see below. Inclusive monotheism is a more appropriate term than Cook's (and others') use of syncretism.

[44] Herodotus 3.27–30; Καμβύσης δέ ὡς λέγουσι Αἰγύπτιοι αὐτίκα διὰ τοῦτο τὸ ἀδίκημα ἐμάνη ἐὼν οὐδὲ πρότερον φρενήρης (3.30). See note 15.

[45] See Boyce, "Persian Religion," 1.288.

[46] Gray, "Foundation of Persian Empire," 4.24–5.

all choices of temple administrators.[47] This privilege was key to Darius' control of the power of the Egyptian priests, whose power was explicitly tied to the large amount of revenue they generated.[48]

With Xerxes I we are fortunate to possess an inscription regarding his destruction of temples in conquered countries,[49] wherein the king destroys the temples because "they performed festivals to the evil gods." Xerxes destroys these temples, forbids the performance of the rites, and performs a proper sacrifice to *Ahura Mazda*. The inscription ends with a word to the wise: "Whosoever you are in future days who thinks as follows: 'May I be prosperous in this life and blessed after my death' do live according to this law which *Ahura Mazda* has promulgated: 'Perform religious rites *only* for *Ahura Mazda* and for the cosmic order reverently'" (emphasis mine). At first blush this text paints Xerxes as motivated purely by piety. However, it is clear that his destruction of temples was due to concerns other than piety. The inscription speaks of Xerxes' purification of temples in the same group of countries wherein he puts down rebellion. Indicative of Xerxes' priorities, the inscription treats the rebellion in these countries before turning to their impiety. After his destruction of the Esagila in Babylon, Xerxes allowed the priests there to continue to worship on the ruins without hindrance, and after he destroyed the Acropolis he ordered the Greeks to sacrifice on the ruins. Herodotus makes the curious observation that Xerxes may have felt guilt or may have been given a vision regarding the destroyed temple on the Acropolis that led him to order worship on its ruins.[50] M. Boyce sees the acts at the Esagila and Acropolis as political, while the inscription is motivated by piety.[51] These two motivations cannot be so easily separated and

---

[47] See E. Bresciani, "Egypt, Persian Satrapy," in *The Cambridge History of Judaism* (2 vols.; ed. W.D. Davies and L. Finkelstein; Cambridge: Cambridge University, 1984) 1.358–72, esp. 361.

[48] Such an imperial attempt to control the economic power of the Egyptian cult was no new thing in the Persian period. It can be seen as one of the main factors surrounding Ahkenaton's so-called monotheistic reform and his establishment of a new capital and cult center at Amarna in the 14th century.

[49] *ANET*, 316–7.

[50] So Herodotus 8.52–55; εἴτε δὴ ὦν ὄψιν τινὰ ἰδῶν ἐνυπίου ἐνετέλλετο ταῦτα, εἴτε καὶ ἐνθύμιόν οἱ ἐγένετο ἐμπρήσαντι τὸ ἱρόν (8.54).

[51] "Persian Religion," 1.293–4.

applied from one case to another. Rather, they must be seen as a continual interplay between political motives couched in religious terms and religion used for political ends.

The actions of Xerxes I mark a shift in Persian religious policy from the more conciliatory approaches of Cyrus and his immediate successors. Where formerly, the policy was to equate the regional god with the Persian high god *Ahura Mazda*, and for rulers such as Cyrus and Darius to style themselves as restoring proper worship of the regional deities, Xerxes appears to view worship of local gods as false worship and restores the true, exclusive worship of *Ahura Mazda*. It is no longer a case of the Persian administration making the equation of the local god with the high god; rather, in the face of a Persian policy focused exclusively on the high god, it is the task of the worshippers of the local/regional god to make the equation and then to convince the Persians as well. Xerxes' exclusive focus on the Persian high god is further evidenced by the fact that all extant inscriptions dating from Xerxes I to Artaxerxes II mention no other gods but *Ahura Mazda*.[52] It is towards the end of this 80 year period (ca. 486-405) that the destruction of the Elephantine temple, Yedoniah's request and Bagohi's response fall. Yedoniah is making an equation in order to appear to be within the bounds of a policy already at least three quarters of a century old.

5. *A.P. 30 in the Context of Persian Religious Policy*

Seen in the larger context of an imperial policy driven by an inclusive monotheism, the wording of Yedoniah's request stands as a brilliant use of the policy to advance the cause of the Jewish garrison at Elephantine. As leader of a community his concern is to reestablish their cult place.[53] In an effort to have a sympathetic ear for his appeal, Yedoniah, in addition to an offered bribe, equates

---

[52] See Cook, *Persian Empire*, 147.
[53] For both religious and economic reasons. See the collection list of A.P. 22 in which Yedoniah collects the large sum of 318 silver shekels for the temple of יהו. This is five times more than the largest dowry paid at Elephantine and roughly twice the size of any known legal fines; see Porten, *Archives from Elephantine*, 73-5.

the local god יהו[54] with Ahura Mazda through use of the appellative אלהא שמיא. This would have been necessary since Persian
imperial policy at the time named no other gods but *Ahura Mazda*
in official texts and had ceased making such equations between regional deities and the high god. In earlier times, the imperial administration already might have equated the local Jewish god with the
god of heaven, but by the time of Yedoniah's letter it is his respon-
sibility to make this equation for the Persians. The imperial policy
is also evident in Bagohi's directive to rebuild the temple to the god
of heaven without mentioning יהו by name.[55] Yedoniah's political
savvy is matched by Bagohi's who, recognizing the need to maintain the goodwill of the Jewish garrison who are servants of the
empire, orders the temple to be rebuilt, but forbids the animal
sacrifice that perhaps caused Widranag and the priests of Khnum to
destroy it in the first place. Their motivation must remain speculative, however, since Widranag and the priests apparently had caused
a non–religious disturbance at Elephantine by destroying royal
storehouses (cf. A.P. 27).[56] Bagohi's actions are in concert with the
precedent of the religious policy of Xerxes I, dominated by political
expediency couched in the language of monotheism. As such, one
need not delve into issues of theological reflection regarding the

---

[54]   That יהו is a local god is clear by the frequent appellative יי ביב found in the
Elephantine documents.
[55]   Cf. also the Aramaic copy of the Behistun inscription of Darius I found at
Elephantine (Cowley, *Aramaic Papyri*, 248–71) that contains numerous occurrences
of the phrase בטלה זי אהרמזד with בטלל אלה שמיא in A.P. 38:5 as well as the
frequent use of "under the shadow of Ahura Mazda" in the Xerxes inscription. See
Cook (*Persian Religion*, 374) for evidence regarding Elephantine's place in the
larger life of the empire, despite its remote location. Cook notes that presence of
the Behistun text, Phoenician winejar handles and Elephantine's important location
on the second cataract mean that "we are not entitled to regard the Jewish colony
as some secluded, parochial community, living a sequestered life, maintaining such
religious conceptions as the early founders had brought with them, and untouched
by, if not ignorant of, events in the world outside" (366–7). Contra Vincent (*Religion d'Éléphantine*, 99) for whom "La petite colonie juive n'a rien d'une académie
de sages orientaux, ce sont de pauvres gens, attachés à la foi de leurs ancêtres et ils
en gardent précieusement le trésor mélangé malheureusement de beaucoup de
scories ... Ils n'ont ni les loisirs, ni la culture intellectuelle, ni la fréquentation des
cercles mosaïques qui leur permettraient d'élaborer un semblant de théologie."
[56]   See the discussion above.

application of the appellative "god of the heavens" by Jews to their god. This usage is rather to be traced to the more pragmatic, secular and observable context of the early Persian empire.

The equation of יהו with אלהא שמיא in this particular instance is not generated by theological reflection and cannot function in this period as evidence of Jewish worship of a universal high god with regional refractions, although it testifies to the already clearly observable Persian policy of inclusive monotheism begun by Cyrus and modified by Xerxes I.[57] The Jews of Elephantine commended themselves to and swore oaths by יהו, חרם, אנת, בתל, אשם, אלהא שמיא among others, with a particular deity being chosen as the *context* demanded.[58] That יהו was the premiere deity of their pantheon is indisputable; the temple is dedicated to him. However, offerings were collected for other deities as well (cf. A.P. 22). What we see in A.P. 30 is a usage dictated by a pragmatism that seeks the appearance of adherence to an imperial religious policy that itself is

---

[57] See Galling (*Studien*, 149): "Diese Motive werden nicht selten von der 'Weltanschauung' der Achämeniden abgeleitet, die u.E. jedoch nur eine sekundäre Rolle spielt ... die Aktionen und Reaktionen des persischen Hofes ganz konkrete gesamtpolitische Erwägungen ausgelöst worden sein;" Vincent (*Religion d'Éléphantine*, 142-3): "Il y avait surtout trop d'intérêts pratiques et matériels en jeu pour que les scribes qui régnaient dans les bureaux et rédigeaient les protocoles, ne dissumulent pas les divergences cultuelles pour ne mettre en lumiére que les ressemblances et à la faveur de cette unification, non seulement défendre et protéger, mais encore favoriser let intérêts religieux, ethniques ou nationaux qui pouvaient leur être chers. Il n'est pas douteux que les Juifs aient profité de ces bonnes dispositions ... on comprend que les colons juifs de Ieb aient essayé de profiter des bonnes dispositions des autorités perses à l'égard des dieux célestes. Ils ont accentué la confusion, en affectant de se servir dans leur correspondance officielle d'une expression à double sens. Ils ont tenté ainsi contre des païens attardés dans l'adoration d'un dieu bélier d'obtenir des maîtres de l'heure l'autorisation de reconstruire leur temple;" and Thompson ("Intellectual Matrix") in this volume.

[58] See Porten (*Archives from Elephantine*, 150-8) regarding Jews taking oaths by a plethora of deities according to context. Thus, the Jewish woman Mibtaiah swears by Sati in the divorce from her Egyptian husband (A.P. 14:4). By way of analogy, Smith's observation on the data theophoric elements in names may yield regarding religious practices is valid here: "to name a child for a god gave no assurance that when the child grew up it would worship its namesake" ("Jewish Religious Life," 222). That is to say, the child is named for a particular god based on the situation of its parents, whose motivations may or may not have been religious.

dictated by pragmatism. Gods referred to in salutations *can* furnish information regarding deities worshipped by the sender, the recipient or both. Apart from this, these *nomina divina* may also be an indication of the type of relationship that existed between the two parties, or they may be meaningless protocol that is, nonetheless, a necessary part of the letter (e.g. the use of "sincerely," or "yours truly" in modern letters).[59] To ask questions of theological signification of texts that are clearly not dealing with issues of theological speculation disregards the genre of the texts under study and the limits that genre sets on the type of data a text can and cannot yield.

---

[59]   See *opera citata* above in notes 9 and 36.

Scenes from the Early History of Judaism

Philip R. Davies

Judaism and Judaisms

The perception of Judaism in the Second Temple period has undergone a marked change in the last few decades. It is now frequently represented as a pluriform phenomenon; indeed, so much so that it has become commonplace to speak of the existence not only of various forms or types of Judaism but even of several "Judaisms" before rabbinic Judaism emerged as the authorized (though still not the only) form.[1]

This new profile has emerged from research in different areas. The idea of a single or "normative" Judaism that held the field earlier this century has persisted in some quarters, but has been steadily undermined for several decades. The rediscovery and subsequent re-evaluation of Jewish and early Christian apocalyptic literature that flourished early in this century led to a dichotomy between "rabbinic" and "apocalyptic" Judaism that for a long time absorbed the attention of scholarship, especially a New Testament scholarship that was seeking to define the precise relationship between Jesus, the early Church, and their Jewish background.[2] Among Old Testament/Hebrew Bible scholars, the thesis of Plöger, which was reformulated by Hanson, that two streams of Judaism were present from the early part of the "postexilic" period, has been quite influ-

---

[1] It is important to bear in mind that the Judaisms that preceded the emergence of rabbinic Judaism were not obliterated but persisted; indeed, they continued in some cases to influence the development of Judaism (e.g. Gnosticism, Hekhalot literature, Kabbalah, and Hasidism).

[2] Especially influential on a whole generation was the thesis of E. Käsemann that Christian theology derived from "apocalyptic" Judaism; see "The Beginnings of Christian Theology" (ET), *Journal for Theology and Church* 6 (1969) 17-46. J.J. Collins, *The Apocalyptic Imagination* (New York: Crossroad, 1984) is subtitled *An Introduction to the Jewish Matrix of Christianity*.

ential.[3] Both scholars represented the dichotomy as one between "theocratic" and "prophetic" groups or "streams," in which rabbinic Judaism's supposed emphasis on legalism placed it on the "theocratic" and "non-eschatological" side. It was necessary to this kind of analysis, especially Hanson's, that the eschatological/prophetic/apocalyptic stream was peripheral, and that the other element was therefore dominant, sociologically "central," and normative.

More recent developments have disposed of this dichotomy. First of all, the relationship between the rabbinic literature and the Judaism(s) of the first century CE has been redefined: rabbinic Judaism is now treated by the majority of scholars as a 2nd century CE phenomenon that cannot be read back into the Second Temple period and which, moreover, as a system of thought and practice, has its own discrete points of origin beyond the Second Temple period.[4] There is currently no consensus as to the nature, role or importance of the Pharisees — or, indeed, their relationship to rabbis. Second, the Dead Sea Scrolls, whether they are to be integrated into a single sectarian ideology or contain substantial amounts of literature from various sources within Judaism, have widened the range of ideas and practices recognizable as "Jewish."[5] The combination of cultic,

---

[3] O. Plöger, *Theocracy and Eschatology* (trans. from German; Oxford: Blackwell, 1968); P.D. Hanson, *The Dawn of Apocalyptic* (Philadelphia: Fortress, 1975). For a survey and critique of this view, see my "The Social World of Apocalyptic Writings," in *The World of Ancient Israel* (ed. R.E. Clements; Cambridge: Cambridge University, 1989), 251-71.

[4] I refer in particular to the work of Jacob Neusner, who adopted the terminology of "Judaisms" partly as a consequence of his conclusion that rabbinic Judaism, the "Judaism of the Two Torahs" that came into being during the first two centuries of the Common Era had no single precursor. He has also sought to compare and contrast some features of these Judaisms. See e.g. his essay, and the others, in W.S. Green (ed.), *Judaisms and their Messiahs in the Beginning of Christianity* (New York: Cambridge University, 1987). For an account of the use and abuse of rabbinic material in the study of first century Judaism, see E.P. Sanders, *Paul and Palestinian Judaism. A Comparison of Patterns of Religion* (London: SCM, 1977) 33-75.

[5] In contrast to the situation twenty years ago in Qumran scholarship, there exists no consensus on this point at present. For the purposes of this essay, whether the Scrolls express one or more Judaisms is not important, though it is universally conceded that the range of ideas present in the Scrolls can hardly be the exclusive property of one sect, whatever sect it might have been (and here

legal, eschatological and apocalyptic elements in this archive has demonstrated clearly that the Judaism of the period cannot be easily sociologically (or ideologically) divided by means of these categories. Finally, if further evidence of great diversity were needed, the vast amount of so-called pseudepigrapha dating from this period provide a ready store of examples.

The outcome of these developments is the now widely shared (though admittedly not unanimous) perception that what is called "Judaism" in the period before the fall of the Second Temple (and in effect a good deal later) was in reality a set of cultural/religious options. Sometimes they overlapped, sometimes they competed, and they ranged from what sociologists might nowadays call "civic religion" to quite exclusive sects. It is no longer possible to maintain unchallenged the notion of a "normative" Judaism in the Second Temple period,[6] although there remains a lively debate about what E.P. Sanders has described for the period 63 BCE-66 CE as a "common Judaism."[7] The extent of basic practices and, to a lesser extent, beliefs shared by many Jews does not, however, amount to a "Judaism," any more than observing the first day of the week, Christmas and Easter amounts to a Christianity; but the question of common practice will be addressed at the end of this essay.

Whether or not "common Judaism" is an appropriate term, the idea of a "common denominator" of Judaism, philosophically as well as historically, needs to be addressed. The replacement of the concept of "Judaism" by the concept of "Judaisms" solves one problem only to create another, perhaps even more fundamental one-namely what it was that made any "Judaism" a Judaism. On this question a good deal is taken for granted in modern (as in older) scholarship, and some disagreement is also evident. The nature of

---

there now is no agreement, either).

[6]   It should be acknowledged that there remains some dissent. Among the few who have contested this view are H. MacCoby, but his premises and methods of argumentation have induced little scholarly confidence in, or assent to, his conclusions. See his *Revolution in Judea: Jesus & the Jewish Resistance* (2nd ed.; New York: Taplinger, 1980).

[7]   See also the recent debate between C.A. Evans, ("'Mishna and Messiah' in Context: Some Comments on Jacob Neusner's Proposals," *JBL* 112 [1993] 267-89) and Neusner ("The Mishna in Philosophical Context and Out of Canonical Bounds," *JBL* 112 [1993] 291-304).

this problem can be illustrated neatly through two recent books on Judaism in the Second Temple period. One is G. Boccaccini's recent account of what he calls "Middle Judaism,"[8] which affirms that "Judaism is to be seen not as an ideologically homogeneous unit but ... as a set of different ideological systems in competition with one another" (13-4) and which characterizes "Judaism" as a "genus" (18-20). The other is L.H. Schiffman's history of Second Temple Judaism,[9] which states in conformity with the new paradigm that "Judaism is not a monolithic phenomenon," and speaks in the next sentence of "all these 'Judaisms'"(1), but which nevertheless prefers to speak thereafter of "approaches" to (one) Judaism that stand "in a dynamic and interactive relationship to each other" (4).[10]

What, in the case of Boccaccini, is common to these "different ideological systems" that makes them "Judaisms," or, in the case of Schiffman, what is the "Judaism" that all of these interacting manifestations "approach?" Even if "Judaism" is, as Boccaccini says, something of a generic term, the genus itself requires a definition, which is not given. In Boccaccini's treatment the essential nature of "Judaism" emerges differently, and indeed, only implicitly. At first glance, since the title of his book, *Middle Judaism*, requires an "Early Judaism" of some kind, and since the character of Middle Judaism, according to Boccaccini, is divergence, "Early Judaism" ought to describe some common starting point for that divergence. If an attempt were to be made to identify the contours of that "Early Judaism" that is implied by Boccaccini, one or two hints could be followed: for example, he refers to Ben Sira as "reaffirming the centrality of the covenant and the retributive principle" (80). Although he remarks that Job and Qoheleth challenged this centrally affirmed notion, the word "centrally" looks very much as if it is functioning here rather like "normative," with Job and Qoheleth representing dissenting and marginal viewpoints. Again dealing with

---

[8]   G. Boccaccini, *Middle Judaism: Jewish Thought 300 BCE to 200 CE* (Minneapolis: Augsburg-Fortress, 1991).

[9]   L.H. Schiffman, *From Text to Tradition: A History of Second Temple and Rabbinic Judaism* (Hoboken: KTAV, 1991).

[10]   The irony of this choice of term is probably unintentional: "Approaches to Ancient Judaism" was Neusner's title for a series of books that he and others edited and wrote.

Ben Sira, Boccaccini speaks of "the postulates of a theology of the covenant being reaffirmed," defining these postulates as "the freedom of human will and the retributionary principle" (116). Here again there is a hint of a normative "Early Judaism" in the guise of a "covenant theology." But it is nonetheless uncertain whether, despite these remarks, Boccaccini intends to commit himself to a definition of "Early Judaism"; it is clear to me both from some of his writings but chiefly from private conversations with him, that he is not prepared to identify any single "Early Judaism";[11] if so, then we are left without an account of what "Early Judaism" was, and thus, without a definition of the genus "Judaism," historically speaking, though Boccaccini seems to suggest something rather like Deuteronomism as a "central" feature of it.

Schiffman, on the other hand, gives a direct definition of "Judaism": "the collective religious, cultural and legal tradition and civilization of the Jewish people" (1). This might be interpreted as a tautology, if the word "collective" means no more than "sum total," i.e. "whatever Jews do"; but it seems fairly clear that Schiffman means instead some kind of unity, or at least cohesion. His notion of "tradition and civilization" comes into view when he is discussing the penetration into Yehud of "Hellenistic cultural values." He speaks of the "rural peasantry" of Yehud having "no intention of abandoning their ancestral way of life for the new cultural symbiosis" (71). (It is interesting that Schiffman describes this way of life as "Hebraic" rather than "Jewish"; he is perhaps trying to avoid tautology here!) Shortly before this, too, he writes of the "religious tradition" that the "Hellenizers" were challenging (68). Finally (98), where he is discussing "sectarianism" he observes that these divergent expressions of Judaism should not be taken as "independent Judaisms" because that term "ignores the vast body of commonality which united them around adherence to the law of the Torah" (98).

---

[11] Boccaccini's "postulates" of free will and retribution, which for him characterize "covenant theology," both lie just as obviously at the heart of the ideology of ancient Near Eastern wisdom writing generally and are reflected in the book of Proverbs. Yet Proverbs has no "covenant" concept. Why does Boccaccini then think that Ben Sira, as a wisdom teacher, is echoing Deuteronomistic ideas rather than the basic premises of wisdom teaching? Behind his interpretation of Ben Sira might be suspected the common assumption that the earliest form of Judaism was some kind of "biblical religion."

Here the language is a bit evasive: he does not want to repudiate "Judaisms" entirely, so he adds "independent." He also appears to regard the "ancestral way of life" as centering on the Torah. It seems reasonable, then, to ascribe to Schiffman the view that the various "approaches" to Judaism are versions of a common heritage, whose core is the Torah, and which can be defined over against the "Hellenizing" influences that tried to distort it. This perspective should be seen as justifying the central argument of Schiffman's book (against Neusner, though this is not explicit) that rabbinic Judaism is continuous with earlier "approaches" to Judaism and deeply rooted in the preceding Jewish tradition.

If I am interpreting both Schiffman and Boccaccini correctly, they appear to diverge quite significantly in their assessment of "Judaism." Schiffman has replaced "normative Judaism" by "collective Judaism," but the change is hardly more than linguistic. There is in his account a "Jewish tradition" from which various "approaches" developed. Boccaccini's presentation of "Middle Judaism" as manifold and divergent does not, on the other hand, explain what the various Middle Judaisms diverged *from*, and in fact leaves one wondering what these often quite different Judaisms could have had in common. But both scholars seem to agree on one thing, namely, a *descriptive* rather than a *prescriptive* approach to "Judaism(s)." But there is another difference between the two scholars of some relevance: for Schiffman, Jewish civilization is a matter essentially of the practice of the population. Boccaccini's agenda, however, is "Jewish thought" rather than a religious system: his "Middle Judaism" is defined by a set of thinkers and writers, not by a culture or a common tradition. It is a "Jewish thought," a cluster of intellectual systems expressed by individual authors. His "Judaism" is constituted by literary relics, and accordingly, he could presumably argue for an "Early Judaism" that similarly was expressed by literary works. But which literary works would be chosen? The biblical literature is hardly reducible to any kind of religious core, or religious system.

In the end, then, there is a divergence over the very *nature* of "Judaism" in these two works, and (as will be argued presently) it is not a divergence that can be left aside. There is a substantive issue here: did Judaism arise and develop as traditional social practice (with the peasants at times to the fore), or as a religious system or systems developed by intellectual reflection? And if we wished to answer "both," we could not avoid asking how the relationship between the two rather different phenomena is to be understood and expressed. There is, then, much of a fundamental nature that needs to be said on the problem of Judaism — not merely what its content was, but what sort of a thing it was in the first place. However desirable according to the canons of logic, neither of these questions can be disposed of in advance of exploring the origins of "Judaism," because only by such an historical investigation can it be discovered what "Judaism" came to be. But our investigation can at least start without a definite *a priori* conception of what it ought to have been, or what it claimed to have been.

Juda-ism and Judaism

As Neusner, Boccaccini and others have demonstrated, by concentrating on the doctrinal and literary aspects of "Judaism" in the last two centuries BCE, a diversity of ideas sufficient to justify the use of the "Judaisms" can easily be exposed. And yet, the replacement of "Judaism" by "Judaisms," rather than resolving the issue of what "Judaism" is, exacerbates it. The plural "Judaisms" requires some definition of "Judaism" in the singular, in order itself to have any meaning. Nevertheless, this does not mean that Schiffman's programmatic description of "Judaism" as "the culture of the Jewish people" can simply be accepted as valid. This formulation supposes that the "Jewish people" logically precedes "Judaism," whereas many Jews in the ancient world became so by voluntary or compulsory conversion to a religion that previously existed, so that in their case it was adherence to "Judaism" that made them "Jews." Schiffman's formulation also means that the origin of Judaism and of the Jewish people are one and the same question. Yet even he does not call the Israelites of the "preexilic" period "Jews." But if he had said (as indeed he may even have meant) that "Judaism is the culture of the people of Judea," he would have provided us with a proposition worth exploring. Even if "Judaism" came to embrace many non-Judeans (in the strict sense), it remains likely that the culture of Yehud/Judea must lie in some way at the origins and early development of "Judaism." In order to avoid tautology and introduce linguistic and historical precision, I shall therefore apply the distinction between "Jewish" and "Judean." Although in Hebrew (יהודי)

nor in Greek (ιουδαιοι) there is a *linguistic* distinction between the two meanings, the terms are not synonymous in English, nor in most other modern languages in which Jewish scholarship is conducted; nor, in fact, was it synonymous in the ancient languages either; when Paul called himself a "Jew," he may have understood it to mean "Judean" in an ethnic sense, but he did not understand it to mean that he came from Judah.

To begin, a historical distinction can be made between "Judaism" and "Judaism" by examining the word ιουδαισμος itself. The term implies a self-conscious cultural and religious identity and appears first several times in 2 Maccabees where, as Schwarz notes, it "parallels and contrasts with 'Hellenism' (*hellenismos*) and even 'foreignism' (*allophylismos*)."[12] As Schwarz also rightly notes (13), it is only when such a concept as "Judaism" comes into consciousness, that is, becomes conceptualized, that there is a need argue about what that concept denotes. Up to that moment, it may be a matter either of loyalty to a particular Temple and cult, or residence in Yehud/Judea, or perhaps of membership in a society ethnically defined in some way, or any combination of these. But the conscious "-ism" is a prerequisite, or at the least a symptom of the emergence of Judaism. Indeed, it is also a prerequisite of "Juda-ism" as a concept rather than as an unreflected way of being. Schwarz notes that "as long as 'being Jewish' [in my terminology, 'being Judean'] was basically a matter of place or race, there was no reason to assume that all should agree about belief or practice, any more than all French or all women do."[13] "Juda-ism" and "Judaism" imply the self-consciousness of a system of belief and/or practice, as opposed to unreflected participation in the culture or cultures of Yehud/Judea. What does this mean? It means that no genus of "Judaism" is logically and historically possible until the emergence of "Juda-ism" as a concept looking for a definition. And Juda-ism, the idea of a Judean way of life, does not necessarily entail "Judaism" or "Judaisms," though it implies them insofar as "Juda-ism" comes to be defined in different ways by different Judeans. To put

---

[12] D. Schwartz, *Studies in the Jewish Background of Christianity* (Tübingen: JCB Mohr, 1992) 11. See also Hengel, *Judaism and Hellenism* (2 vols.; London: SCM, 1974) 95-7.
[13] Schwartz, *Studies*, 13.

it as simply as possible, three stages can be posited: a Judean culture that has not yet been conceptualized and that therefore is not a "Juda-ism"; "Juda-ism," which constitutes the culture of Judea as an object of definition, and finally "Judaism" and "Judaisms," according to which "Juda-ism" develops into something more than (but also different from) the "culture of Judea." "Judaism," then, has a prehistory, and without understanding that prehistory no attempt can be made to begin writing the history. All three stages certainly cannot be merged under the single heading of "Judaism" without leaving "Judaism" itself ultimately inexplicable.

A study of the origins and prehistory of "Judaism" is quite possible along critical and historical lines, so long as the above distinctions are adopted at the outset.[14] The *origin of Judaism* is contained within the history of "Juda-ism," which itself has a moment of conception (in both senses) within the cultural history of Yehud/Judea. Recognizing that Judaism *has* a beginning, not in the mists of antiquity or in some other inaccessible source, but in historical and cultural events and processes, is an important first step in a *historical* approach to this religion.[15] Despite its stories about itself, Judaism did not begin at a "point," whether with Abraham, Moses or Ezra. The history of Judaism is not the history that Judaism has itself generated. Its characterization of itself as a "revealed" religion,[16] as timeless, is a theological claim, and not a historical one (as the rabbis understood much better than many modern scholars). Historically, it came into being by means of distinct cultural processes. It will not do to skate over these historical processes by appealing to a "tradition" that cannot be shown. Tradition is a product of a series of discrete developments and innovations that, nevertheless, becomes conceptualized by members of a society and by scholars as implying a repository of an essence that, though modified, does not undergo a change of character. My own view is that

---

[14] It is clear from these remarks that I would regard Hengel's *Judaism and Hellenism* to be conceptually inadequate in respect of what he calls "Judaism," which he nowhere defines as he does "Hellenism." On the other hand, his work opens the way towards treating "Judaism" (even "Juda-ism") as a product of "Hellenism."

[15] I am unhappy about the description "religion" but let the reader take this in its widest possible sense.

[16] "Judaism is fundamentally a revealed religion," Schiffman, *From Text to Tradition*, 17.

as a historical term rather than a purely sociological or theological one, it is virtually useless, and what it claims to represent should be analyzed dynamically in such a way as to expose its conception and evolution. Certainly, the implications that the terms carried of some essence that is somehow beyond the particularities of history must be rejected. The various "Judaisms" or "approaches to Judaism" discussed earlier have to be seen as part of the *development* of Juda-ism and Judaism, not as mere variations on an already established "tradition" whose essence is given in some undefined past. The practical wisdom of a Ben Sira, the mantic wisdom of the followers of the Enoch cult, the beliefs and rites of the Samaritans and the regimented lifestyle of the יחד all have to be fitted into the history of Judaism that needs to be constructed, in which "Judaism" is not a "given" at the outset (nor at the end, for that matter) but something that participates fully in the ever-changing flux of human thought and behavior.

False Origins

An account of the origins of Judaism, including its prehistory, needs first of all to clear away a number of assumptions and theories that do not pass critical reflection and yet serve very commonly as agreed starting points. A majority of scholars apparently accepts the view that the production of scriptures and the activities of Ezra and Nehemiah were important early stages in the formation of Judaism. It is first necessary, then, to see how far either of these two factors belongs to the origins of Judaism.

Scriptures

The notion that the Jewish scriptures provide an account of the earliest form of Judaism, or form its historical foundation, is unworkable on a number of grounds. First, the scriptures do not have their own intrinsic religious system. Their contents cannot be transcribed into a coherent set of beliefs and practices without the aid of an *external* framework of systematic theology that controls a hermeneutical process, such as is the case with both rabbinic Judaism and Christianity. The possible religious systems that could be derived from the scriptures are numerous.

Second, the scriptures cannot have described, or arisen directly from, an actual historical religious system, far less one that can be reconstructed from its contents. Such an assumption, which often seems to be present in scholarly accounts of Judaism, ignores the distinction between a culture and a literature, between a way of life and a set of ideas preserved in the writings of unknown authors, between the literature that became the scriptures of later Judaism and the actual lifestyle of Judeans. "Community of faith" is one common way of overriding this distinction, implying that all the scriptural writings emerged and were shaped by a society conscious of its own values and desirous of expressing these in writing. Preliterate societies do not work this way. Literary sources, necessarily coming from the educated elite, as the Jewish scriptures do, might in certain restricted cases represent an attempt to prescribe social practice, but literature of the kind found in the Jewish scriptures is not the means by which the literate seek to influence the behavior of the illiterate, or the rulers the behavior of the ruled. The religion to be practiced by an agrarian society will lie almost entirely outside the area of literary discourse. Peasants who have neither the facility nor the time to read or write books cannot be presumed to have lived according to the doctrines of learned literature; they themselves have left no reliable written record of their beliefs. The historian is only able to deduce their culture from archaeological research. In the Iron Age, the culture of the peasant seems to have been polytheistic, concerned with fertility and based on local and domestic shrines. Its folklore would probably have comprised such things as local legal practices, local stories about ancestors and places, and a collection of proverbial sayings. Even if all the foregoing observations were rejected, it would remain unlikely that peasant religion would have been concerned with torah, purity and the workings of the cult, or speculation on the origin of evil; nor would it have included a national historiographical tradition concentrating on the deeds of kings and prophets. The Jewish scriptures as representative of a Jewish society at any time is historically impossible.

Third, not all Judaisms seem to have taken scriptures as their basis. The literature of Enoch, Tobit and Ben Sira does not do so, nor the Mishnah. The Hekhalot literature does not, either; indeed, most of the works translated in Charlesworth's two-volume *Old Testament Pseudepigrapha* do not. Moreover, many of the writings that explicitly base themselves on scriptural texts (e.g. the Qumran פשרים) arise from forms of religious belief or cultural behavior that

are minimally represented in the scriptures, such as messianic ex-
pectation or the belief that future events can be divined from texts.
The scriptures function as an important part of most ancient Judaisms, but they did not, *as scriptures*, create Judaism. That does not
mean that as part of the created culture of Judah they did not play
an important role in the cultivation of Juda-ism.

Fourth, scriptures, as a corpus, and as religiously authoritative,
do not necessarily predate Second Temple Judaism. Many of these
writings are widely accepted as products of the Second Temple
period. But the view that torah and prophecy are already firmly
established in written (not necessarily final) form by the end of the
Babylonian exile needs to be challenged because it is precarious. I
have argued elsewhere, as have others[17] that the books of the Jewish Bible are not from the Iron Age, or even from the so-called
exilic period, but from the Persian and Hellenistic periods. It is fairly widely conceded that all of these books in their present form
must have come from this time. I have argued that the society constituted in Yehud in the 5th century BCE onwards generated, in the
literature now preserved in the Bible, its own literary tradition, including its history, wisdom teaching, cultic poetry and prophetic
corpus. Even accepting this thesis only in part, it has to be conceded that the formation of this later-to-be-biblical literature and the
formation of a Judean culture in the Persian period are contemporary processes, in which the literature is not prior to the culture, but
part of its expression. One is unjustified in programmatically setting
the biblical literature, or any substantial part of it, as something
that Second Temple society inherited rather than something it created.

The accumulation of the arguments just given makes it impossible to affirm that as a body of literature, or as individual works,
written and rewritten, the writings adopted as the Jewish scriptures
articulate an early stage of Judaism; they do not describe a religious
system, they are not a blueprint for the religion of Judaism, they
are not a description of a culture or expression of a tradition. They

---

[17] I am here drawing on the perspective outlined in my *In Search of 'Ancient
Israel'* (JSOTSup 148; Sheffield: JSOT Press, 1992) esp. 94-161; see also N.P. Lemche, "The Old Testament — a Hellenistic Book?" *SJOT* 55 (1992) 81-101 for a more
radical position.

are part of the intellectual process by which Juda-ism was articulated, and later, when adopted as a religious scripture, they played a vital role in the definition of most Judaisms, including, eventually, rabbinic Judaism. But from the historical point of view, the relationship between Judean culture, Judaism, and the scriptures is one of a fascinating and complex interaction. It is truer to say, if that relationship were to be simplified, that Judaism adopted the literature as scripture rather than that the scripture preceded and determined Judaism; the notion of a scripture without a Judaism is nonsensical, and until and unless scriptural, the literature could not play any decisive role in the formation of a "Judaism."

Ezra and Nehemiah

A second foundation of Judaism commonly offered by the relevant scholarly works is the work of Nehemiah and Ezra. These two, and especially Ezra, are commonly held to mark the beginning of Judaism; the reading of the law, the (re)making of a covenant, the establishment of social and religious exclusivity represent either the beginning or the rebirth of a religion constituted by an exclusive, ethnically-defined, law-bound relationship between a people and its deity. The essential historicity of the events described in the two books has rarely been questioned; the famous exception of C.C. Torrey[18] has attracted few supporters. Even Morton Smith abandoned most of his instinctive scepticism at this point and treated the accounts of these books as substantially historical reportage, even though he recognized a good deal of divergence from what he construed as the real state of affairs. Significantly, he suggested that the events related to a community within the society, the self-styled "children of the Exile."[19] Other scholars have also regarded this early "Judaism" as pertaining to a select group — Weinberg calls it

---

[18] C.C. Torrey, *Ezra Studies* (Chicago: University of Chicago, 1910).

[19] M. Smith, *Palestinian Parties and Politics that Shaped the Old Testament* (New York: University of Columbia, 1971); see also, however, his "The Dead Sea Sect in Relation to Ancient Judaism," *NTS* 7 (1961) 347-60 for an early perspective on the early "sectarian" character of Judaism.

a *Bürger-Tempel-Gemeinde*[20] — whose culture was gradually adopted
by the society of Yehud as a whole, and indeed, presumably by
those in Samaria too, a factor that is given too little attention. Such
a process, by which a certain culture and organization spread from
an elite group outwards to encompass a society, may well be essentially correct. But the source material, namely the books of Ezra
and Nehemiah, presents difficulties for historical reconstruction that
have always been recognized. To begin with, there is no general
critical consensus about the chronology of the two figures. This is
a result of the confusion caused by the books themselves, which
keep the two characters largely apart from one another but apparently date Ezra to about the same time as Nehemiah. There appears
no way in which these difficulties can be resolved, as long as historical reconstruction remains the primary agenda of scholarship on
these books.

From the point of view of the historicity of the events described
in these books, serious doubts have to be entertained. The stories of
Nehemiah and Ezra do not commend themselves as reliably informative; their contradictions and the overt symptoms they bear of
editorial attempts to overcome some of these inconsistencies lead
one to question how far, as accounts of the origin of "postexilic"
Judean society, they are to be treated as historiographical. The present form of these books points to the original independence of the
Ezra and Nehemiah materials, and the connection of the two figures is rather slim. At what point were Ezra and Nehemiah associated? Both Ben Sira and the author of 2 Maccabees know of Nehemiah, but neither mentions Ezra. In the case of Ben Sira, this is an
extremely eloquent silence. The only justifiable conclusion from
this silence about Ezra is that he remained separate from Nehemiah
until the end of the 2nd century BCE at the earliest. Had Ezra and
Nehemiah been historically associated, the fact that the literary evidence does not associate them until centuries after their ascribed
dates is inexplicable. Certainly, Ezra seems to fall under the greater
suspicion, since he is unattested elsewhere until the 1st century CE.

---

[20] See the convenient collection of Weinberg's essays in his *The Citizen Temple
Community* (JSOTSup 151; Sheffield: JSOT, 1992) and the further discussion in
P.R. Davies (ed.), *Second Temple Studies 1: Persian Period* (JSOTSup 151; Sheffield:
JSOT, 1991).

But even in the case of Nehemiah, the enmity expressed towards the Samarians suggests that the book has a secondary theme in denying any legitimacy to these would-be temple builders and may be evidence that the narrative postdates the separation of the Judean and Samarian Yahwistic communities and the building of a Samari-(t)an temple. Although a firm date for these events cannot be set, recent trends in scholarship suggest that they did not occur until the Hellenistic period.[21] In fact, how small or great any historical kernel may be cannot really be assessed: the imprecisions in these books are widely accepted; their historical reliability remains a matter of charitable assumption.[22] To speculate endlessly and fruit-lessly about the possibilities of events for which there is as yet no other evidence and about the authenticity of "official" documents of which no other copies exist and which we know cannot in any case all be entirely authentic is to strain at gnats while swallowing a camel.

Some recent trends in Ezra and Nehemiah studies, however, of-fer a departure from questions such as the priority of one or, other, the identity of Ezra's lawbook, the nature of the reforms of Nehe-miah, or the authenticity of the Aramaic documents. Greater atten-tion is being been paid to their literary and ideological aspects.[23] The recent and widely-supported challenge to the view that these books belong to the Chronicler's work has also reopened the ques-tion of their purpose. Consequently, attention is being diverted away from the historicity of the details and towards the more

---

[21] See the discussion and bibliography in J.D. Purvis, "The Samaritans and Ju-daism," in *Early Judaism and its Modern Interpreters* (ed. R.A. Kraft and G.W.E. Nickelsburg; Philadelphia: Fortress and Atlanta: Scholars, 1986) 81-98.

[22] I am here consciously advancing beyond my own remarks in *In Search of 'Ancient Israel'*, 75-93 and esp. 86, where my use of the Nehemiah-Ezra material was criticized for failing to meet the critical standards I was demanding of others. I hope that my approach here comes closer to those standards.

[23] See e.g. T.C. Eskenazi, *In an Age of Prose: A Literary Approach to Ezra-Nehe-miah* (SBLMS 36; Atlanta: Scholars, 1988); D.J.A. Clines, "The Perils of Autobio-graphy" in *What Does Eve Do To Help? and Other Readerly Questions to the Old Testament* (JSOTSup 94; Sheffield: JSOT, 1990) 124-64; J.C. VanderKam, "Ezra-Nehemiah or Ezra and Nehemiah?," in *Priest, Prophets and Scribes. Essays on the Formation and Heritage of Second Temple Judaism in Honour of Joseph Blenkinsopp* (ed. E. Ulrich *et al.*; JSOTSup 149; Sheffield: JSOT, 1992) 55-75; D. Kraemer, "On the Relationship of the Books of Ezra and Nehemiah," *JSOT* 59 (1993) 73-92.

promising quest for the historical circumstances that might account for the production of such narratives. If such a new agenda for historical research has yet to become fully explicit, it is surely more productive for the historian of Judaism to accept the clear evidence that these books are far removed from the time they describe and to ask about the function of stories and of characters such as these in such a later period. Indeed, this approach also seems the best way to account for the literary form of the books of Ezra and Nehemiah. Such an approach might begin with the observation that the two books, or the tales attached to the two characters, claim to describe *the origin of Judaism*; two stories, which inherently contradict one another by assigning functions to each that undermine the functions of the other, have been flimsily entwined by an editor, and no earlier than the 2nd century BCE. Hence, it appears plausible that *competing* claims about the origin or the true founder of "Judaism" (and in each case the "Judaism" is differently conceived) have been reconciled editorially, with the happy result not only that these ancient rivals were accommodated into a single and perhaps mutually acceptable legend, but also, unhappily, that modern and so-called critical historians are chasing historical scenarios that never existed. An investigation into these books, then, needs to be first focused on the end of the 2nd century BCE or perhaps later, when a hitherto unknown (to our extant sources) Ezra confronted Nehemiah for the post of founder of Judaism. From here can be explored the subsequent point at which a literary compromise was reached to the satisfaction of both sets of proponents, who thereafter could not deny one without the other. But it can be said that, thereafter, Ezra seems to have been the more popular figure. Perhaps this superiority suggests simply that the "Ezraite" definition of Judaism prevailed, as indeed, it seems to have in the form of rabbinic Judaism, whereas the builder of the walls of Jerusalem under imperial patronage perhaps looked suspiciously like a predecessor of Herod the Great.

This historical agenda can be carried further by involving another account of the origins of "Judaism," which has not found its way into the biblical literature, and yet another "founder." It is contained in the *Damascus Document* (CD), whose date of composition is probably not too far removed from that of the Ezra story.[24] According to the *Damascus Document*, the exilic punishment on Israel led to the restoration of a remnant, to whom the true divine will about sabbaths, feasts and laws was given. While the rest of Israel went astray, this chosen remnant remained to await the divine judgement on Israel and on the Gentiles, anticipating salvation and vindication for themselves.[25] The revelation of the law and the foundation of this "true Israel" is credited to a figure known as the "Interpreter of the Law" (דרש התורה). The account is different in scope, in literary form and in some details, from both Ezra and Nehemiah. But these differences are mostly attributable to the literary genre in which the story is embedded, and to the fact that CD's "Judaism" is yet again different from that implicitly advanced in either Ezra or Nehemiah. The similarities between the three accounts are even more striking and significant; they presuppose the same story of Israel's "preexilic" past (though the historical narrations of that period have quite different emphases)[26] and the exile as punishment for that past. All three accounts, significantly, speak of a covenant with the members of the elect group that is based on a lawgiving, and all three allude to a process of interpretation of that law and deal with issues of holiness and separation from "outsiders" (and indeed from other Judeans, the "people of the land" or "builders of the wall"). In these respects the accounts all reflect a certain common perspective on "Judaism."

CD seems to belong broadly to the same ideological circle as Jubilees, Enoch and Daniel, which, in addition to other resemblances they share, deny that any "restoration" took place immediately after the end of the "exile" and ignore or belittle the building of a Temple at about that time. These works are datable to the period

---

[24] CD and "Damascus Document," strictly speaking, refer to the medieval manuscripts of a text known to have originated in the same way as many of the Qumran texts. Unfortunately, it is impossible to reconstruct with certainty any supposedly "original form" from the Qumran fragments, despite assertions to the contrary. Much of the Qumran material simply does not overlap. For a survey of the Q material and its readings, see M. Broshi (ed.), *The Damascus Document Reconsidered* (Jerusalem: Israel Exploration Society, 1992).

[25] For fuller discussion see my *The Damascus Covenant* (JSOTSup 25; Sheffield: JSOT, 1982) 56-104.

[26] Nehemiah 9; CD 2.14-3.12.

suggested earlier for the appearance of Ezra as a contender to Nehemiah, and betray a conscious conflict over the matter of the "origins" of Israel. It seems pertinent to recall the theory of Smith that the Nehemiah covenant was, like that of CD, a sectarian one. Rather than understanding the history of Judaism to begin with a firm historical tradition, what is found is a range of competing traditions, clustering around the same period, with only Nehemiah attested before 200 BCE as a builder of Jerusalem (Ben Sira 49:13).

The case of Ezra and Nehemiah represents, therefore, a microcosm of the issue outlined earlier about the relationship between scriptures and Judaism: a literary text cannot be taken as a matter of course, whether scriptural or not, in isolation as an historical basis for explaining the origin of Judaism; rather, the context of that literary work must first be found, and in this case the material itself reflects a certain stage in the evolution of Judaism(s). When critically examined, Ezra and Nehemiah presuppose the existence of what they are supposed to be founding and can provide information only about a period much later than the Persian era, contributing to a quite different story about the origins of "Judaism."

Regarding "Juda-ism" in the Persian period, however, the self-designation of the colony of Elephantine as "Judeans" and the preservation of a culture that is both similar to Iron II Judah but which also shows traces of local assimilation in custom and personnel are interesting features revealed in the letters that have been excavated at the site. Since it had been probably been founded under the Assyrians, few if any of this military colony were native Judahites or Judeans. "Judean" identity is perhaps to be taken as ethnic in the technical sense and not necessarily in the strictly genealogical sense, since an *ethnos* is a community that assumes an identity that genealogy only *expresses*. It is likely that if the Elephantine garrison had been originally composed of Judahites, all its members over the succeeding generations, whatever their origin, automatically would have assumed the label and the identity "Judean", including their choice of cult and of personal names. This is known to have been the case with other military colonies in the Hellenistic period. Such cases, if established, provide one example of the spread of "Juda-ism" beyond Judah/Judea, in which the evolution of Judaisms in Judah played a fairly peripheral or at least indirect role. It would accordingly be misleading to speak of the culture of these colonies as a "Judaism" undifferentiated in nature from other "Judaisms." In this paper, however, I cannot even begin to deal with such intriguing cases of "Judaism." I merely wish to underline that other than this archive, which is not even from Judah anyway, very little is known as yet about the culture of native or non-native Judeans in the 5th century BCE beyond arti-factual (including some inscriptional) evidence.[27]

Scenes from Judah in the Hellenistic Period

Hecataeus of Abdera

From about the beginning of the Hellenistic period (ca. 300 BCE), several references to Judeans by non-Judean authors are known. Of these the most interesting, and the most discussed, is that of Hecataeus of Abdera.[28] A summary of his accounts of Judean history and constitution is preserved in the work of the 1st century BCE plagiarist Diodorus Siculus (40.3);[29] a further excerpt from his book "written entirely about the Jews," is preserved in Josephus,[30] but the extent of its authenticity remains disputed, and it will not

---

[27] K. Hoglund's *Achaemenid Imperial Administration in Syria-Palestine and the Missions of Ezra and Nehemiah* (SBLDS 125; Atlanta: Scholars, 1992) is an excellent study of the period, except for its assumption that the stories of Ezra and Nehemiah are historically reliable. It also suffers from an agenda based on the biblical narratives. The Elephantine garrison, as far as their archive shows, wished to re-build their temple to Yaho/u, to which end they sent letters first to the sons of the governor of Samaria, then to the governor of Judah. They venerated other gods and goddesses and apparently did not know of Passover (contrary to what is often asserted).

[28] There is a convenient summary of the literature and issues in L.L. Grabbe, *The Jews from Cyrus to Hadrian* (2 vols., Minneapolis: Fortress, 1991) 1.173; for this particular account see 216-8. Text, translation and discussion are in M. Stern (ed.), *Greek and Latin Authors on Jews and Judaism*, 1.20-35); further discussion in Hengel, *Judaism and Hellenism* (3 vols.; Jerusalem: Academy of Sciences and Humani-ties, 1974) 1.255-6; 2.169 and E. Schürer, *The History of the Jewish People in the Age of Jesus Christ* (3 vols.; rev. edn; ed. G. Vermes, F. Millar and M. Goodman; Edin-burgh: T.& T. Clark, 1986) 3.1.671-7.

[29] The ascription by Diodorus (or by Photius? Diodorus' text is preserved in Photius' *Bibliotheca*) of these comments to Hecataeus of Miletus (ca. 500 BCE) is generally taken as an error.

[30] *Contra Apionem I*, 183-204; see Stern, *Greek and Latin Authors*, 1.35-44, who takes it as basically authentic, as does the revised edition of Schürer.

be considered here. According to the preserved testimony, a pestilence in Egypt at some time (Hecataeus gives no chronological clues) prompted the inhabitants to expel certain strangers who practised alien rites; of these deportees, some landed in Greece, but the larger number in Judea, which was then uninhabited. They settled under the leadership of Moses, who founded several cities, including Jerusalem, where he established a temple. He also set up "forms of worship and ritual," laws, and political institutions. He divided the people into twelve tribes, forbade images to be made of their sole deity, and appointed priests, who were to be not only in charge of the cult but also political leaders and judges. Thus, he says, "the Jews have never had a king" but are ruled by a high priest, who enjoys great power and prestige. Moses also instituted a military education and led the people to many conquests against neighboring tribes, after which he apportioned the land equally, but reserving larger portions for the priests. The sale of land was forbidden, specifically so as to avoid oppression of the poor by the rich through accumulation of land. The people were also enjoined to reproduce. In marriage and burial their customs differed from those of others, though their traditional practices were disturbed under the Persians and Macedonians. The Judeans' laws claim to have been words heard by Moses from God.

It is immediately apparent that at least superficially this account demonstrates some Hellenistic features. For instance, Moses appears as a typical colony founder. There is also a patently Egyptian legend underlying the account of the origin of the Judeans in Egypt; In a passage almost certainly reproduced from Hecataeus, Diodorus elsewhere (1.28.1-3) reproduces an Egyptian legend or myth that most of the civilized world came about through colonization from Egypt: thus Belus led colonists to Babylon, Danaus to Greece, and others to Colchis and Judea.[31] A few elements of Hecataeus account are also traceable in Manetho's stories preserved in Josephus, notably the name Moses and the immediate connection between the departure from Egypt and the foundation of Jerusalem.

But how accurately might this account reflect (a) the profile of Judean culture at the end of the 4th century and (b) the account of

---

[31]   For the text and translation, see Stern, *Greek and Latin Authors*, 1.169.

their history that the Judean themselves had? It has been widely surmised that Hecataeus must have had some Judean information, whether from Judeans living in Egypt or from those in Judea itself. A study of this account by D. Mendels has proposed that Hecataeus' account is fairly accurately preserved and reflects Judean ideas emanating from priestly circles from his own time.[32] Mendels' contention is based on correspondences between the account and the situation described in Ezra and Nehemiah, which he takes to be a reliable portrait of Yehud in the Persian period. Although I have earlier argued against this view, many of Doron's observations and arguments nevertheless suggest that Hecataeus was fairly closely reflecting the state of affairs in Judea during his own time. Mendels notes that the Judeans are said to have occupied a land that was "utterly uninhabited" after leaving Egypt. This, as he notes, conflicts with the Pentateuchal tradition, but is in accordance with the ideology represented in Nehemiah and Ezra that maintains that the returnees from exile had come to an empty land. He cites Nehemiah 2-4 and Judith 5:19; but as noted by R.P. Carroll[33] the ideology of the "empty land" appears even more emphatically in Jeremiah 32 and Leviticus 25-27 and so can be seen as a perception outside the books of Ezra and Nehemiah. These books, on the contrary, do not stress the concept of the "empty land"; indeed, in them we meet the "people of the land" on several occasions, though in an entirely negative sense. Hecataeus' view, then, is reflected in some biblical texts, giving support to Mendel's contention that Hecataeus reports a perspective of the land as having been "empty" from the point of view of the immigrants who would have been the ancestors of his informants.[34]

---

[32]   D. Mendels, "Hecataeus of Abdera and a Jewish 'patrios politeia'," *ZAW* 95 (1983) 96-110.

[33]   "Textual Strategies and Ideology," in *Second Temple Studies I: Perisan Period* (ed. P.R. Davies; JSOTSup 151; Sheffield: JSOT, 1992) 108-24.

[34]   The argument could be pressed further: such an attitude points to a strongly imperialistic or at least colonial mentality on the part of the immigrants and strengthens the suspicion that they were not conscious of being (and perhaps were not in reality) of the same stock and nationality as those who lived in the land being colonized. The strenuous efforts of the writer of Isaiah 40-55 to persuade the Judeans that the newcomers really were "daughters of Zion" suggests that the indigenous inhabitants (specifically, their hitherto ruling classes) were not convinced

As for Moses' having founded Jerusalem and other cities, Mendels suggests that because of the authority of Moses during the Persian period and particularly the authority of his "law," Hecataeus may have understood Moses also to have been a city-founder. To support his explanation, he claims that the role of David is underplayed in Ezra–Nehemiah. Rather than focusing on unconvincing parallels in Ezra–Nehemiah, there are other divergences from what became the canonical version of Judean history that need to be considered together and not piecemeal. Moses is credited with conquest, with the creation of twelve tribes and with the division of land. These activities correspond in some measure to the story in the book of Joshua, where, however, another hero is credited with conquest and land allotment. The statement that the Judeans had always been ruled by priests and never by a king is blatantly contradicted by the canonical history as well as by Ezra–Nehemiah, where references are made to David (Ezra 3:10), a king of Israel who built the temple (Ezra 5:11), Solomon (by name, Neh 13:26), and Israelite "kings" generally (Ezra 4:20 — in a letter from the Persian king that many scholars consider authentic; 9:7 and Neh 9:32). This is an interesting state of affairs: Hecataeus' source did not seem to know of the books of Samuel, Kings or Chronicles but did know of some stories that appear in Joshua, though differently ascribed. He also knows of something like an "Exodus". It cannot be insisted that the reliability of Hecataeus' information is simply erratic. Since there is no evidence to the contrary, this account may just as well preserve a precious insight into the early stages of the formation of the Pentateuchal tradition, a national history of the people of Judea in the process of being written (and created), and — most curious of all — clustering around a hero with an undoubtedly Egyptian name. Was Hecataeus garbling the book of Exodus, or the other way round? Since neither story appears to accord with the archaeologically-derived historical knowledge we have at present, this will not be an easy question to answer![35]

---

of shared roots with the new immigrants, either.

[35] Deuteronomy, after all, has the Moses who has led the Israelites out of Egypt legislating for the constitution of the people. Does Moses' death belong in the original Deuteronomy, or is it introduced when that book is inserted into the larger historiographical context? An original form of Deuteronomy could easily be

Quite apart from our lack of ability to date the formation of the Pentateuchal tradition, some degree of credence ought to be given to Hecataeus's account simply because he appears to be quite accurate in other details regarding the Judeans' account of their history. He knows that the laws governing cult and ritual are ascribed to Moses and even that Moses is claimed to have heard them from God. In calling this cult monotheistic and aniconic he is presumably also observing correctly. He even knows that Moses appointed judges (see Numbers 11)!

He is also correct, as far as is known, about the high priest being the ruler of the Judeans, and his observations about land tenure fit with what most scholars believe was the practice — at least during the monarchic period. Of course, the sorts of changes in land tenure often posited for this earlier period are just as plausibly set in the Persian and Hellenistic periods, so that some, or even all of the "prophetic" material in the Bible protesting at the accumulation of land must at least be considered as possibly emanating from this later period.[36]

Finally, there is the matter of military education. The widespread use of Jews as mercenaries is well-known from the Assyrian period (when the Elephantine colony was set up) to the Hellenistic period. The likelihood that Judeans were trained in the military arts is quite high, in view of this and of their initial success during the Maccabean wars, when a quite effective militia seems to have been organized. In any case a military aspect to Judean culture is probably betrayed in its literature, in the elaboration not only of the military victories in Joshua and the "holy war" ideology of Deuteronomy and Deuteronomistic writings, but also in the depiction of the Israelites in the wilderness as a nation-army. That material strongly suggests a self-image of Judeans as a nation of warriors. In-

---

reconstructed on the basis of Hecataeus' information.

[36] For a detailed analysis of the relevant prophetic texts, though in the context of very conventional datings, see most recently R. Kessler, *Staat und Gesellschaft im vorexilischen Juda. Vom 8. Jahrhundert bis zum Exil* (VTSup 47; Leiden: Brill, 1992). The implications of land tenure for the development of Judean society in the Second Temple period are discussed by H. Kreissig, *Die sozialökonomische Situation im Juda zur Achämenidenzeit* (Schriften zur Geschichte und Kultur des alten Orients 7; Berlin: Akademie, 1973); H. Kippenberg, *Religion und Klassenbildung im antiken Judäa* (SUNT 14; Göttingen: Vandenhoeck & Ruprecht, 1978).

deed, one title given to their deity, יהוה צבאות, probably means "Yahweh of armies" (whether astral or earthly is not very important: probably both).

The account of the Judeans by Hecataeus furnishes an extremely important, and certainly undervalued, source of information about the culture, and especially about the historiographical activity of Judah at the dawn of the Hellenistic era. If Hecataeus is as reliable in all matters as he is in those that can be tested, his work reflects "Juda-ism" at a relatively early stage of formation; the Temple cult, priesthood and a distinctive land tenure system have been established, but only a rudimentary history has yet been formed to explain who these "Judeans" are, where they came from, and how they got their deity. Between the beginning of the 3rd century and its end, when Ben Sira wrote his scroll, the extent to which practices, beliefs and historiography have developed can perhaps be traced. The more or less contemporary descriptions by Theophrastus, Clearchus and Megasthenes[37] should also be consulted. Rather than an ancient Judean "tradition," a dynamic process of ideological formation is revealed, the end product of which is a conscious "Juda-ism," a developed identity of which any Jerusalem *literatus* can be proud. No doubt the impact that the Ptolemaic administration made, notably in respect of economic exploitation, urban development and bureaucratic intrusion even into the rural areas, facilitated that development by presenting Judeans with a culture in the face of which their own identity needed to be more strongly defined and articulated.

Ben Sira

Ben Sira (end of 3rd century BCE) is a key figure in the evolution of Judaism, both because of the time and place he occupies and also because of the influence his writings had in different kinds of Judaism. A wisdom teacher whose work belongs to a well-known Near

---

[37] Theophrastus (ca. 370-285 BCE) describes Judeans as philosophers, performing burnt offerings, looking at the stars while praying, and fasting. Clearchus (early 3rd century), like Theophrastus, classes the Judeans as "philosophers" and traces their origin to India; Megasthenes, too, (ca. 300) associates the Judean philosophers with India (anticipating Max Weber?).

Eastern genre,[38] he was also devoted to the cult and the priesthood of Jerusalem. He was aware of a Mosaic lawbook, the "book of the covenant of the Most High God" and also spoke of "the law" (תורה), which will be considered presently. He was familiar with the cultural world of Hellenism, which he did not oppose, though his writings demonstrate above all a fusion of the traditional ethos of wisdom with something more specific, a Jewish, or Judean culture.[39]

The kernel of Ben Sira's culture, his "Juda-ism," is the temple and priesthood itself; but Ben Sira shows himself familiar with native Judean literature, which he not only has read, but can imitate and which he intends to augment through his own writing (see 24:30-31). He attests to a Judean education, whose curriculum, whatever Greek elements it contains, includes native literature in the "national tongue" of Hebrew. This literature and its contents he has absorbed and is passing on as "wisdom." Thus, by his time Judah must have possessed a substantial body of writing in its own language (whether a living language or a book language), which continued to be taught and learned but which also was extended. How did this literature come about, and what was Ben Sira's knowledge of it and attitude to it?

The Judean literature that became in the end "scripture" was hardly originally conceived for this purpose, not least because there was no concept of "scripture" nor was there yet a religious system that would require it. This literature has achieved the status it has in Ben Sira's time by being adopted by the educated as part of a

---

[38] In this section I am developing some of the material to be found in my *In Search of 'Ancient Israel'*, 134-54; conversely, some matters receive a fuller treatment there than they do here.

[39] The traditional ethos of wisdom I take to be empirical, non-nationalistic, ethical and thoroughly represented by the writer of Qohelet. Indeed, a study of Jewish philosophy might well start with this text, perhaps the oldest Judean philosophical text that exists. Qoheleth does not deny the traditional wisdom dualism between wise and foolish, but he does deny that these are synonymous with the religious categories of righteous and wicked. In a fuller study it would have been possible to analyze his ideas for evidence of a growing awareness of a development towards a religious rationalizing of wisdom, possibly one of the deepest and earliest roots of what would emerge as "Judaism." But this must await another study.

Judean school curriculum,[40] and *this* status *is* consistent with the aims of its creation. For behind its production and development lie two distinct motives: one was to generate a cultural and social identity, the other to refine that identity and oppose it to the identities that other cultures and peoples were furnishing for themselves. If the matrix for the initial formation of this literature is the Persian period, it has to be allowed that it was the Hellenistic matrix that expanded, shaped and refined that corpus. The outcome of this activity is the production of a "tradition" of a similar kind to the "highland tradition" of Scotland or the druidic fantasies of Welsh bards, or indeed, the stories and ritual of the United States of America known as Thanksgiving. The invention of an identity, which these storis and rituals accomplish, is part of the creation of nationhood. Its creation and sustenance are often left in the care of the wise men, the elders, such as Ben Sira.[41]

It must be made clear that Ben Sira does not know the five books that now constitute the Pentateuch in their now canonical form. He is more knowledgeable about Adam and Enoch than the modern reader of Genesis would be; he may well be ignorant of Genesis 2-3 and seems not to have heard of either Ezra or of Joseph's exploits in Egypt. It is as clear that Ben Sira does not regard this literature as what might now be termed "scripture." He does not cite proof texts from the literature, nor does he exegete passages from it.[42] Commentators generally assume, nevertheless, that he identifies "wisdom" with "law" and by "law" (תורה) they assume he

---

[40] On the Jewish school, see Hengel, *Judaism and Hellenism*, 76-83.

[41] On the production of history in connection with "nationhood" and its cultural roots and implications, see J. Van Seters, *In Search of History: Historiography in the Ancient World and the Origins of Biblical History* (New Haven and London: Yale University, 1983).

[42] "Ben Sira hat in seinem Buch weder ein zusammenhängendes Stück des A.T. ausgelegt, noch hat er beabsichtigt, ein Glaubensbekenntnis umfassender Art abzulegen. Er hat die Schriftstellen und biblischen Redewendungen einfach für seine Gedanken verwendet. ... Ben Sira eine Schriftauslegung befolgt hat, die einem griechisch geschulten Leser verständlich war." Middendorp, *Die Stellung Jesu Ben Siras zwischen Judentum und Hellenismus* (Leiden: Brill, 1973) 90-1. An interesting case is 3:1-6, where Ben Sira exhorts children to honor their father and mother; he even says that it is the Lord's will. Yet he represents this as his own advice, and does not say that this is a divine written commandment. The "commandments" (1:26) and "words" (2:15) are not synonymous with scripture.

means the five books of Moses, the earliest body of Jewish scriptures. This is unlikely. First, Ben Sira's discourse lays primacy on wisdom, with which the "fear of the Lord" is more or less synonymous. Nowhere does he write that this wisdom is coextensive with a prescribed body of writing, not even his own. The "law which Moses commanded" is probably only Deuteronomy (in some form), since (1) this book is the only book that claims to be "commanded" by Moses,[43] (2) Ben Sira's use of the terms "words" and "commandments" (1:26; 2:15) echo particularly the vocabulary of Deuteronomy;[44] (3) the phrase "law that Moses commanded" is in parallel to "book of the covenant of the Most High" (24:23), which, as a single "book" comprising a covenant, can only be Deuteronomy. This conclusion would suggest in turn that the Mosaic "constitution" to which Hecataeus referred was also some form of Deuteronomy.

It is true that Ben Sira regards the words of Moses as commandments of God, just as Hecataeus wrote that the Judeans regarded the words of Moses as heard from God. But, does he regard Moses' writings as from God in an essentially different way from his own words, which, according to the same discourse (24:30-32) are "prophecy" and elsewhere are "wisdom" and will be a "bequest to future generations," (24:33) just as Moses' words were (24:23)?[45] "Torah," as Ben Sira uses the term generally, is no more the summation of divine wisdom than are Ben Sira's own words. True, he uses the word תורה to refer to the "law of Moses," but more often he means not some concrete Mosaic lawbook but something more abstract. Thus, for instance, in 41:8 he condemns those who have "forsaken the תורה of the Most High God." "Wisdom" and "law" are for Ben Sira synonymous, where "law" approximates to the Stoic meaning of νομος and wisdom consists in discovering and living according to

---

[43] The phrase, including the words that follow, is probably a quotation from Deut 33:4.

[44] See also 42:2: "do not be ashamed of the law and covenant of the Most High," a *hendiadys* referring to the Mosaic lawbook. It is one of a list of things of which not to be ashamed, however.

[45] I cannot help but think of 2 Tim 3:16; possibly "all scripture/literature is divinely inspired, etc." refers there to a distinct body of writings — but does the author here exclude his own work? If so, he was subsequently proved wrong!

it. Thus, Ben Sira's use of תורה equates it with wisdom, and that תורה can be concretely manifested in a particular form of teaching, be it his own or the book of the covenant by Moses. But it does not seem that תורה has yet acquired the sense of a technical term for a collection of writings. In 39:1 both senses are used: the "law of the Most High" that Ben Sira's scribe studies is the goal of all wisdom and embraces not only the contents of many writings but also empirically learned laws, while the "law of the Lord's covenant" (39:8) is specifically a book, and — as suggested earlier — most probably Deuteronomy.

It is incorrect, then, to find in Ben Sira a Jewish teacher who already sees the study of scripture and its interpretation as the essence of his Judaism. The effect of this misunderstanding is to retroject a later development onto an earlier period and thus to ensure that this development, the emergence of the category of "scripture," will be interpreted out of its proper historical context. For Ben Sira, the demarcation between "scripture" and "interpretation" is not yet a valid one; his understanding of "Judaism" is that it is the fullest expression of divine wisdom, the fulfilment of the "law of the Most High God." This includes due worship in the cult, respect for the "covenant" that is expressed in the law of God as given to Moses, and study of prophecy and wisdom. His own words do not stand over against a "scripture" as an interpretation of them, but alongside the Judean literature, as part of it.

Ben Sira's Judaism is not a revealed religion in Schiffman's sense: "... based on the belief that God revealed himself to the Jewish people through the agency of Moses." If that were so, Ben Sira's book would not be, as it so obviously is, a genuine book of wisdom, such as the *Wisdom of Solomon* is not. A comparison of the two writings is highly instructive. Ben Sira's Juda-ism draws on the Mosaic covenant book for its political manifesto and on other writings for a cultural resource; but the cult and priesthood are emphasized as the symbol of national unity and identity, and wisdom is the basis of its ethic. Ben Sira's תורה is not the תורה of later Judaism, as many modern scholars (including *both* Schiffman *and* Boccaccini) suppose.

Juda-ism in Conflict

The importance of the Maccabean revolt for the definitive transition from Juda-ism (as arguably found in Ben Sira) to Judaism is that it took the form of a *religious* war. Whatever the root causes of that conflict, which were at least as much economic and political as religious, Antiochus IV was seen by the Judeans who resisted him to have attacked the foundation of Juda-ism, its major symbols of national identity, the highpriesthood (in which he was not, of course, the initiator), and the cult. Inevitably, a cultural conflict became a religious war: 1 Maccabees represents the protagonists as Israel on the one hand and the "nations" on the other, and narrates this conflict as a replay of the time of the Judges. Similarly, the author offers the Maccabees to the readers as descendants, literal and spiritual, of the zealously xenophobic and anti-idolater Phinehas.

Nevertheless, this nationalistic and xenophobic level is not the only one that 1 Maccabees, an account of the war according to a keen promoter of the Hasmonean dynasty, sustains. Alongside the conflict between Israel and the nations is set another, between "apostates" and "pious" within Judea. Naturally, righteousness lies with the victors: a dispassionate assessment is no more to be expected than historical accuracy in an historian of this period. Some apparently fundamental elements of Judaism emerge here as key issues in the religious struggle — circumcision, diet, sabbath, holy books. These are identified as the features upon which Antiochus' attempts to eliminate Judean culture were focused (apart from the obvious case of the Temple cult). These practices (presumably fundamental to Schiffman's "traditional Judaism") become dominant characteristics of Judaism in due course. Yet, do they constitute that clearly recognizable Judaism which, according to 1 Maccabees, Antiochus recognized and tried to destroy, which "hellenizers" tried to reform, and which others defended with their lives? Was the Maccabean war about the preservation of such practices, as definitions of an agreed "Judaism?" It needs to be recognized that for *some* Judeans these practices were apparently not fundamental. At the same time, the historical circumstances, social context and ideological agenda of the Jewish accounts of the Maccabean war must be borne in mind. The most cherished prize of the victor is the right to define the history of the past, and all the Jewish sources for the Maccabean period (Daniel excepted) stem from well after the establishment of the

Hasmonean dynasty, thus reflecting what were subsequently understood or perhaps decreed to have been the issues involved in the de-
fence of "Judaism." In other words, the Judaism that was success-
fully "defended" was the Judaism of the victors, not simply "the
people of Judah" but those among the people of Judah who fought
and won (or, perhaps, those who led those who fought and won).
Those things that Judeans came to revere as the trophies of independence are represented as the issues over which the struggle was
joined. Circumcision, dietary customs, sabbath observance and holy
books emerged as issues that for the Hasmoneans, or their various
supporters, especially defined Judaism; but the possible status of
these practices before the Maccabean period needs to be considered.
Was it the case that the victors stood for a clearly accepted definition of Judaism, or did their success enable them to impose the definition that they wished? How much of the unity of "Judaism"
that the Hasmoneans achieved is to be retrojected? Given the nature
of the evidence, this question cannot be answered very fully, yet it
is important that it be asked, if only to avoid being ensnared as
historians in the propaganda of the past and being misled into en-
dorsing a view of Judaism that is not critically based.

Circumcision is prominent as a custom which, according to 1
Maccabees, some Jews tried to conceal, others abandoned, and the
Maccabees enforced. The custom was practised among many people
in the Levant during all preceding periods, and while a distinguish-
ing feature of being Judean, it was not entirely distinctive; certainly
it cannot always have been an outward sign of the covenant of god
and people that it later came to be.[46] What caused it to become a

---

[46] The evidence from the Bible is intriguing and worthy of a detailed study.
Deuteronomy and Jeremiah contain the expression "circumcision of the heart," a
Deuteronomistic *topos*. A further Deuteronomistic (?) text, Josh 5:2, contains an account of a circumcision of all Israelites after crossing the Jordan. Although Josh 4:2
ascribes to this operation some importance, circumcision is not connected with
any covenant ceremony nor given any religious rationale. Exod 4:26 provides an
aetiology of some sort, which continues to defy explanation, though it has suggested to some commentators that circumcision was thought to be connected with
marriage and that failure to circumcise might cause divine retribution. The key
text is Gen 17:10-14, where circumcision is named as a mark of the covenant. Unfortunately, this passage cannot be dated, and so the process of connection between
circumcision and covenant remains obscure.

central feature of Juda-ism, and the major religious symbol of all Judaisms — and when?[47] As an initial attempt to answer, it can be noted that circumcision became a mark of difference only when publicly shown, and that it was in the Hellenistic city (as 1 Maccabees implies), and particularly the gymnasium, the bath and the stadium, i.e. where nudity was the norm, that the circumstances arose in which the traditional habit of circumcision might become an issue of loyalty or identity. Nudity was normal and natural among Greeks, and circumcision was seen by them as a deformity. Judeans who encountered this cultural contradiction (hardly a majority, one supposes) could become for the first time self-conscious about circumcision, regarding it a cultural aberration and not a norm. They could react in one of two ways: give it up or cover it up on the one hand, or reassert it with pride as a mark of their own culture. If circumcision had been universally perceived as an inalienable mark of Judaism, then those who abandoned or neglected it were abandoning Judaism. However, it is not clear that circumcision was so perceived by Judeans collectively before the Maccabean conflict. More significantly, perhaps, those Judeans who resented Hellenism, and especially its culture of nudity, could oblige other Judeans to resist it by enforcing circumcision upon them. Circumcision would thus serve as both an expression of anti-Hellenism and also a measure against it.

These observations make possible the following sketch of the history of circumcision: even before the Hellenistic period it was a common practice among Judeans and several other neighboring peoples. With the advent of Hellenism, the custom was being mocked, and in time it was being broken by those who accepted the view that it was deformity. The practice of nakedness in Jerusalem itself exacerbated the situation and led to certain groups not only exalting circumcision as the highest mark of "Juda-ism" (because of its degree of incompatibility with features of Hellenism) but, when open conflict broke out, forcibly imposing circumcision on other

---

[47] According to the 5th-century Herodotus, "the Phoenicians and Syrians in Palestine themselves confess having learned it from the Egyptians" (2.104.3); see the text and discussion in Stern, *Greek and Latin Authors*, 1.1-3. This does not have to be a true claim; the report confirms, however, that the custom was followed in the Levant and not regarded as a peculiarly Judean phenomenon by outsiders.

Judeans. Simultaneously, circumcision might have been an obvious target of Antiochus IV (though I suspect that the measure banning it may have been invented by the Judean historians). With the establishment of the Hasmonean dynasty, whose support included some groups who were strongly pro-circumcision, the new rulers enforced the old custom of circumcision, extended it to conquered neighbors and enabled it to emerge in various Judaisms as the most important index of all, the mark of Jewish membership of the covenant. It is difficult to see any other context for the emergence of circumcision into such prominence, and the dating of this development, if correct, is extremely important in reassessing the origin and early development of Judaism.

Official Judaism

Let us now return to the question of scriptures. Here I find helpful the analysis by Neusner of the distinction between what he calls "testament" and "torah."[48] "Testament" refers to a religious system, or a text or texts, that does not have a potential for engendering a total religious system, whereas torah does. Neusner traces the evolution from testament to torah in the case of the scriptures over the period 500 BCE-700 CE. However, a similar kind of distinction might be made on a more limited scale between a testament that belongs with a certain group and operates only within a restricted social and temporal boundary, and a body of texts that is given the status of a national symbol, and thus acquires the possibility of becoming the nucleus of a religious system that embraces "Israel" in a fuller sense than any testament. In an interesting study of the Temple Scroll,[49] Wayne O. McCready has argued that this document represents an attempt at creating the "Jewish worldview" for which many looked to them. Hence, while the Hasmoneans created the matrix for a "Jewish worldview" through their establishment of a politically united and independent "Israel," they did not in fact

---

[48] Testament to Torah (Englewood Cliffs, NJ: Prentice-Hall, 1988).
[49] "Sectarian Separation and Exclusion — the Temple Scroll: A Case for Wholistic Religious Claims," in Origins and Method: Towards a New Understanding of Judaism and Christianity. Essays in Honour of John C. Hurd (ed. B.H. McLean; JSNTSup 86; Sheffield: JSOT, 1993) 360-79.

fulfil this potential, and it was left to "sectarian" groups to articulate that vision, and inscribe the "torah."

In large measure I think that Neusner's distinction and McCready's application of it to a specific case, clarify the issue of scripture as it developed in the Hasmonean period. Neusner is correct in insisting that the development of a fully-fledged "torah" does not occur until much later than our period, but McCready is probably correct to see in what we call "sectarian" circles the earliest attempts to define a torah, albeit for a group that consciously set itself against the political and religious authorities of their time. The Temple Scroll itself, and the attempt which is evident in the *Damascus Document* to organize a community around the laws of "scripture" show, nevertheless, that a certain body of literature was taken by all Judeans as a benchmark, against which all systems had to be judged. It is, I suggest, in the aftermath of the Maccabean revolt that dissenting groups can attack each other on the basis of their understanding and application of an agreed set of texts. The establishment of such a bench mark is not indicative of a consensus which somehow emerged among Judeans, but the outcome of a political and social act of uniformity, by which I mean one politically imposed (though not against dissent) and accepted by all Judeans. The attempts to turn the writings thus declared definitive of "Judaism" into torahs of "Judaism" can first be seen in the Dead Sea scrolls, but do not succeed in defining a total and abiding religious system until the completion of the social and intellectual architecture which the rabbis undertook.

The process by which "literature" became "scripture" can be documented. We have seen that the "book of the law of Moses" had apparently achieved such a status by the time of Ben Sira (and probably earlier), and there were other books that he read, knew and venerated. But Josephus is able to say in the first century CE that "we have twenty-two books"; we know that the Jews had many more, including some used by Josephus himself. Is he inventing a convenient alphabetic figure, or is some authority responsible for deciding how many, and what they are? If so, from what time does such an authority exist, and why would such a decision require to be made? 2 Macc 2:13 narrates that Judas collected the "scattered books" just as Nehemiah had once done "to found his library"; according to 1 Macc 1:56-57 they had been targets for destruction by

Antiochus. It is a reasonable inference from this text that the Hasmoneans set up a library of books which were regarded as "holy";
such a policy both matched the library-building of other cities (e.g.
Alexandria, Rhodes) in the Hellenistic world (and so again we find
Judaism developing in imitation of Hellenism!) but also of establishing a literary archive capable of functioning as a cultural canon, and
indeed, as it turned out, a religious canon too; culture and religion
are rather hard to distinguish in the Hasmonean period, because the
cultivation of a religious norm was unavoidable. The restoration of
independence under a new priestly and later royal dynasty claiming
to have been chosen by God as deliverers and having succeeded
with the help of groups with different aims could not help making
decisions about religious and cultural norms. Parties devoted to different definitions of "Judaism" had to be appeased, controlled, or
marginalized; it appears that several changes of allegiance took place
as those called "Sadducees" and "Pharisees" came in and out of favor
with the rulers, while other groups, represented in the Dead Sea
Scrolls, removed themselves from the established cult and priesthood and either preserved or invented other versions of "Judaism."
While "Judaism" had been defined in the mid-2nd century by external conflict, now it was being defined by internal conflict, with the
possibility of an "authorized" form of practice because of political
independence. Thus, specific Temple rites, festivals, calendar, taxes,
laws — everything "Jewish" was a matter of political decision and
could not be avoided. The Hasmoneans were forced to make explicit a "Judaism" — and indeed, they apparently exported it to
their neighbors in the process of political expansion in Palestine.
From this moment on, there are not only several "Judaisms" but
authorized and unauthorized Judaisms, central and peripheral Judaisms, priestly and non-priestly Judaisms, because of the identification of certain religious practice with the state. The banner under
which the Maccabees and their allies had fought was now enshrined
at the centre of their political ideology — "Judaism."

"Common Judaism"

In a recent volume devoted to Judaism, E.P. Sanders has attempted
to express its essential uniformity for the period of Roman adminis-

tration.[50] He describes what he calls "common Judaism," a picture based largely on the Mishnah and Josephus and thus inevitably representing certain beliefs and practices at the expense of others. His attempt to find what was common in Judaism, what made Judaism "Judaism," is nevertheless an important contribution to the problem discussed above and intended, it seems, as a further challenge to those scholars who wish to find different competing Judaisms in the first century CE. Unlike his earlier volume on Palestinian Judaism,[51] this book attempts to grasp the realia rather than the theory of Judaism, and Sanders plausibly suggests the Temple as a practical and symbolic expression of "Judaism" for many people during the period of Roman administration, including the reign of Herod. This exercise is marred only by the inclusion of a chapter on "common theology," which attempts to explore what the "common Jew" thought when performing the "common acts." The more a scholar addresses the texts, the products of the literate, the further away one moves from the "common Jew" and the more divergence is found It is precisely in practice that convergence is most readily encountered, but precisely because conformity of practice obscures and relegates disparity of belief; it does *not* exhibit conformity of belief.

Insofar as Sanders claims a fairly wide degree of conformity *in practice* among Palestinian Jews in (mainly) the 1st century CE, he is probably correct. I have suggested that this conformity was imposed as part of the reconstruction of an independent Judah. The Temple cult is in any case one of the oldest and most important ingredients of "Judaism" and capable in most cases of retaining loyalty in practice regardless of philosophical differences.

It also must not be forgotten that under the Romans, including under Herod the Great, political circumstances may have been such as to encourage both greater loyalty to the Temple itself and greater divergence of philosophy corresponding to different perceptions of Jewish identity and aspirations under imperial rule. How far Judeans expressed their resistance violently during this period is dis-

---

[50] *Judaism, Practice and Belief 63 BCE-66 CE* (London: SCM and Philadelphia: Trinity International, 1992).
[51] *Paul and Palestinian Judaism.*

puted.[52] Whatever the overt political manifestations, assertion of sovereignty under direct foreign rule is likely to have taken the form of increased attachment to national symbols, of which the Temple was the most obvious. The examples of popular loyalty to the Temple and its cult are many (as Sanders points out). Ironically, they confirm Herod the Great's policy, as a Roman client, of re-building and enlarging the Temple. Thereby Herod aimed to con-solidate the cultural unity and the pacificity of his Judean subjects, just as by his displays of munificence outside his territories, he sought to consolidate an empire-wide "Judaism" as a secure and re-spected philosophy within the Hellenistic culture of its environ-ment and to bind the Judean *ethnos* outside Judea to its Palestinian "homeland" and its "king." Virtually all of the elements of Sanders' "common Judaism" gain their rationale from the Temple. This in-creased fervor for the Temple carried through a process that can be observed from the beginning of the current quest. The Temple cult had long been a central feature of Judean life, but perhaps only in the 160s BCE did it become explicitly a symbol of resistance to Hel-lenism and a focus for the raising of Juda-ism to consciousness, in opposition to those who would readily diminish its status and in the last resort bring it to ruin. By the 1st century CE, it was now the central and uniting symbol for every form of Judaism, including the Diaspora. The symbols of the Temple — holiness, agricultural festivals, tithing, priesthood, divine presence, atonement — became so pervasive that its removal in 70 CE necessitated the creation of a Judaism based on those symbols. It will be for another essay to ar-gue that adherence to תורה was not an alternative to the Temple cult, but a supplement to and extension of it.

Conclusions

My suggestion in this paper has been that the emergence of Judaism can be traced by a series of discrete historical developments and was characterized by distinct phases, beginning with the formation of

---

[52] See, for example, D.M. Rhoads, *Israel in Revolution: 6–74 C.E. A Political His-tory Based on the Writings of Josephus* (Philadelphia: Fortress, 1976); R.A. Horsley, *Jesus and the Spiral of Violence: Popular Jewish Resistance in Roman Palestine* (Minne-apolis: Fortress, 1987); M.D. Goodman, *The Ruling Class of Judaea* (Cambridge: Cambridge University, 1987).

cultural habits and customs, then the cultivation of those as a distinct way of life in opposition to "Hellenism" and finally, as a set of competing and ever more religious definitions of that culture. The catalyst for the last development was the religious character that the "Maccabean revolt" was given and the subsequent embroiling of the Hasmoneans in religious (not exclusively cultic) matters through their adoption of a religious ideology in support of their bid for power, their assumption of the high priesthood, and the lobbying of groups with whom they had been obliged to associate in their bid for power. Juda-ism, by which I mean the culture that all those who called themselves Judeans adopted as their mark of identity, increasingly took on the form of a religion.

The picture I have sketched is rather simplified, both because of the paucity of the evidence and also because of the scope of the discussion. I have, in any case, been attempting not to rewrite single-handedly a new history of Judaism, but to establish the thesis that it ought to be approached by certain methods and using certain kinds of evidence. I have also ignored non-Palestinian Judaism. Outside Palestine, Judaism assumed varied forms, such as those that Hellenistic associations and societies took, or as a philosophical system that absorbed Stoic, Platonic, Pythagorean and Epicurean metaphysics and ethics. (Nor do I mean to imply that these developments were exclusively non-Palestinian). But the Temple cult in Jerusalem remained the one uniting force, later to be replaced by other systems, in which its symbolism was retained or displaced, such as the rabbinic law: yet this process was gradual, and it must be remembered that other Jewish temples existed in the Hellenistic period in Elephantine, Leontopolis, Araq el-Emir, Gerizim and Cyrenaica, some of which may have outlasted the one in Jerusalem. Of the elements in Judaism that have been overemphasized by Christian scholarship, scripture is the most prominent. Only among certain kinds of Judaism (Christianity, some writers of Dead Sea Scrolls, the Alexandrian allegorists, probably other non-Palestinian members of the Jewish *ethnos*), did the Jewish literature serve important dogmatic and philosophical purposes. Rabbinic Judaism embraced it only in the 2nd century CE as a canonical expression of Judaism.

In the end, the emergence of Judaism in all its forms is a topic of immense scope and complexity. It appears for the most part to have come to *assume the form of* a religion (more properly, "religions"), though it had roots that spread more widely, and never, until this day, has it been adequate to define Judaism exclusively as a religion. The elements that formed and defined it — cult, culture, nationalism, Hellenism, reaction to Hellenism, political independence, loss of Temple, the imposition of the *fiscus iudaicus*, which required Judaism to be defined in a way that was not previously necessary, and Christianity, first as a sect, later as imperial power — all these factors can to a greater or lesser extent be mapped as influences on the history of Judaism. Such a history of Judaism, which is not merely a history of Jewish writings or of Jewish thought but a cultural history, can be written, but the more the variety is probed the less can any single essence of "Judaism" be grasped. In the 20th century, Judaism can be found as a religious denomination in the USA, in the Yeshiva, in the Eastern European *stetl,* in various forms of Zionism (social, religious and imperialist), as a nation-state, or as a recognizable and influential sub-culture in Hollywood or New York. "Judaism" remains to this day an idea, or a cluster of ideas, worked out in forms that are sometimes related and sometime not. To say that Judaism came into existence as an idea and has remained such is an overstatement, but perhaps a useful antidote to the many accounts of it that assume it to be much simpler or restricted a phenomenon than it was, or indeed that it still is.

Tracking Observance of the Aniconic Tradition Through Numismatics

Diana V. Edelman

Introduction

Coins minted for the province of Yehud/Judea during the Persian period through the end of the Hasmonean dynasty provide some useful parameters in the quest to determine the history of the development of the aniconic tradition. The coins cannot be used to establish the date of origin of the Second Commandment; they can only provide direct and indirect evidence for the observance and enforcement of a prohibition against divine images within Yehud/Judea in different periods. The commandment may or may not have been in existence during periods when divine images were produced; the production of images of deities on provincial coins could have been due to the nonexistence of the aniconic commandment at the time or simply to a nonchalant attitude among a large or influential segment of the population toward an existing prohibition. In addition, the two levels of prohibition contained within the current wording of the Second Commandment need to be borne in mind in the ensuing discussion. On the one hand, there is a clear prohibition against images of gods other than Yahweh, based on the latter's jealous nature. On the other hand, there is an implied prohibition against images of Yahweh as well.[1] It is possible that the his-

---

[1] For the view that the Second Commandment in both Exod 20:4-6 and Deut 5:8-10 prohibits only certain categories of iconography based on representations of creatures, the planet bodies or vegetation, but presumes that Yahweh was correctly represented iconographically in a composite image that mixed anthropomorphic and animalistic traits, see the earlier article by B. Schmidt ("The Aniconic Tradition: On Reading Images and Viewing Texts.") I completed my article before reading Brian's and so did not utilize the distinction he has proposed between legitimate and illegitimate iconographic representations of Yahweh as a basis for my discussion. Instead, I am working from the perspective that the Second Commandment came to be understood as a blanket ban on images of Yahweh. I will

tory of observance of aniconism in Yehud/Judea developed at different times in respect to these two different levels.

Caution must be exercised in using coins as a form of testimony.[2] It is not always possible to determine under whose authority they were minted in Yehud/Judea. Non-Yahweh-worshipping authorities could have chosen to place on coins symbols and representations that were not consistent with aniconic standards during the existence of the Second Temple. On the other hand, had the aniconic tradition been firmly ensconced within the practice and life of the Yahweh-worshipping provincial elite and/or the populace at large, it is unlikely that a non-Yahwistic or non-Jewish official would have offended the sensibilities of his subjects by minting coins that broke with local religious law for use within the province. Even if he did not accept that law personally, he would have run the risk of reprisal and possible revolt, which could have ended his political career.

It would seem that a non-Yahwistic or non-Jewish offical would only have chosen to offend the sensibilities of his subjects deliberately as an act of repression or reprisal in response to some sort of nonacceptable behavior or action on their part. Thus, it would seem that under normal circumstances, the ethnoreligious background of the authority in charge of minting would probably not have deter-

---

just note that the only apparent depiction of Yahweh in the numismatic evidence, the coin from the British Museum, would not be consistent with the authorized mixed iconography; it bears a portrait of Yahweh as a fully human figure. It might serve as evidence for the existence of competing iconographic traditions for Yahweh prior to the creation of the Second Commandment. Alternatively, it could indicate a struggle among competing iconographic traditions for control of the cult, or an acceptance of a prohibition against non-mixed forms to represent Yahweh in the cult but a feeling that it was then legitimate to use a human form in the non-cultic sphere.

2   Other representational art as well as extrabiblical texts describing the beliefs of adherents to the cults of Yahweh in this period are equally important sources that should be examined in addition to the coins. Unfortunately, I was unable to include them in the present study. All depictions need to be evaluated in the same way images on coins will be here. All characterizations of Jewish religion by non-Yahwistic or non-Jewish writers must be carefully scrutinized and not accepted at face value. Their testimony must be converted to evidence by placing all statements made within their historical and social contexts and by realizing the potential biases of both the writers and their sources.

mined the iconic or aniconcic nature of coins. Instead, the key factor would have been the widespread acceptance of an aniconic tradition among the social elite or the general populace of the province. The ethnoreligious background would have become important, however, in a situation where punishment of the population of the province would have been a factor. If the Second Commandment were being observed as a prohibition against images of Yahweh in addition to other deities, coins should have been aniconic regardless of the background of the governor. If, however, it were being observed only as a prohibition against depictions of deities other than Yahweh, coins bearing images of Yahweh but not of any other deity could have been produced by either a native or foreign-born governor.

A. *The Persian Period*

The extant corpus of coins minted in the Persian province of Yehud provides unambiguous proof that at least one physical depiction of Yahweh and representations of other deities were produced during that period. At least twenty-three published coins bear the face of Athena on one side and her sacred animal, the owl, on the other, while one specimen seems to bear an image of Yahweh.[3]

The coins depicting Athena are based on an Athenian prototype. Changes are minor: inferior style and a change of language in the inscription. Similar imitations of Athenian coins, the so-called Philisto-Arabian coins, have been recovered from Gaza and other mints in the Near East and have been dated to the period ca. 400-333 BCE.[4] The imitation of Athenian coinage in particular among the wide range of coins being produced by various Greek cities is probably due to the dominance of Athens in the confederacy of Greek states that had been formed to resist Persian invasion early in the 5th century BCE. It appears that in 449 BCE, Athens issued a decree that required all members of the confederation to use the weights

---

[3]   For pictures of the coins, see Y. Meshorer, *Ancient Jewish Coinage* (2 vols.; Dix Hills, NY: Amphora Books, 1982) 1.115-6, pls. 1-3. Many more are now known, although I do not have a current count.

[4]   *Ibid.*, 15, 17. For specific coins, see G.F. Hill, *Catalogue of the Greek Coins of Palestine (Galilee, Samaria, and Judaea)* (Oxford: Horace Hart, 1914) 176-83, pls. xix.8-12; xx.5-6 and lxxiv.

and measures of Athens, including its coinage.[5] This monopoly
lasted until Lysander captured Athens in 404 BCE and explains why
Athenian coins have been found at 5th and 4th century sites within
the Persian empire as geographically diverse as Al Mina in Syria,
Babylon, Malayer in Iran, and Chaman-i-Hazouri in Afghanistan[6]
and outside the empire in Tunisia, Spain, and India.[7] At the same
time, it explains why the authorities in Yehud would have chosen
to model their local currency after the well-recognized and widely-
accepted Athenian coinage, which had become the standard currency for Mediterranean trade.[8]

The Persians, having apparently adopted their system of coinage
from Croesus in Lydia in the mid-6th century BCE, were unable to
enforce a standard currency throughout their growing empire. Beginning in 450 BCE, Artaxerxes I authorized certain cities to issue
their own money. Cities located in coastal Asia Minor and Syria,
which were far removed from the Persian homeland and in constant
contact with the Athenian fleet, were especially granted the right to
mint their own coins.[9]

---

[5]   So C. Seltman, *Greek Coins. A History of Metallic Currency and Coinage down
to the Fall of the Hellenistic Kingdoms* (2nd ed.; Methuen's Handbooks of Archaeology; London: Methuen & Co., 1965) 155; contrast the earlier understanding that
the decree was issued in 454 found, for example, in J.G. Milne, *Greek Coinage* (Oxford: Clarendon, 1931) 64-6.

[6]   G.K. Jenkins, *Ancient Greek Coins* (New York: G.P. Putnam's Sons, 1972) 78.

[7]   Seltman, *Greek Coins*, 110.

[8]   An alternative explanation has been proposed by B. Kanael ("Ancient Jewish
Coins and their Historical Significance," *BA* 26 [1963] 40). He has suggested that
coins that were to be used primarily for the payment of mercenaries were modelled after types current in the home countries of the soldiers. The imitation of
Athenian coins would suggest then that the province of Yehud employed Greek
mercenaries — a situation that cannot be proved or disproved on the basis of current information, but which seems less probable than the first explanation that
equates the adoption of Athenian prototypes with a desire to imitate coinage that
had become the standard medium in Mediteranean trade. It should also be noted
that in Tarsus at least, coins used to pay mercenaries bore images of soldiers on
one side. Two types are known: either a Persian soldier with spear, bow and
quiver, or a Greek hoplite in a posture of defense (C. Kraay, *Archaic and Classical
Greek Coins* [Berkeley and Los Angeles: University of California, 1976] 281.) On
analogy then, had Yehud needed to pay mercenaries, it might have minted coins
bearing images of mercenaries, following established practice.

[9]   Milne, *Greek Coinage*, 11-2, 80.

Persian coinage typically features on one side a picture of the Persian king in a half-running, half-crouching position. He wears the royal robe, the crown of war, and carries various weapons, usually a spear, strung bow, quiver with arrows, and dagger. The first such Achaemenid coins, minted by Darius I, had no design on the other side. The same tradition was continued under Xerxes, Artaxerxes I, Darius II and Cyrus the Younger, with occasional imprints on the otherwise blank side whose designs are too indistinct to be identifiable. Beginning with the coins of Artaxerxes II and continuing under Artaxerxes III and Darius II, the imprints begin to be clear enough to identify on occasion. The designs include a series of wavy lines, a crouching lion or bull facing left, and two contiguous circles with symbols inside.[10]

The Persian practice of depicting the ruling king broke with the long-standing Greek tradition of placing the depiction of the local patron god on coins.[11] The latter practice had been used throughout the Greek world, including its colonies, and had been adopted by neighboring regions, like Lydia. Other cities in the Persian empire that were granted the right to mint their own coins were free to choose the designs to go on the face of the currency; there was no imperially imposed set of symbols. It seems as though many cities chose to imitate the early Greek and Phoenician coins of the 6th and 5th centuries BCE. They often substituted their own local deity and its representative symbol when they did not copy the depiction of the Greek or Phoenician gods outright.[12]

The appearance of the representation of the goddess Athena on the official coinage of the province of Yehud indicates that the authorities in charge had no objections to the depiction of a female deity in their realm. Had the Second Commandment been taken seriously at this time by the native religious or lay leaders of the community or the people at large, it is highly unlikely that the civil

---

[10] For the coins, see M. E. Babelon, *Les perses achéménides. Les satrapes et les dynastes tributaires de leur empire. Cypre & Phénicie. Planches* (Catalogue des monnaies grecques de la bibliotheque nationale; Bologna: Arnaldo Forni, 1980) pls. 1 and 2.

[11] *Ibid.* For the Greek practice of depicting a deity, often a portrait of the head only, see Milne, *Greek Coinage*, 109.

[12] For examples of such coins, see Hill, *Catalogue of the Greek Coins of Palestine*, pls. xix and xx.

authorities, whether native born or non-native Persian appointees, would have chosen to mint such coins. Since they were free to use whatever images they wanted for their coins, their use of the goddess Athena must be seen to reflect a nonchalant attitude toward any prohibition against the representation of gods other than Yahweh that might have existed at this time.

The coin that appears to depict Yahweh is a silver drachm or quarter shekel in the collection of the British Museum.[13] It bears on one side within a square border of dots a bearded deity seated on a winged and wheeled throne. He is wearing a long garment that drapes from his chest to wrap around his waist and extends to his feet. On his outstretched left hand sits an eagle, falcon, or hawk. The inscription יהד appears in archaic Aramaic script above the god's head. In the lower right corner of the border is the profile of a somewhat grotesque, bearded face. The other side of the coin bears a bearded human head in three-quarter pose, facing right, wearing a crested helmet with a bay wreath on it, enclosed in a solid circular border. The coin's provenance is unknown; it was found in the early 1800's (see *Fig. 2* on page 225).

Past discussions of the coin have readily concurred that the seated figure with the bird is a deity, although his precise identity has been disputed. An identification with Dionysis has been proposed on the basis of the winged seat and the presence of the satyr-like face in the corner,[14] while an equation with Triptolemos has been suggested on the basis of the winged seat alone.[15] I. Lévy has interpreted the images on both sides as representations of the Cilician deity Hadranos,[16] while a number of scholars have proposed

---

[13] The coin was first published in T. Combe, *Veterum populorum et regum numi-qui in Museo Britannico adservantur* (London: British Museum, 1814) 242 no. 5; pl. xiii, 12. For early discussions of it, see Hill, *Catalogue of the Greek Coins of Palestine*, lxxxvi-lxxviii; 181 no. 29; xix. 29. For an excellent recent discussion and clear picture of both sides of the coin, see Meshorer, *Ancient Jewish Coinage*, 1.21-30 and pl. 1.1.

[14] For a good summary of the history of this position, see H. Kienle, *Der Gott auf dem Flügelrad: Zu den ungelösten Fragen der "synkretischen" Münze BMC Palestine S. 181, Nr. 29* (Göttinger Orientforschungen VI, 7; Wiesbaden: O. Harrassowitz, 1975) 38.

[15] For a convenient summary of the discussion, see *ibid.*, 36.

[16] I. Lévy, "Dieux siciliens," *RevArch* 34, III (1899) 276-7.

an equation with Ba'altarz, who is depicted on the coins of three Cilician satraps.[17] H. Kienle raises the possibility that the deity might logically represent Ahura Mazda, with the winged wheel being a most graceful expression of the winged solar disk. He notes that the coin could have been used for a represssive function by the Persian authorities.[18]

The most popular position equates the figure with Zeus in light of the common the depiction of that deity as an enthroned bearded god with an eagle on his hand, often with his himation draped in the manner found on the coin.[19] A.B. Cook has argued, however, that the portrait represents Yahweh under the guise of a solar Zeus.[20] He has compared it with an onyx of unknown provenance bearing a youthful, beardless Zeus-figure enthroned with a scepter, thunderbolt, and eagle, which bears the legend ΙΑΩ ΣΑΒΑΩ on its reverse. In addition, he has cited examples from magical texts from the Hellenistic era that equated Yahweh with Zeus at times and with Helios at other times.[21] An identity of the figure with Yahweh has also been affirmed by M.J. Price,[22] B. Kanael,[23] Y. Meshorer,[24] E.R. Goodenough,[25] C. Seltman,[26] and ultimately, H. Kienle.[27]

L. Mildenberg has proposed that the deity represents a general conception of male deity comprehensible to many people in the

[17] For a summary of this position, see Kienle, *Gott auf dem Flügelrad*, 46.
[18] *Ibid.*, 52.
[19] For advocates of this position, see *ibid.*, 34.
[20] A.B. Cook, *Zeus. A Study in Ancient Religion* (2 vols.; [Cambridge, 1914] New York: Biblio and Tannen, 1964) 1.232-7.
[21] *Ibid.*
[22] M.J. Price, *Coins and the Bible* (London: V.C. Vecchi & Sons, 1975) 10. His comment that Yahweh "is depicted in a manner that would be more suited to one of the deities of their Persian overlords" is misleading; Yahweh is depicted in the guise of Zeus, a Greek deity, not in the guise of Ahura-Mazda, who appears in a winged solar disk.
[23] Kanael, "Ancient Jewish Coins," 41.
[24] Meshorer, *Ancient Jewish Coinage*, 1.25.
[25] E.R. Goodenough, *Jewish Symbols in the Greco-Roman Period* (13 vols.; Bollingen Series 37, 1-13; New York: Pantheon Books, 1953-1968) 1.271.
[26] Seltman, *Greek Coins*, 154.
[27] Kienle, *Gott auf dem Flügelrad*, 68-74.

western part of the Persian empire rather than a specific deity.[28] His conclusion rests primarily on the "syncretistic nature" of the depiction, a characterization that rests in turn on his description of the elements as a deity in a long himation (hence Greek) holding an Egyptian falcon, with the head of Egyptian Bes facing left, and a legend in Aramaic, the official language of the Persian empire.[29] The Egyptian origin of the bird, whose species is not clear, and of the somewhat grotesque face is not widely accepted. The bird appears to be a hawk, eagle, or falcon and has no particular Egyptian affinity in its depiction, while the face could just as easily be that of the Greek satyr Silenus, who appears on a number of coins from Syria and Asia Minor.[30]

Mildenberg's proposal also seems to contradict his further observations that "coinage in the western part of the Persian Empire is of a *local* character..."[31] and that "the unique drachm and all of the minute coins just discussed are local issues struck in and for Judea by consecutive provincial administrations."[32] His second statement is more accurate: the legend יהד indicates that the drachm in question was struck for use within the Persian province of Yehud spe-

---

[28]   L. Mildenberg, "Yehud: A Preliminary Study of the Provincial Coinage of Judaea," in *Greek Numismatics and Archaeology. Essays in Honor of Margaret Thompson* (ed. O. Mørkholm and N.M. Waggoner; Wetteren: Cultura Press, 1979) 183-96, esp. 184. While not discussing this coin in particular, A. Kindler seems to share the same sentiment that no coin from Yehud bearing the image of a male deity is to be construed as a depiction of Yahweh. He states, "All these types show religious and cultural influence from outside Palestine. Consequently they cannot be regarded as evidence of local cults" ("The Greco-Phoenician Coins Struck in Palestine in the Time of the Persian Empire," *INJ* 2 [1963] 25). Both conclusions seem to build upon the early argument of G.F. Hill in connection with this coin. He warned that it was not to be taken as evidence for the existence of a cult of Yahweh in the place of minting because it belongs to the category of Philisto-Arabian coins, which are characterized by varied types and imagery drawn from a range of cultures that were likely to attract the people among whom they circulated. "None of these so varied types can be regarded as evidence of local types" (*Catalogue of the Greek Coins of Palestine*, lxxxvii-lxxxviii).
[29]   Mildenberg, "Yehud," 184.
[30]   For bibliography about the identification of this face, see conveniently, Kienle, *Gott auf dem Flügelrad*, 40.
[31]   Mildenberg, "Yehud," 184, n. 9.
[32]   *Ibid.*, 191.

cifically, and not in the western part of the Persian empire at large. Some of these coins may well have circulated outside of Yehud. It seems implausible, however, to argue that the local minting authorities would have deliberately chosen to put a general conception of deity on the province's coins rather than the specific god of the province in order to make them more acceptable to neighbors in the event they came into contact with them and used them. The primary target audience of the coins were inhabitants of Yehud. The widespread use of Athena and her owl on coins minted in a number of local provinces in the western part of the empire indicates that there was no need felt to develop a "koine" artistic tradition to represent generalized conceptions of categories of male and female deities.

The real underlying basis of Mildenberg's refusal to identify the male deity on the drachm from Yehud as Yahweh seems to be revealed in his admittance that "The design is indeed offensive to the eyes of today's Jews."[33] While he goes on to admit that "This may not have been the case in Judea during the period of Persian rule,"[34] he is unable to accept the latter alternative for personal religious reasons, unlike his colleagues Meshorer and Kanael. The former responds to Mildenberg's proposal in the following way: "The natural tendency to assign to the Jewish community a purely spiritual conception of their God may be very much removed from the reality of the second temple period."[35] The latter simply remarks, "We may have in this coin evidence of assimilatory and syncretistic tendencies among the Jewish aristocracy in the fourth century."[36]

The identity of the enthroned deity as Yahweh is primarily indicated by the coin's point of origin as legal tender within the province of Yehud. His depiction in a pose and in dress that is commonly used for Zeus in Greek art and coinage would appear to be the result of either the conscious imitation of a prototype unknown at present, or of the use of a Greek engraver to produce the die cast for the drachm. As noted already by C. Clermont-Ganneau in 1880, however, the winged wheel upon which the deity is seated is not a

---

[33] Ibid., 184, n. 7.
[34] Ibid.
[35] Meshorer, Ancient Jewish Coinage, 1.25.
[36] "Ancient Jewish Coins," 41.

typical Greek feature and calls to mind the vision of Yahweh enthroned in Ezekiel 1 and 10.[37] This then would seem to be a local
Yehudian adaptation of the standard Greek portrayal of the head of
the pantheon, designed to introduce iconographic elements more
commonly linked with Yahweh, Zeus' equivalent. The inclusion of
the bird of prey as Yahweh's attribute animal is consistent with the
imagery of Yahweh as an eagle in Exod 19:4.[38]

The significance of the profile of the grotesque bearded face in
the lower right corner of the side with the seated deity is difficult
to determine. The most plausible explanation would seem to be to
identify the face as the symbol or badge of the issuing magistrate.
There developed during the 4th century BCE the practice of placing
by the side of the main image on a coin a small symbol, badge or
initial that represented the magistrate who had issued the money, as
a guarantee of its standard.[39] The practice became common in
many Greek city states at this time.

It is generally agreed that the lighter weight of the silver drachm
under discussion in relation to other Philisto-Arabian coins as well
as its rendering of the portrait on the reverse side in three-quarter
profile suggests a date of issuance ca. 380-360 BCE.[40] The latter
practice was fashionable in the eastern part of the Mediterranean
during the first half of the 4th century BCE.[41] Such a date is like-

---

[37] *Receuil d'archéologie orientale*, Vol. 8 (Paris: E. Bouillon, 1924) 301. The idea
first appeared in print in E.J. Pilcher, "A Coin of Gaza, and the Vision of Ezekiel," *Proceedings of the Society of Biblical Archaeology* 30 (1908) 49-52.

[38] H. Kienle would add to this reference Deut 32:11 and Ps 91:4, which I do not
find to be clear-cut references to eagles. In addition, he notes the appearance of a
golden eagle on the temple of Herod and the sculpture of an eagle on the gate at
Araq el-Amir in Transjordan, an unfinished structure built by the Tobiad Hyrcanus that may have been a temple of Yahweh (*Gott auf dem Flügelrad*, 69). The
eagle on Herod's temple may be pertinent. For a detailed discussion of the eagle as
a Jewish symbol, see Goodenough, *Jewish Symbols in the Greco-Roman Period*,
8.121-42.

[39] So Milne, *Greek Coinage*, 104-5.

[40] So especially, Mildenberg, "Yehud," 184-6, whose arguments are accepted by
Meshorer, *Ancient Jewish Coinage*, 1.26.

[41] Meshorer, *ibid.*; Hill, *Catalogue of the Greek Coins of Palestine*, 181, no. 29. M.
Robertson places the revival of the practice, which was used initially in the second
half of the 6th century BCE, earlier, in the second half of the 5th century BCE (*A
History of Greek Art* [2 vols.; Cambridge: Cambridge University, 1975] 1.360).

wise consistent with the development of the practice of guaranteeing coin standard through the use of symbols or initials of the issuing authority.

According to the proposed dating, the grotesque bearded profile would be the identifying signet of Bagohi, the general of Artaxerxes II (404-359 BCE) and governor of Yehud. Other Philisto-Arabian coins that seem to be contemporaneous with the silver drachms bear the letter ב or letters בי written in Hebrew, Aramaic, or Phoenician script. These letters would seem to reflect the practice of guaranteeing coin standard through the use of the issuing magistrate's initial(s). They confirm that the practice was in use by Bagohi, the governor of Yehud. While the silver drachm from Yehud would be the only example known to date of Bagohi's use of a symbol in place of his initials, such a substitution would not be out of character with the general practice at the time. It might have been the result of the preference of the engraver for a magistrate's symbol instead of his initial(s). Should the grotesque figure in profile be correctly identified as Bes or Silenus, it can be noted that two other Philisto-Arabian coins minted under Bagohi bear images of Bes or Silenus on them, suggesting but not necessitating a preference for this protective deity by Bagohi.[42]

The bust on the other side of the silver drachm under discussion can plausibly be identified as a portrait of Bagohi, the governor of Yehud. This identification, first suggested by Meshorer,[43] seems more likely than the range of alternative views, which include an identification with the Cilician god Hadranos, Minos, the legendary founder of Gaza, the Persian satrap Pharnabazos or Datames, the war god Ares, or a stylized depiction of a mercenary.[44]

The latter proposal presumes that the coin was minted in order to pay mercenaries stationed in or employed by Yehud.[45] There is no evidence of the use of Greek mercenaries in Yehud during the governorship of Bagohi, although the scantiness of testimony cannot rule out this situation. The possibility has been raised that the

---

[42] For the coins, see Hill, *Catalogue of Greek Coins of Palestine*, pl. xx.1-3; Meshorer, *Ancient Jewish Coinage*, 1.27.

[43] *Ancient Jewish Coinage*, 1.27.

[44] For these alternatives, see conveniently, Kienle, *Gott auf dem Flügelrad*, 25-9.

[45] So also by implication, Kanael, "Ancient Jewish Coins," 40-1.

coin was minted in connection with military preparations for the invasion of Egypt during the reign of Artaxerxes II in 391-389 BCE, and again in 379-374.[46] According to Xenophon[47] and Plutarch,[48] the bulk of the army for the first invasion was gathered in Syria by Pharnabazus, satrap of Dascyleium, Tithraustes, governor of Sardis, and Abrocomas, satrap of Syria. The army for the second invasion was also assembled in this region by Pharnabazus' successor, Datames.[49] Thousands of Greek mercenaries were hired for both campaigns, which would have required the minting of new coins for payments.

Since Yehud and other territories under the governorship of Bagohi were en route to Egypt, they might have also been expected to supply troops for the engagements. It is equally possible, however, that they would have been commanded to provision the standing armies instead, being the closest Persian outpost to Egypt. Had Bagohi been expected to hire mercenaries for either campaign, we might expect similar coins with a bust of a mercenary to have been produced in other mints under his authority, but this does not seem to have been the case.

As noted early by E.J. Pilcher, many of the coin's features resemble those found on a didrachm from Tarsus issued by Pharnabazus sometime between 379 and 374 BCE and a direct relationship between the two needs to be considered.[50] Both bear the profile of a bearded human on one side and the portrayal of a deity in the guise of enthroned Zeus, wearing a himation draped over one shoulder, on the other. The directions the images face, however, are reversed. On the Tarsus coin, the deity's hand rests on a scepter instead of being extended and holding a bird of prey. The throne is not winged and has a bunch of grapes beneath it. It is possible that this coin served as the model for the Yehud coin. The coin from Tarsus was probably issued to pay mercenaries in connection with the second invasion of Egypt in 374. These coins could easily have made their way into Yehud with mercenaries travelling overland en

---

[46] So Kienle, *Gott auf dem Flügelrad*, 17 n. 31.
[47] *Anab.* ii.4.8; iii.4.13; 5.17; iv.3.4.
[48] *Artox.* 12.1; 27.4.
[49] So Xen., *Hell.* vi.3.12-14; 4.31; 5.2-3; Plut., *Ages.* 28.
[50] "A Coin from Gaza," 46, 48.

route to the war or who traversed Yehud after the war on their way back north.

Portraits of rulers or satraps were first introduced on coins in Asia Minor toward the end of the 5th century BCE, ca. 425 BCE. The early busts tend toward an ideal type rather than individual characterization and have well-kept beards, a tiara or helmet, and often an inscribed name. By 375-350, true portraits appear.[51] The portrait on the other side of the silver drachm would be consistent with the tendency to idealize rather than render accurate portraits, which was just beginning to be superceded by individual portraiture in the period in which the coin in question is thought to have been minted, 380-360 BCE. Bagohi's status as a general would favor his depiction with a helmet rather than a crown. The Greek style of the helmet is consistent with the Zeus-like portrayal of Yahweh on the other side of the coin, suggesting that the engraver of the die cast for the coin was either imitating a coin whose engraver used Greek stylistic devices or was personally of Greek origin.

Since the coin bearing an image of Yahweh seems to date to the governorship of Bagohi, a further consideration of the career of this Persian official and his attitude toward Yehud needs to be undertaken to determine whether he might have deliberately depicted Yahweh as a means of repressing or countering a local aniconic tradition. Such a possibility has been raised by H. Kienle, although he ultimately rejects the idea.[52] Josephus reports that Bagohi was good friends with Yeshua, the brother of the high priest of Yehud, Yohanan, and that he promised to make the former high priest in his brother's stead. As a result, Yeshua picked a fight with his brother, but ended up being killed inside the temple in the process. Bagohi then is said to have used this situation as a pretext to enter the temple himself, thereby defiling it, and is to have made the population suffer seven years for the death of his friend, making

---

[51]   So i.e. Milne, *Greek Coinage*, 109; Kraay, *Archaic and Classical Greek Coins*, 271.
[52]   Kienle, *Gott auf dem Flügelrad*, 52.

them "slaves" by having them pay fifty drachmae from the public treasury for every lamb offered in the daily sacrifices.[53]

Bagohi's friendship with Yeshua, a member of the family of the high priest, should have led him to respect any aniconic traditions that may have existed in Yehud during Yeshua's lifetime, unless Yeshua had been a Persian collaborator who was willing to ignore religious prescriptions in favor of Persian policy. The possibility cannot be dismissed that Bagohi specifically sought the friendship of Yeshua for political reasons, in order to put him into power as the high priest in place of his brother, who may not have been sympathetic to Persian policy.[54] After Yeshua's death, however, he could have deliberately countered any aniconic sentiments as part of his punishment process by issuing the coin bearing the image of Yahweh, to be used to purchase the deity's daily offerings in the temple. Is there any evidence to support this possibility? Not really. However, the date and significance of a series of minute silver coins needs to be considered in this connection. They may illustrate the deliberate substitution of alternate images for Athena and her owl, raising the possibility that an aniconic tradition was being honored during Bagohi's governorship.

The first coin is blank on one side but bears the owl of Athena in typical stance on the other. In place of the usual olive sprig in the left field, a lily appears, and below it, a rosette. There is no

---

[53] R. Marcus, *Jewish Antiquities, Books IX-XI* (Cambridge: Harvard University, 1966) 459-61; XI.297-301. A.T. Olmstead has concluded that Bagohi assessed the steep price for the sacrificial animals because he found animal sacrifice repugnant, as evidenced by his advice to the Elephantine community to abandon the practice of animal sacrifice as a means of gaining permission to rebuild their temple (*History of the Persian Empire* [Chicago: University of Chicago, 1948] 398). Animal sacrifice was an integral part of old Persian religion and Zoroastrianism, so that Bagohi, an official representative of the Persian administration, would have had no reason to object to its practice in Yehud. His advice would seem to stem from his knowledge of Egyptian aversion to animal sacrifice, which seems to have led to the destruction of the first Elephantine temple. Contra also then, G.W. Ahlström, who suggests that the promise by the Elephantine community not to sacrifice animals in the new temple may have been made to conform to the religious policies of the Persian administration and its worship of Ahura Mazda (*The History of Ancient Palestine from the Palaeolithic Period to Alexander's Conquest* [JSOTSup 146; Sheffield: JSOT, 1993] 871).

[54] This possibility is raised by Ahlström, *History of Ancient Palestine*, 873-4.

inscription. A second coin bears a lily on the front and Athena's owl on the reverse, with traces of an inscription that is no longer legible. A third coin is closely related to the second; it has a lily on the front, but substitutes a bird with outstretched wings for the owl on the reverse. The inscription יהד is located above the right wing.[55] A crude rendition of the third coin has been found.[56] A fourth coin, known from three examples, bears the head of the Persian king wearing a kidaris in profile, facing right, on the side where the profile of Athena would otherwise appear. On the reverse, her owl is replaced by the same bird with outstretched wings that appears on the third coin. The bird's head faces right in two examples and left in the third. The inscription יהד appears in the field beside one wing in each example.[57]

Meshorer has argued cogently that these coins constitute a single series that are derived from the standard Athenian coin bearing a portrait of Athena on one side and her owl, an olive sprig, and the first three letters of the name Athens, on the other. The earliest of the three types would seem to be the first, in which the portrait of Athena has been eliminated in favor of a blank surface. On the reverse side, the owl has been maintained, but the olive sprig has been replaced by a lily and the three Greek letters replaced by a rosette. The removal of the portrait of Athena would be consistent with the prohibition against any representation of gods other than Yahweh in the Second Commandment, while the substitution of the lily for the olive sprig on the first coin might reflect an attempt to remove another symbol that was too closely linked with the goddess in favor of one that was more appropriate to the cult of Yahweh in Yehud.[58] With these two changes, the owl was able to be "neutralized" and could remain simply as a decoration without any religious

---

[55]   For the coins, see conveniently, Meshorer, *Ancient Jewish Coinage*, 1. pls. 1.1A, 3, and 10. He states that ornithologists have identified the bird as a *falco sacer*, the hunting falcon (*ibid.*, 39).

[56]   See conveniently, *ibid.*, 1. pl. 2.8a.

[57]   See Meshorer, *Ancient Jewish Coinage* 1. pl. 2.9, 9a, and 9b. Two of the coins appear enlarged, with clearer details, in Mildenberg, "Yehud," pl. 21.12 and 13.

[58]   For the symbolism of the lily within the cult, see Goodenough, *Jewish Symbols*, 3.184-239.

or symbolic content.[59] Alternatively, the blank surface may simply be the result of bad minting and so have no implications for the issue of the observance of aniconic restrictions.

After this initial adaptation, further changes were made. The lily was removed from the side with the owl and made the main decoration on the other side, replacing the portrait of Athena, and her owl was either maintained or replaced by a bird of prey with spread wings. The latter adaptation might have been an attempt to replace the owl with a bird that was more closely associated with Yahweh.[60] A second variation involved the substitution of the head of the Persian king for the portrait of Athena and the substitution of a bird of prey for her owl. Although no name of the issuing authority appears on any of the coins in the series, the fourth type indicates a date of production under the Persian administration.

Was this series of minute coins issued for use primarily within the temple precincts? Such an explanation would be consistent with the use of the lily in place of Athena, as a symbol of the temple and its deity, Yahweh, or the blank in place of the expected portrait of Athena if the latter change was deliberate rather than accidental. It would not necessarily be true, however, for the coins bearing the portrait of the Persian king. The issue to be determined then is whether the minute coins bearing the lily or a blank in place of Athena predated the coin bearing the depiction of Yahweh and the minute coins bearing the portrait of the Persian king, were contemporaneous with them, or postdated them. Can we establish two contemporaneous sets of coinage within the province, one devoted to religious affairs and one to civil affairs? Should the series of aniconic minute coins predate the coin with image of Yahweh but still fall within the governorship of Bagohi, it could be argued that Bagohi minted the coin with the depiction of Yahweh as a deliberate means of upsetting the sensibilities of Yohanan and the priesthood after Yeshua's murder. Should the series postdate the coin, it might serve as an indication that Bagohi decided to make a

---

[59]   For the coins and the recognition that these are the earliest in the series, see Y. Meshorer, *Jewish Coins of the Second Temple Period* (Tel Aviv: Am Hassefer 1967) 38.
[60]   The falcon probably would have borne the same symbolic value as the eagle since both are birds of prey; see n. 36.

concession to an aniconic tradition to which he had not been sensitive earlier, or at least allowed money to be used within the religious sphere to conform to religious prescriptions against the depictions of deities.

At present, there is no way to establish a firm chronology for the series of minute coins that avoid a depiction of Athena in relation to the coin with the depiction of Yahweh. It needs to be noted, however, that another series of minute silver coins that bear the name of Bagohi's successor, Yehezkiyah, contain two specimens that are also blank on the side where the portrait of Athena would normally occur, but bear her owl on the reverse with the inscription in paleo-Hebrew, יחזקיה הפחה. Alongside these two coins are four that bear full-face portraits of Athena on one side and her owl on the back, with the accompanying inscription יהזקיה הפחה.[61] Did Yehezkiyah issue a series of minute coins that contained six variant types of coins, some aniconic and some iconic, some with his name and some without? Or, do the six types of related coins belong to two series, the first of which was issued by Bagohi and the second by Yehezkiyah, who continued the aniconic tradition only briefly before restoring Athena to her familiar place? Since there is no way to confirm that the coins bearing blanks on one side and the name of Yehezkiyah alongside the owl on the other are the first in the series as opposed to the last, the issue of the date of the two sets of minute coins must remain open. Again, however, the blanks in this series may simply have resulted from bad minting.

It is perhaps significant that the lily series are all minute coins of small denominations in contrast to the coin bearing the image of Yahweh, which is a larger drachm. Y. Meshorer has suggested that this distinction in weight indicates that in the closing years of Persian rule, between ca. 350 and 332 BCE, coins were struck contemporaneously by both Persian authorities and the autonomous Jewish

---

[61] For the coins, see Meshorer, *Ancient Jewish Coinage*, 1.pl. 2.10aBZ, 10c, and 10, 10a and 10b; pl 3.11a and 11b. In his addendum, Meshorer has corrected his reading of #11 on pl. 2 from יחזקיה הפחה to יוהנן הכוהן, "Yohanan the priest," whom he identifies with the high priest Yohanan II of the mid-3rd century BCE. The iconography is identical to that used by Yehezqiyah ("Ancient Jewish Coinage. Addendum I," *INJ* 11 [1990-1991] 104).

administration, the religious leadership in Jerusalem. He would attribute the larger drachm to the Persian authorities and all the minute coins to the local religious leadership, who had received authorization from the Persian provincial administration to issue coins but were restricted to smaller denominations.[62]

Based on his understanding of the development of the minute series, Meshorer's proposal tends to be undercut by two factors. First, as argued above, there is good reason to date the drachm with the depiction of Yahweh to the governorship of Bagohi, while Meshorer has dated the minute coins to Yehezkiyah. It is possible, nevertheless, that contrary to his own conclusion, the first series of minute coins that do not bear Yehezkiyah's name were issued by Bagohi, so that his proposal that the coins were issued contemporaneously by two different authorities, local and governmental, might still be valid, even though it cannot be proven at this time. The proposal seems to be further undercut, however, by the minute coins that bear the name of Yehezkiyah and which also give his title, הפחה, "governor." They belie his argument that the minute coins represent the religious authorities of Jerusalem instead of the official Persian administration in the period from 350-332 BCE; Yehezkiyah was the head of the Persian administration in Yehud during this time. If Yehezkiyah were continuing the tradition of minute coins begun by Bagohi, then it is unlikely that that the first series of coins would have been issued by the local religious authorities rather than the representative of the Persian administration, Bagohi. The inclusion of the one type of minute coin that bears a portrait of the Persian king would tend to corroborate the view that the first series of minute coins were issued by a representative of the Persian administration.

L. Mildenberg proposes a tentative date of 350-340 BCE for the first series containing the lily and the portrait of the Persian king, which would date them some ten to thirty years after the drachm and the minute coins that bear the profile of Athena on one side and her owl on the other. He does not state whether he believes the first group dates from the governorship of Bagohi or of Yehezkiyah. His criteria for dating are by necessity too general, however,

---

[62] Meshorer, *Jewish Coins of the Second Temple Period*, 36-8.

to allow certainty and do not permit satisfactory resolution of the issue at hand.[63]

The minute coins issued under Yehezkiyah that include full-face portraits of Athena are crude adaptations of a style of portraiture that became popular in the 370s BCE. The three-quarter or full-face depiction of a female deity with spiked hair standing out from her head like sunrays seems to have been developed in Syracuse by Eukleidas as an image of Athena, but was quickly adapted by other die-cutters in Syracuse to depict their local deified nymph, Arethusa.[64] Although the date of the original portrait of Athena is not able to be determined, it is thought that the adaptations by Kimon to represent the nymph Arethusa appeared on commemorative coins issued after the defeat of the Carthaginians by Dionysis I in 405 BCE.[65] Both types became popular elsewhere in the empire during the first half of the 4th century BCE, as evidenced by their appearance on at least one coin minted by Pharnabazus, satrap of Tarsus, between 379 and 374, a number of coins minted between 378-372 BCE by Datamas, satrap of Cilicia, and a series of coins issued by Datamas' successor, Mazaios, sometime between 361 and 333 BCE.[66] Similar portraits also appear on Achaemenid coins of uncertain dates from Lycia and Hierapolis,[67] and from Rhodes, Thessaly and Clazomenae.[68]

Another series of minute silver coins issued by Yehezkiyah bears on one side a portrait of the governor, without helmet or wreath, and the head and front legs of a winged, roaring lion on the other side. The latter depiction resembles that found on one side of a series of minute coins issued by Datamas' successor, Mazaios, except for the wings.[69]

---

[63]   Mildenberg, "Yehud: A Preliminary Study," 187-8, 191.
[64]   So Robertson, *History of Greek Art*, 1.360.
[65]   *Ibid.*
[66]   See conveniently, Babelon, *Perses achéménides*, pls. IV and VI.
[67]   For photos of these coins, see conveniently, *ibid.*, pls. IV-VI; X; LI.
[68]   For photos of these coins, see conveniently, Seltman, *Greek Coins*, pls. xxxiv.10-2, 15; xli.12, 13; lxi.13-5; xxx.13-5.
[69]   See conveniently, *ibid.*, pl. V and Meshorer, "Addendum I," pl. 18.10, 10a.

Summary

During the Persian period, at least one official coin of the province of Yehud bore an image of Yahweh.[70] It appears to have been minted during the governorship of Bagohi. Because of insufficient data, it is impossible to decide whether or not this coin was issued by the non-Jewish governor in defiance of a local aniconic tradition that was already being extended to include Yahweh. In light of Josephus' report of Bagohi's involvement in a fight for control of the high priesthood, the possibility that he issued the coin as a repressive measure cannot be ruled out.

In addition, other coins bearing the portrait of Athena and her attribute animal, the owl, and Athena/Arethusa appear to have been issued for use in Yehud during the governorships of both Bagohi and his successor, Yehezkiyah. In contrast to the coin bearing an image of Yahweh, their presence is to be explained either in terms of the nonexistence of the Second Commandment at this time or as a nonchalant attitude by the local Yehudian elite or populace in general about the prohibition against representation of deities other than Yahweh. Their production in two different styles under two separate governors, one a worshipper of Yahweh and one not, tends to indicate that the series issued by Bagohi cannot be explained as a possible further example of a deliberate act by the governor to anger the local population as a form of punishment or repression after the murder of Yeshua. At the same time, however, the production of minute coins that might have deliberately avoided the depiction of Athena by substituting a lily or leaving one side blank, and which also might have attempted at times to neutralize the owl or replace it with a bird more associated with Yahweh, suggest that there might have been periods during the governorships of one or both men during which some sort of aniconic pressure was being brought to bear by a faction within the community. Alternatively, the blanks may simply have resulted from bad minting and the introduction of new symbols or motifs may not have been moti-

---

[70] Y. Meshorer has informed me that he now knows of another Persian-era coin from Yehud depicting Yahweh: an ear appears an one side with a shofar, representing the hearing-god motif and the obverse bears a falcon with the inscription, יהד (private communications. For details, see his forthcoming article, "Two Outstanding YHD Coins," *Eretz Israel* 25, Hebrew with English summary).

vated by explicit aniconic concerns, but merely a desire to develop a local coinage that no longer imitated Athenian prototypes.

B. *Ptolemaic Coins*

The coins issued under the authority of the Ptolemaic rulers for use in Yehud continue the tradition developed under Bagohi and reused by Yehezkiyah on one set of minute coins of portraying the civil authority on one side and a divine attribute animal on the other. An eagle with outstretched wings graces most of these coins, whose other sides feature a male head in profile, facing right more often than left. The provincial name appears in paleo-Hebrew letters, spelled in a range of ways: יהד, יהדה, and יהוד.[71] Another series bears the head of a horse in place of the portrait of the Ptolemaic ruler and a dove facing left, with its head turned right, looking over its wing on the reverse side, in place of the eagle. The provincial name is spelled יהודה in paleo-Hebrew script.[72] The number of coins dating to this period, which covers roughly 312-198 BCE, is relatively small, so the available sampling may not represent the full range of coin types.

The dating of the first series bearing the head of Ptolemy I seems best placed during the reign of Ptolemy II Philadelphus (284-249 BCE). This king continued the coin type that his father had introduced ca. 300 BCE that bore the portrait of Ptolemy I wearing the aegis of Zeus around his neck on one side and an eagle standing on a thunderbolt on the other. Ptolemy I was also responsible for introducing a weight standard for the currency of his empire that contrasted with the Attic standard used elsewhere in the Greek world. Both his original coin type and his standard of weight were used throughout the years of the Ptolemaic dynasty.[73] As Y. Meshorer

---

[71] See conveniently, Meshorer, *Ancient Jewish Coinage*, 1.117, 184 and pl. 3.

[72] *Ibid.* Meshorer has corrected his earlier view that the horse head was that of a feline in light of a new example of this coin whose image is clear ("Addendum I," 115).

[73] For details, see G.K. Jenkins, "The Monetary Systems in the Early Hellenistic Time, with Special Regard to the Economic Policy of the Ptolemaic Kings," in *The Patterns of Monetary Development in Phoenicia and Palestine in Antiquity. Proceeding of the International Numismatic Convention, Jerusalem, 27-31 December, 1963* (ed. A. Kindler; Tel Aviv: Schocken, 1967) 58-62.

has argued, it is unlikely that Ptolemy I would have granted minting privileges to the province of Yehud/Judea since he conquered
Jerusalem and enslaved its residents. Contrary to his father, however, Ptolemy II redeemed Jewish slaves with his own money, com-
missioned the translation of the Torah into Greek, and dedicated
ceremonial objects to the Temple in Jerusalem.[74] Unlike other
mints in Syria issuing coins under Ptolemy II, the coins of Yehud/
Judea did not place the name and title of the king or queen next to
the eagle or provide a regnal year or a minting authority's mark,
allowing a more accurate dating of the coins.

The dating of the second series bearing the horse head on one
side and the bird facing left with its head turned right cannot be
established on the basis of current criteria and data. No royal names
or dates are included.[75] Thus, it is uncertain whether it predates
the first series, is contemporaneous with it, a postdates it.

Whatever the date of the first series, it is significant that the portraits of Ptolemy I on the few extant examples appear to have been
altered from their Egyptian counterparts to eliminate symbols of
deification, yielding portraits of mere human individuals instead of
a deified ruler. The characteristic aegis of Zeus that adorns the neck
of Ptolemy I on successive generations of Ptolemaic coins minted in
Egypt as well as Syria and other outlying Ptolemaic holdings is
missing from the portraits on the coins of Yehud/Judea.[76] Traces

---

[74] *Ancient Jewish Coinage*, 1.18-9, 184.

[75] Meshorer originally proposed a dating scheme based on the spelling of the provincial name (*Ancient Jewish Coinage*, 1.18-20), but new coins have overturned his
theory. It is possible that this series dates to the period of Alexander the Great
(private communication).

[76] The aegis appears regularly in busts of Ptolemy I on coins from Joppa, Gaza,
Ace/Ptolemais, Sidon, and Tyre. Coins issued in Joppa from 261-248 under Ptolemy II that are not depicted on plates are not specifically said to bear the aegis. The
few published examples from his reign from mints in Cos and Salamis show him
with the aegis, even though its presence is not mentioned in the accompanying description. I cannot confirm, therefore, whether or not it is present or absent in the
20 examples from Joppa and Gaza. It is definitely present on coins issued within
Egypt proper and in other provincial areas. See R.S. Poole, *A Catalogue of Greek
Coins in the British Museum: The Ptolemies, Kings of Egypt* (Bologna: Arnaldo Forni,
1977) 34-5, nos. 125-44. The aegis is present on portraits of Ptolemy I minted under Ptolemy III Euergetes I (*idem*, 48-53, nos. 18-23, 25-28[?], 31-43, 56[?], 63, 74[?])
and Ptolemy IV Philopater I (*idem*, 64 no. 25).

of it remain as a decorative raised band or border at the bottom of the neck. In one case, the plaited pattern is even maintained, but the band is thin and lacks the characteristic knot in front that defines the necklace as the aegis of Zeus.[77] The use of this decorative raised band on a portrait of Berenike I in addition to busts of Ptolemy I provides strong evidence of its adapted nature.[78] No portraits of Berenike on Egyptian coins have her sport the aegis; this was a privilege limited to the divine, male ruler.

Given the small size of the coins, it could be argued that the engraver(s) ran out of space or decided not to replicate every last detail from the larger coins and that the omission of the knot of the aegis is insignificant — a mere oversight. I think, however, that a corroborating point tends to favor the view that the omission was deliberate and not a mere oversight. Unlike other Syrian mints, Yehud/Judea never produced any of the series of coins begun by Ptolemy I and continued by Ptolemy II (III and IV) that bore a portrait of Zeus on one side and the eagle on a thunderbolt on the other. Examples of this series were minted in Ptolemais under Ptolemy I,[79] in Tyre under Ptolemy II,[80] in Tyre, Ptolemais and Joppa under Ptolemy III,[81] and in Tyre under Ptolemy V.[82] It seems unlikely that the Ptolemies would have prevented the coining of this type in Yehud when they allowed it elsewhere in the outlying areas of their holdings. The failure of coins bearing a portrait of Zeus to be minted in Yehud must therefore lie with the local officials, who may have objected to its depiction of Zeus. Should the alternate series of coins bearing the head of the horse in place of the portrait of Zeus or of the deified Ptolemy I date to the Ptolemaic era, they could provide further corroboration for the deliberate removal of Zeus' aegis from the portrait of Ptolemy I. They are unique to Yehud/Judea. This point may be related to the previous one: the second series of coins may have been a concession by Ptolemy II to Jewish aniconic sensibilities, allowing them to substi-

---

[77] Meshorer, *Ancient Jewish Coinage*, 1.184.1.
[78] *Ibid.*, 1.117, pl. 3.15a.
[79] Poole, *Catalogue of Greek Coins, The Ptolemies*, 34, no. 123.
[80] *Ibid.*, 32, nos. 102-7.
[81] *Ibid.*, 53-4, nos. 64-73, 75-9.
[82] *Ibid.*, 73 nos. 56-9.

tute the horse series for the Zeus series. In this case, the removal of
the eagle on the thunderbolt in favor of the dove might indicate
that the former image had objectionable religious connotations as
well. Perhaps it was too closely associated with Zeus, in spite of its
use in biblical imagery in connection with Yahweh, leading to the
substitution of the dove, which also had specific symbolic connections with Yahweh.[83]

A third point should be addressed: why do the coins from Judea
lack the name and title of Ptolemy I in association with the eagle
on the thunderbolt, in contrast to the common practice elsewhere
in Egypt and outlying provinces? One Judean coin may reflect this
practice in a highly abbreviated way: it contains the Greek letters
BA between the Hebrew inscription יהדה and the eagle on the
thunderbolt.[84] The BA may refer to the pre-261 BCE title used of
Ptolemy I, βασιλεύς, "king," in contrast to the later title, σωτήρ,
"savior."[85] Nevertheless, there is a clear tendency to avoid either
title, as well as to avoid the monarch's name.

The desire to avoid use of the title σωτήρ is easily explained as
a conscious rejection of the deification of this king, even after
death. Since its avoidance can be seen to represent a refusal to recognize the divine status of Ptolemy I, the portrait of Ptolemy I on
the front of one series of Ptolemaic coins issued in Judea can be
interpreted as a human portrait of a civil authority. The apparent
removal of the divine aegis from these portraits would be consistent
with the failure to identify Ptolemy I as deified "savior."

The reason lying behind the possible desire to avoid the use of
the title "king" for Ptolemy I is less clear-cut, especially since it may
be used somewhat cryptically on the one coin mentioned above.
On the one hand, there may have been no objection to this title.
On the other, it may not have been used because the Jewish authorities were aware that the Ptolemies had adopted the old Egyptian
concept of divine kingship, viewing the king as a god incarnate. In
this case, they would not have wanted to accede to this ideology

---

[83] For the religious symbolism of the dove, see Goodenough, *Jewish Symbols*, 8.27-
46.
[84] Meshorer, *Ancient Jewish Coinage*, 1.184.
[85] For this change made by Ptolemy II, see Poole, *Catalogue of Greek Coins. The
Ptolemies*, xxv.

that countered their own long-standing tradition of human kingship and which also produced an unwanted divinity alongside Yahweh. It may be significant that no Judean coins bear portraits of Ptolemy II or his queen Arsinoe II, the monarchs living during the time of minting, unlike other Syrian mints. In light of the mistreatment that Judeans experienced under Ptolemy I, it is surprising that they would choose to mint coins bearing his portrait rather than that of his more sympathetic successor, Ptolemy II. Is this use of the dead founder of the dynasty on Judean coinage rather than the living ruler due to an aversion to the concept of divine kingship?

In light of the foregoing points, it may be significant that there is no clear example of the use of the aegis of Zeus on Judean coins bearing the portrait of Ptolemy I. It would seem that this was not a mere oversight, but a deliberate attempt to eliminate symbols of deification from the standard portrait on the nation's currency. It is consistent with the failure to name the king as σωτήρ, and possibly also as βασιλεύς. It may also be consistent with the elimination of the coin type bearing a bust of Zeus in favor of one with a horse, although it is possible that the first two anomalies are the result of an objection to the concept of the divine king while the third is an objection to the depiction of deities other than Yahweh.

Summary
On the basis of the scanty published evidence now available, it seems that the prohibition against the representation of gods other than Yahweh was being taken seriously within Yehud/Judea during the first half of the third century BCE by the authorities in charge of minting coins for the province. It is probably significant that the mint in Yehud/Judea removed the symbols of deification from the bust of Ptolemy I as well as his titles that bore divine overtones, creating a human portrait of the dead king that was acceptable to the religious sentiments of the province. Should the series of coins bearing a horse's head on one side and a dove on the other also date to the Ptolemaic era, it might provide further support for an avoidance of representation of gods other than Yahweh. The horse's head might have replaced a portrait of Zeus that appeared on coins in other outlying areas. It is less certain whether a prohibition against the representation of Yahweh was also in effect.

While it appears that the Ptolemies moved toward a standardiz-
ation of coins to a few types, Ptolemy II apparently was not so
rigid as to require every province to adhere to his standard prototypes without exception, as the lack of the aegis of Zeus, the substitution of a dove for the expected eagle, and the replacement of the
portrait of Zeus with a horse's head attest. The changes made to
standard Ptolemaic imagery in Yehud/Judea seem to have arisen
from the desire to avoid depictions of gods other than Yahweh. It
might be argued that they provide indirect evidence for a policy
that strove to avoid depictions of Yahweh as well, although such a
conclusion is not beyond dispute, since all the changes can be explained in terms of the avoidance of images of gods other than
Yahweh, as stated above.

C. *The Seleucid Period*

Judea does not appear to have been granted the right to mint coins
under the Seleucids before the local Hasmonean dynasty came to
power during the reign of Antiochus VII (137-129 BCE). Thus, they
would have used standard Seleucid currency minted at various sites
within the empire for their taxes and daily transactions from 198-ca.
135 BCE. During the reigns of Antiochus I-III, they would have
found on their coins portraits of the three kings, without beards.
The other side would have borne a picture of Apollo, the patron
god of the royal dynasty, seated on an omphalos or leaning on a tri-
dent.[86] Beginning with Antiochus IV, the portrait of the king gained symbols of divinity, depicting him no longer as a mere mortal
but as a reigning god. At the same time, the image of Apollo was
replaced by one of the enthroned Zeus Nikephorus, probably in a
move by that ruler to choose a deity acceptable to Greeks and
Asiatic peoples alike in place of one who had appealed to Greeks
alone.[87] Among his successors down through Antiochus VII, only

---

[86] For a good general survey of the divine imagery on Seleucid coinage, including
its political nature and the changes introduced in the late Seleucid period, see J.
Zahle, "Religious Motifs on Seleucid Coins," in *Religion and Religious Practice in
the Seleucid Kingdom* (ed. P. Bilde *et al.*; Studies in Hellenistic Civilization 1; Aarhus: Aarhus University, 1990) 125-39.

[87] So H. Seyrig, "Antiquités syriennes 29. A propos du culte de Zeus à Séleucie,"
Syria 20 (1939) 300.

Antiochus VI Dionysis (145-142) chose to portray himself as a god; the others all had self-portraits as humans, portraits of famous rulers from the past, especially Alexander, or gods. It should be noted, however, that they all continued the common practice of depicting a deity on the reverse side from the portrait, or occasionally, figures from mythology. Deities featured include Apollo, Tyche, Artemis, Nike, Zeus, Pallas Athena, Athene Alkis, Poseidon, and Eros, while mythological figures include Europa, the Dioscuri, young Dionysis, and Demeter.[88] The images of the mortal kings would not have offended the Jewish population of Judea, but the images of a divinized Antiochus IV and Antiochus VI and the wide range of deities would have broken the prohibition against images of deities other than Yahweh in the Second Commandment, had it existed in this period. A tendency to avoid depictions of deities other than Yahweh was noted for the preceding Ptolemaic period. Without the ability to mint their own coins, however, the population would not have any choice but to use the coins, despite their bearing what might have been deemed objectionable iconography.

The first coins minted in Judea under the Seleucids were struck by John Hyrcanus I in 131-129 BCE, during the reign of Antiochus VII Sidetes.[89] On one side the coins bear an anchor flanked by the inscription ΒΑΣΙΛΕΥΣ ΑΝΤΙΟΧΟΥ ΕΥΕΡΓΕΤΟΥ. The reverse side

---

[88] See conveniently, P. Gardner, *Catalogue of Greek Coins. The Seleucid Kings of Syria* (Bologna: Arnaldo Forni, 1963) 44-75 with corresponding plates. The wide range of deities is the result of the policy introduced under Antiochus IV that allowed nineteen cities within his kingdom to mint semiautonomous and autonomous copper coins; for details, see O. Mørkholm, "The Monetary System of the Seleucid Kings until 129 B.C.," in *The Patterns of Monetary Development in Phoenicia and Palestine in Antiquity. Proceedings of the International Numismatic Convention, Jerusalem, 27-31 December, 1963* (ed. A. Kindler; Tel Aviv: Schocken, 1967) 82-6.

[89] Y. Meshorer now thinks that a coin previously attributed to the reign of Antiochus VIII might date instead to Antiochus IV Epiphanes (private communication). The coin bears on one side a portrait of the king with radiated crown, facing right. The other side features a lily inside a circle of dots with the inscription BA-LK. For an example, see Meshorer, *Ancient Jewish Coinage*, 1.40, pl. 56.7. If he is correct, this coin type would be the earliest known to have been minted in Judea under the Seleucids, although Meshorer is not certain that the coin was from Jerusalem even.

depicts a lily in a circle of dots.[90] The anchor replaces the traditional portrait of the ruler and the lily, the depiction of a deity. It once was surmised that the anchor was used because of its close associations with the Seleucid dynasty; the founder, Seleucid I, apparently had a birthmark in this shape.[91] It is now surmised, however, that the anchor represents Judea's control over the port city of Joppa, which Jonathan had conquered in 148 BCE, for which tribute money was being rendered to Antiochus VII as part of the settlement to end the latter's siege of Jerusalem.[92] There is no reason to choose between these alternatives; both probably were influential in the decision by Hyrcanus I to use the anchor on one side of the coins minted during his tenure of office.

The lily was a common ornamental design used on buildings during the Hasmonean period and seems to have been considered a local emblem.[93] It had already been used during the Persian period on the series of small denomination coins issued by Yehezqiyah in place of the owl, the symbol of Athena. Its resuscitation under Hyrcanus I for use in place of the common depiction of a deity need not be construed as a deliberate act of imitation of the earlier coinage, but certainly reinforces the idea that the lily had long-standing symbolic value in connection with the cult of Yahweh. Under the Hasmoneans, it seems to have become a favorite motif, whose widespread use may have broadened its original symbolic connection with the cult to become a local emblem for the incipient Hasmonean state.

The coins minted under Hyrcanus I that bear the name of his overlord, Antiochus VII Sidetes, provide indirect, but inconclusive proof of the avoidance of the depiction of Yahweh as well as other

---

[90] Meshorer, *Ancient Jewish Coinage*, 1.39.
[91] So e.g., Seltman, *Greek Coins*, 227; G.F. Hill, *Historical Greek Coins* (Chicago: Argonaut, 1966) 119.
[92] So e.g., Goodenough, *Jewish Symbols*, 1.272-4; M. Avi-Yonah, "The Historical Background of Palestine in the Light of the Recent Archaeological Discoveries," in *The Patterns of Monetary Development in Phoenicia and Palestine in Antiquity. Proceedings of the International Numismatic Convention, Jerusalem, 27-31 December, 1963* (ed. A. Kindler; Tel Aviv: Schocken, 1967) 113; Meshorer, *Ancient Jewish Coinage*, 1.62.
[93] So Meshorer, *Ancient Jewish Coinage*, 1.62. For a full discussion, see Goodenough, *Jewish Symbols*, 3.184-239.

deities. The lily parallels the use of local emblems on contemporaneous coinage minted elsewhere, such as the palm tree for Tyre, the dove for Ashkelon, and the galley for Sidon, so its presence need not imply a deliberate avoidance of the depiction of a deity. It could simply reflect a preference for developing a national emblem for the newly created state as Seleucid power in the region of Syria-Palestine waned. On the other hand, given the ancionic tendency in Judea during the preceding Ptolemaic era, it is likely that the desire to avoid the depiction of Yahweh was a motivating factor in the decision to place a national emblem on the side that often bore a depiction of the local or empire god.

The next Seleucid coins were minted in Jerusalem during the reign of Antiochus VIII, Epiphanes. One type is known. It bears a portrait of the king, with radiated crown, facing right on one side, and the other, a bunch of grapes enclosed inside a circle of dots.[94] This coin is significant for a couple of reasons. First, the radiated crown was used by Antiochus IV and Antiochus VI as a symbol of divinity, so it is surprising to find such a depiction on a coin minted in Judea. Its presence can be explained in various ways. The coin could have been an official or semiautonomous issue on which the portrait was not negotiable. Alternatively, the radiated crown was not an issue, either because its meaning was not recognized or was simply ignored by the Judean authorities, or because the authorities at the time had no objections to its divine symbolism.

The bunch of grapes represents a new, alternative emblem for the Hasmonean state.[95] The presence of the local emblem rather than the depiction of one of the favored empire gods tends to suggest that these coins were semiautonomous issues rather than official issues.

The coins of Antiochus VIII provide mixed testimony about the status of the enforcement of the aniconic tradition. On the one hand, there is no depiction of Yahweh, but instead, the emblem of the bunch of grapes. On the other hand, there is a portrait of a deified Seleucid ruler. The first factor tends to suggest that the ancionic tradition was in force and included avoidance of depictions

---

[94]   Meshorer, *Ancient Jewish Coinage*, 1.41.
[95]   For the symbolic meaning of grapes as a product of the vine, see Goodenough, *Jewish Symbols in the Greco-Roman Period*, 5.99-111.

of Yahweh; the second tends to suggest that it was not being observed for gods other than Yahweh. Since these coins were minted
after the formal establishment of a state of Judea in 140 BCE, it is
possible that there was no need felt to counter the claims of the
nominal overlord. In contrast to the situation in the preceding
century with the Ptolemies, the Jewish authorities may now have
been secure enough about the correctness of their view of non-
divine kingship that they felt no compulsion to eliminate the radiated crown from the portrait because it threatened to spread a
misleading ideology. They may essentially have ignored it, treating
it as a misguided view of "others" that had no bearing on their own
state's ideology.

Summary

The few coins minted in Judea during the Seleucid period show a
clear tendency to replace the normal depiction of a deity on one
side of the coins with a local emblem: the lily or a bunch of grapes.
Since other Syro-Palestinian cities also developed this practice, the
substitution cannot have been exclusively motivated by a desire to
avoid the depiction of Yahweh. However, since images of local gods
appeared on some series issued by these cities instead of the local
emblems, a practice not followed in Judea, it seems likely that the
decision to use a local emblem rather than a depiction of Yahweh
or one of the favored empire gods was motivated to some degree by
adherence to the aniconic tradition.

The appearance of the portrait of a deified Antiochus VIII seems
to contradict the aniconic tendency deducible from the use of the
local emblems. Perhaps the local Judean authorities were unaware
of the symbolic meaning of the radiated crown, or perhaps they
were compelled by their overlord to put this image on the front of
this issue of semiautonomous coinage. A third possibility is that the
Judean authorities were aware of the symbolic meaning of the
crown, but felt that it did not pose an ideological threat since they
were a state once again, albeit still a nominal vassal of the Seleucids,
and the imagery associated with this "foreign" overlord would not
be taken seriously among the Jewish population of the new Hasmonean state.

D. *The Independent Hasmonean State*

Coinage minted under the Hasmonean dynasty from sometime after 129-37 BCE is consistently aniconic.[96] During the entire period, there is even a marked tendency to avoid placing a bust of the reigning high priest/king on the side where traditionally, such a portrait appeared. Instead, the name of the official is written out inside a wreath, together with his title(s). The practice of using a local emblem in place of the traditional depiction of the local god is also continued.

John Hyrcanus I minted three series of coins that can probably be dated after the establishment of the independent state. The precise date for this event is uncertain; while the council of the Jews proclaimed an independent state in 140 BCE, it is traditional to date the actual gaining of independence after the death of Antiochus VII in 129 BCE. However, an even later date might be indicated if the last coin described in the previous section dates from the reign of Antiochus VIII, as suggested by Meshorer.[97] The latter king reigned from 126/5-96 BCE, and the coin bears the regnal year 20, which would date it to 106/105 BCE. Since the circumstances surrounding the issuance of this coin are not clear, it is uncertain whether the independent Hasmonean state began prior to this time or not, and consequently, whether any of the three coin types about to be described predate 106/105 or whether all postdate it. All are autonomous issues.

---

[96] For the dating and attribution of Hasmonean coinage, I am adopting the predominant scheme, which places coins bearing the name Yehoḥanan under John Hyrcanus I and those bearing Yehonatan under John Hyrcanus II. This sequence has been favored for example, by F. Madden (*History of Jewish Coinage and of Money in the Old and New Testament* [London: Bernard Quaritch, 1864] 37-79), Hill (*Catalogue of Greek Coins of Palestine*, xciii-xciv, 184-7), A. Reifenberg (*Ancient Jewish Coins* [4th ed.; Jerusalem: R. Mass, 1963] 3-5), A. Kindler (*Coins of the Land of Israel* [Jerusalem: Keter, 1974] 9-26) and U. Rappaport ("The Emergence of Hasmonaean Coinage," *A.J.S. Review* 1 [1976] 171-86). Originally, Y. Meshorer favored the placing of both types under Hyrcanus II (*Jewish Coins of the Second Temple Period*, 41-7 and *Ancient Jewish Coinage*, 1.35-59), following the work of L. Kadman (*The Coins of the Jewish War of 66-73 A.D.* [Corpus Numicorum Palaestiniensium, 2nd Series, 3; Tel Aviv: Schocken, 1960] 48). In light of new discoveries from Mt. Gerizim, he has joined the majority view ("Addendum I," 106).

[97] *Ancient Jewish Coinage*, 1.40-1.

One type, which would become the standard for the entire dynasty, bears on one side two cornucopias facing each other, with a pomegranate in the center and ribbons tied in the middle of each horn with ends draping downwards. The whole image is surrounded by a circle of dots. On the reverse is an inscription in paleo-Hebrew, encircled by a wreath, that reads in its complete form, יהוחנן הכהן הגדל וחבר יהודים, "Yehohanan the High Priest and the council of the Jews." Not all the letters are present on various die cuts.[98]

The wreath was a symbol of leadership and authority taken over from the Hellenistic world. Although it had strong associations with royalty in the Hellenistic world, being used during coronation ceremonies, it could also be used to represent lesser offices of authority. On the coins of Hyrcanus I, where the wreath encircles the inscription that proclaims the title High Priest, the emphasis does not seem to be on the royal overtones of the wreath.[99] Rather, it seems intended to symbolize the role of Hyrcanus I as the authority over temple rituals. It may have been chosen because of its dual function, however, allowing Hyrcanus to hint at his royal status even though he had agreed not to assume royal titles.

The double cornucopias were another symbol taken over from the larger Hellenistic world, probably as a symbol of fertility, which was then associated with the official religion of the Hasmonean state. In Hellenistic art, Demeter, goddess of the fertility of the soil, carries one or two horns. While in the Hellenistic world the horns would contain pomegranates, vines, or ears of corn, under the Hasmoneans, except the final ruler Mattathias Antigonus, the double cornucopias always appear with a pomegranate between them. This fruit had been used as a decorative motif in the national Yahwistic cult before the exile and so had a long tradition of association with the cult of Yahweh. Under the Hasmoneans the double cornucopias with pomegranate became an official Jewish emblem.[100]

---

[98] For the coins, see Meshorer, *Ancient Jewish Coinage*, 1.136-47, pl. 28-42. He now attributes these to Hyrcanus I ("Addendum I," 106-7).

[99] So Meshorer, *Ancient Jewish Coinage*, 1.63-4.

[100] For the symbolism of the corncopia, see Goodenough, *Jewish Symbols*, 8.106-14. For this Jewish character, see Meshorer, *Ancient Jewish Coinage*, 1.67-8.

The second coin type bears on one side a palm branch[101] with a fillet on top, flanked by the inscription in paleo-Hebrew, "Yehohanan the High Priest and head of the council of the Jews." The other side bears a lily flower between two ears of wheat; the whole design is encircled by a border of dots.[102]

The final series is commemorative in nature, although the event behind it remains uncertain. A crested helmet appears inside a circle of dots on one side, while the reverse bears two parallel cornucopias instead of what would become the standard facing pair. The parallel layout is more typical of Ptolemaic and Seleucid depiction on coinage.[103] The cornucopias are surrounded by the paleo-Hebrew inscription "Yehohanan the High Priest and head of the council of the Jews," Under subsequent rulers, an inscription naming the ruler and giving his titles would come to be placed on the reverse side inside the wreath. The cornucopias and inscription are contained within a circle of dots.[104] In Rome, a similar style helmet was used to symbolize the authority of the high priest, and different crests were used to distinguish the ranks of officers. The use of the crested helmet, would seem, therefore, to represent Hyrcanus I as both high priest and temporal ruler, the latter office being emphasized through the addition of the title ראש, "head."

Although the helmet represents an innovation that would not be repeated by subsequent rulers, it avoids a portrait of the ruler in favor of a more abstract symbol. The decision by Hyrcanus not to place his own bust on his coins is curious, since the prohibition against images applied to deities, not to humans. On the one hand, it could be argued that the avoidance is an indirect indication that Hyrcanus I was claiming some sort of divine kingship for himself. On the other hand, however, the move might have been motivated by a desire not to be associated with such claims, which were being

---

[101] For the symbolism of the palm branch, see Goodenough, *Jewish Symbols*, 7.87-91, 93-108, 110-9, 121-9.

[102] See conveniently, *ibid.*, 1.136-55, pls. 28-53. Some of the coins bear the Greek letter *A* or the monogram *AP* on the side with the lily. Although its meaning is disputed, Meshorer adopts the suggestion of Kanael ("The Greek Letters and Monograms on Coins of Jehohanan the Priest," *IEJ* 2 [1952] 190-4) that it represents a later addition during the reign of Antipater (*ibid.*, 84-5).

[103] So Goodenough, *Jewish Symbols*, 8.106-14, esp. 107.

[104] Meshorer, *Ancient Jewish Coinage*, 1.150, pl. 45.R1 and R1BN.

made by both Seleucid and Ptolemaic rulers in this period. By not
putting his own likeness on the coins, he set himself apart from the
common ideology of the day, thereby avoiding any hint of claims
of divinity for himself. Whatever his reasoning, it was continued by
his successors and into the Roman period, until Philip, Agrippa I
and Agrippa II.

Alexander Jannaeus (103-75 BCE) initially imitated the coins
issued within Judea by Hyrcanus I with the anchor on one side and
the lily in a circle of dots on the other. The only change he introduced was making the inscription bearing his name and the title
king bilingual to include Hebrew as well as Greek.[105] He also continued the coin type that bore the facing cornucopias with pomegranate and ribbons in a circle of dots on one side and the inscription bearing the ruler's name, title of High Priest and a reference to
the council of the Jews enclosed within a wreath.[106] Jannaeus further introduced a series of variations, all of which emphasized his
status as king. One new series reintroduced a palm frond in place of
the anchor,[107] and the inscription המלך יהונתן "Yehonatan, the
king," in Hebrew only.[108] Another series reintroduced the anchor
on one side,[109] surrounded by the Greek inscription ΑΛΕΞΑΝ-
ΔΡΟΥ ΒΑΣΙΛΕΩΣ, "Alexander the king," but placed a star with
the Hebrew inscription המלך יהונתן, "Jehonatan, the king," distrib-
uted between the rays of the star. The entire image was then

---

[105] Meshorer, *Ancient Jewish Coinage*, 1.118 and pl. 4.Aa1-Ab5.

[106] *Ibid.*, 1.123-33, pls. 8-24. B. Kanael proposed that the restriking of the early
coins of Jannaeus that bore the anchor and the lily to bear the name of Jehonatan
and the title "high priest and council of the Jews" on one side and the facing cornucopias on the other was done in order to placate the Pharisees and remove
claims of kingship on the early coins ("Ancient Jewish Coins and their Historical
Importance," 45). Meshorer originally accepted that line of reasoning, but now has
rejected it because of its inability to account for the failure to overstrike other
early coin types that bore the title king (*Ancient Jewish Coinage*, 1.77-8).
[107]

[108] *Ibid.*, 119, pl. 4.B1-B3Sp.

[109] Y. Meshorer has argued that the renewed use of the anchor in this series and
the succeeding one is the result of Jannaeus' annexation of the coastal cities in 95
BCE (*Ancient Jewish Coinage*, 1.62). Even so, he appears to have gone back to a
familiar symbol first introduced by Hyrcanus I, which he also employed on his
first issues, in order to maintain some sense of continuity and identity.

enclosed within a diadem.[110] There were various dies of this design, which varied the number of rays within the star and in some cases, made the inscription within the star in Aramaic instead of Hebrew. He then abandoned the star image in favor of the writing of his name and title in Aramaic within a wreath, "Alexandros, the king," for a brief series.[111]

B. Kanael was the first to recognize that the star with the inscription "Jehonatan the king" was enclosed within a diadem and not merely a circle or wheel.[112] This entire image becomes a substitute for the traditional bust of the temporal ruler who is issuing the coins. Even though the star could have a wide range of symbolism, Kanael is probably correct that the star symbol in the present instance was intended to be associated with the statement in the Song of Balaam that "a star shall come out of Jacob and a scepter shall rise out of Israel" (Num 24:17). Here then, an abstract Jewish symbol associated with kingship was paired with the common Hellenistic symbol of kingship, the diadem, to forge a new symbolic representation of his office as king that would be recognized by Jews and recently converted Gentiles alike.

Judah Aristobulus II continued the coin type initiated by Hyrcanus I and continued by Alexander Jannaeus that bore the paleo-Hebrew inscription, "High Priest and council of the Jews" within a wreath on one side and facing cornucopias with a pomegranate in the middle, encircled in a border of dots, on the other.[113] Given his brief four-year reign (67-63 BCE), it cannot be known whether he might have reinstituted use of the title "king" in time, as Jannaeus had done on his some of his coin series. It is unknown then whether he continued using the favored coin types for the sake of establishing his own legitimacy in the Hasmonean line, or whether he did so deliberately to avoid a claim of royalty, perhaps in response to Pharisaic pressure.

---

[110] *Ibid.*, 1.119-22, pl. 5.Ca1-pl. 7.Cf1.

[111] *Ibid.*, 1.122-23, pl. 7.Da1-Da3.

[112] "Ancient Jewish Coins," 44.

[113] See conveniently, Meshorer, *Ancient Jewish Coinage*, 134-6, pls. 25-7.

220 Diana V. Edelman

While John Hyrcanus II (63-40 BCE) maintained the standard type used by Hyrcanus I, Jannaeus and Aristobulus II,[114] the final Hasmonean ruler, Mattathias Antigonus (40-37 BCE), introduced some innovations during his short rule. On the one hand, he reintroduced the layout used by Hyrcanus I in the commemorative series with the double cornucopias flanked by his titulary written in paleo-Hebrew, although he deleted ראש and went back to the standard setup with his name and the title "High Priest and the council of the Jews." On the reverse, however, he now enclosed within an ivy wreath the Greek inscription ΑΝΤΙΓΟΝΟΥ ΒΑΣΙΛΕΩΣ, "of Antigonus the king."[115] He was the first king since Jannaeus to use Greek on his coins and to claim the title king. Unlike the latter, however, he did not inscribe the royal title in both Greek and Hebrew. The use of the more Hellenistic form of parallel cornucopias might be argued to be consistent with a return to Greek lettering as well, although it is more likely to be the result of his the carrying over of the layout on the coin issued by his forebear and the founder of the dynasty, Hyrcanus I, for the sake of emphasizing his ancestry as a claim to legitimacy.

The use of Greek is certainly to be associated with Antigonus' struggle for recognition as king of Judea during his entire reign against Herod, who had been confirmed king of Judea by Rome. Both rivals used coinage as propaganda to press their political claims to sole rulership. The proclamation of his status as king was written in the international language of Greek so that it could be read by everyone. Two heavier denominations were introduced in addition, probably as a means of impressing the citizenry.

Even more innovative was a newly designed series that featured a menorah on one side encircled by the Greek inscription, ΒΑΣΙΛΕΩΣ ΑΝΤΙ, "king Anti(gonus)." The reverse side featured what has been interpreted to be the table that bears the showbread inside a circle of dots, which in turn is surrounded by the paleo-Hebrew inscription, מתתיה כהן גדול, "Mattathias, High Priest." This is the earliest known depiction of either cultic item. Both symbols emphasize the temple in Jerusalem as the heart of the kingdom of Judea

[114] See Meshorer, "Addendum I," 106. All coins bearing the name ינתן are to be ascribed to Hyrcanus II.
[115] See ibid., 1.155-6, pl. 54.

and may have been chosen to emphasize Antigonus' entitlement by birth to the role of religious leader of the nation, in contrast to the non-priestly heritage of his rival, Herod. At the same time, it might have been designed to emphasize to the Jewish population of Judea that it would be better to have the two offices combined in the person of the high priest who would observe Jewish law rather than having a non-priestly king in charge who might decide to overturn Jewish law in favor of Roman law.

During the same time period, Herod minted coins bearing dates, probably in Samaria. One side bears a circle of dots, inside of which appears the Greek inscription, "King Herod" in varying word order and spellings, encircling a central symbol that varied from series to series. The reverse bore a depiction enclosed within a circle of dots, with no writing. Seven designs have been identified among the front and back combinations: an apex, flanked by two palm branches, a tripod, a shield, a winged caduceus, a poppy head on a stalk, an aphlastron, and a laurel branch or palm branch tied with fillet.[116] Y. Meshorer has noted that five of the symbols are imitations of designs that appeared on Roman republican coins struck in Rome between 44 and 40 BCE. The shield and poppy are not imitations, but probably symbolize military activities and the symbol of the local cult of Demeter and Kore in Samaria, respectively.[117] By contrast with Antigonus, Herod was emphasizing his Roman connections to the people of Judea, probably in a move to remind the people of the strength of his backers and the hopelessness of resistance. The coins of the two rivals declared the futility of resistance to the new outsiders on the one hand, and an appeal to maintain Jewish individuality in the face of such a threat, on the other.

---

[116] See Meshorer, *Ancient Jewish Coinage*, 2.9-10, 17-20.

[117] *Ibid.*, 2.20-2. For another discussion of the symbolism, which emphasizes their nature as symbols of Jewish temple rites and of maritime sovereignty, the army, happiness, and fertility of the soil, see J. Meyshan, *Essays in Jewish Numismatics* (Numismatic Studies and Researches 6; Jerusalem: Israel Numismatic Society, 1968) 85-98. The latter fails to note the strong Roman ideology associated with the objects depicted.

Summary

The Hasmonean rulers observed a strict observance of both aspects of the aniconic tradition: prohibition against images of deities other than Yahweh, and of Yahweh as well. They made a concerted effort not to place portraits of themselves on their coins, breaking with the practice that had begun in the Persian period and which had continued through the Seleucid era. They may have wanted to avoid any application to themselves of the understanding current in the Seleucid and Ptolemaic empires of their days that the king was a living god. Under John Hyrcanus I, a standard coin was produced that emphasized the king's role as head priest, working with the council of the Jews. These titles were written in paleo-Hebrew. Political considerations forced the final member of the line, Mattathias Antigonus, to lay claim to the office of king against Herod and publicize this claim in Greek on coins. Of his predecessors, only Alexander Jannaeus had used Greek as well as paleo-Hebrew in inscriptions and had dared to apply the title of king to himself. Two attempts by Alexander Jannaeus to establish a national emblem for his new state in the form of the lily and a bunch of grapes were abandoned in favor of the two cornucopias facing one another with a pomegranate between them and their ends tied together, which had been introduced by his predecessor, Hyrcanus I. This replaced the usual image of the local deity or its cultic symbol, although in this period other independent states were sometimes also substituting national emblems for deity-related imagery. Antigonus' use of the menorah and the table of shewbread on one series of coins can been seen as an attempt to create new national emblems that were specifically Jewish and which could serve as rallying points against Rome and its appointee as king of Judea, Herod.

Conclusion

The date at which the Second Commandment was formulated, either as a prohibition against images of gods other than Yahweh or as a comprehensive prohibition against any deity images whatsoever, including representations of Yahweh, is uncertain. The foregoing survey and discussion of imagery used on coins minted within the province of Yehud/Judea from the Persian period through the end of the Hasmonean dynasty has revealed that the first possible move to avoid the depiction of gods other than Yahweh in non-cultic contexts[118] occurred in Yehud towards the end of the Persian period, perhaps at the end of the leadership of Bagohi or sometime during the tenure of his successor, Yehezqiyah. At this time, the image of Athena may have been removed from one side of the minute coins in favor of a blank or a lily, and her owl was replaced with an eagle on the other side. It is to be noted, however, that the blank may have resulted from poor minting rather than an intentional decision to remove the depiction of the goddess; Yehezqiyah also issued a series of minute coins that bore a full face portait of Athena/Arethusa. Should the removal of the image of Athena have been deliberate, it seems that in the 340s there might have been a faction within the community that was bringing aniconic pressure to bear, but that it was not yet a majority view. Should it have been a minting mistake, then no aversion to depictions of gods other than Yahweh can be seen to have been in place during the Persian period.

The first deliberate avoidance of depictions of Yahweh on coins has to be placed after the governorship of Bagohi, under whom a drachm bearing a depiction of Yahweh seated on a winged throne in the guise of Zeus was issued. As a non-worshipper of Yahweh, the possibility was left open that he might have minted this coin as a repressive measure in response to negative reaction to his attempt to take control over the temple after Yeshua's murder. It is equally possible, however, that the aniconic law did not yet exist at this time. His Yahweh-worshipping successor, Yehezqiyah, chose not to replace the portrait of Athena with one of Yahweh and chose to place his own bust on another series he issued instead of that of the local deity. This negative evidence must be used with great caution. It could be used to support the view that that both levels of the Second Commandment were being observed by this governor, but

---

[118] B. Schmidt raised the possibility in private conversation that there might have been a cultic image of Yahweh in the temple during some portion of this period and that the ban on images of Yahweh, whether on illegitimate images or any images at all, might have been applied to the secular or non-temple spheres only. As he pointed out, I am not directly addressing the question of an aniconic cult of Yahweh, but rather, the wider social implications of the Second Commandment in non-cultic contexts.

might equally be argued not to bear any particular significance, if an aniconic tradition did not yet exist at this time.

On the basis of the limited evidence now available, it seems as though there was a deliberate move during Ptolemaic control of Yehud/Judea to avoid the depiction of any deity on the locally minted coins. Symbols of deification were removed from the standard portrait of Ptolemy I as well as his title σωτήρ, which made claims to divinity. In contrast to other Syro-Palestinian mints, no portraits of living monarchs were used in Yehud/Judea, which is probably significant in light of the Ptolemies' adoption of the old Egyptian belief in pharoah as a living god. The series of coins that bore the portrait of Zeus was not produced in this province. It is possible but not certain that the series that bore a horse head on one side and a bird facing left on the other, with its head turned right, was developed as a substitute for the Zeus coin type. At this time the date of the series with the horse head cannot be established, however, so any relationship between the two must remain tentative conjecture. Considering the move by the Ptolemaic administration to produce a standard coinage through the empire, these deviations indicate a clear aversion to depictions of gods other than Yahweh and indirectly suggest that representations of Yahweh were also being avoided.

When Judea passed to control of the Seleucids, it did not begin to mint its own coins until the time of Hyrcanus I, after the Maccabean revolt. His coins, minted on behalf of his overlord, Antiochus VII Sidetes, were noticably aniconic. By contrast, those minted on behalf Antiochus VIII Epiphanes, also during his rulership, bore a portrait of the Seleucid king as a god, with radiated crown. How is this discrepency to be explained? Perhaps he was compelled to use the portrait; if not, he may have felt that with the recent reestablishment of Judea as an independent state, their "foreign" ideology was less of a threat. In any event, the coinage minted during the overlordship of Antiochus VIII Epiphanes presents the first clear exception to what has appeared to be an aniconic tradition that had been gaining momentum for almost two centuries.

The aniconic tradition was observed scrupulously on both levels during the period of the Hasmonean state. Even portraits of the reigning high priest/king were studiously avoided, although such depictions should not have broken the terms of the Second Commandment. Given a prevailing ideology of divine kingship in the adjoining Ptolemaic and Seleucid empires, this move may have been strictly precautionary, even though Judean ideology seems to have favored the view of the king as human.

If the above observations are tied to the presumption that the Second Commandment would have been observed throughout its existence, then they would tend to suggest that the aniconic tradition was first introduced as religious legislation at the end of the Persian period or early during Ptolemaic hegemony. If such a presumption is not made, but it is assumed that the tradition dates at least from the late monarchy or the early exile, then it can be noted that there was a nonchalant attitude toward it during the second half of the Persian era, when coins were first minted in Yehud. Only at the end of this period is there the possibility of a faction in favor of the avoidance of depictions of deities other than Yahweh, and its existence remains uncertain. There was also a brief breach in observance during the overlordship of Antiochus VIII Epiphanes, although it remains unclear whether this was a voluntary or involuntary situation. Should no presumption be made about the original date of the Second Commandment or the consistency of its observance once in place, the above review of images on coins minted in Yehud/Judea will merely provide food for thought which, if combined with other studies of Jewish art and symbols and discussions of the religion of those devoted to the worship of Yahweh in extrabiblical sources, might serve as a basis from which to formulate a theory about the two aspects of the aniconic tradition within late forms of Yahwism and early forms of Judaism.

Fig. 2 Persian-era Coin from Yehud with depiction of Yahweh (after Y. Meshorer, *Ancient Jewish Coinage*, 1.21).

Bibliography

J.S. Ackerman, "An Exegetical Study of Psalm 82." Ph.D. dissertation, Harvard University, 1966.

S. Ackerman, *Under Every Green Tree: Popular Religion in Sixth-Century Judah*. HSM 46. Atlanta: Scholars, 1992.

G.W. Ahlström, *An Archaeological Picture of Iron Age Religions in Ancient Palestine*. StOr 55/3. Helsinki: Finnish Oriental Society, 1984.

G.W. Ahlström, *The History of Ancient Palestine from the Palaeolithic Period to Alexander's Conquest*. JSOTSup 146. Sheffield: JSOT, 1993.

G.W. Ahlström, "The Role of Archaeological and Literary Remains in Reconstructing Israel's History," in *The Fabric of History: Text, Artifact and Israel's Past*, 116-41. Edited by D. Vikander Edelman. JSOTSup 127. Sheffield: JSOT, 1991.

G.W. Ahlström, *Royal Administration and National Religion in Ancient Palestine*. SHANE 1. Leiden: Brill, 1982.

R. Albertz, *A History of Israelite Religion in the Old Testament Period*. 2 volumes. Louisville: Westminster/John Knox, 1994.

W.F. Albright, *From the Stone Age to Christianity: Monotheism and the Historical Process*. Baltimore: Johns Hopkins University, 1940.

W.F. Albright, *Yahweh and the Gods of Canaan: A Historical Analysis of Two Contrasting Faiths*. Garden City, NJ: Doubleday, 1968.

P.S. Alexander, "Remarks on Aramaic Epistolography in the Persian Period." *JSS* 23 (1978): 155-70.

K.M. Alomia, "Lesser Gods of the Ancient Near East and Some Comparisons with Heavenly Beings of the Old Testament." Ph.D. dissertation, Andrews University, 1987.

A. Alt, *Der Gott der Väter. Ein Beitrag zur Vorgeschichte der israelitischen Religion*. BWANT 12. Stuttgart: W. Kohlhammer, 1929.

M. Anbar, "Καὶ ποῦ εἰσιν οἳ Θεοὶ τῆς χώρας Σαμαρείας: et où sont les dieux du pays de Samarie." *BN* 51 (1990): 7-8.

D.K. Andrews, "The God of the Heavens," in *The Seed of Wisdom; Essays in Honour of T. J. Meek*, 45-57. Edited by W.S. McCullough. Toronto: University of Toronto, 1964.

N. Avigad, "The Contributions of Hebrew Seals to an Understanding of Israelite Religion and Society," in *Ancient Israelite Religion: Essays in Honor of Frank Moore Cross*, 195-208. Edited by P.D. Miller, Jr., P.D. Hanson and S.D. McBride. Philadelphia: Westminster, 1987.

M. Avi-Yonah, "The Historical Background of Palestine in the Light of the Recent Archaeological Discoveries," in *The Patterns of Monetary Development in Phoenicia and Palestine in Antiquity. Proceedings of the International Numismatic Convention, Jerusalem, 27-31 December, 1963*, 110-16. Edited by A. Kindler. Tel Aviv: Schocken, 1967.

M.E. Babelon. *Les perses achéménides. Les satrapes et les dynastes tributaires de leur empire. Cypre & Phénicie. Planches.* Catalogue des monnaies grecques de la bibliotheque nationale. Bologna: Arnaldo Forni, 1980.

J. Barr, "Philo of Byblos and his 'Phoenician History'." *BJRL* 57 (1974): 17-68.

P. Beck, "The Drawings from Horvat Teiman (Kuntillet 'Ajrud)." *Tel Aviv* 9 (1982): 3-68.

B. Becking, *The Fall of Samaria: An Historical and Archaeological Study.* SHANE 2. Leiden and New York: Brill, 1992.

Z. Ben-Barak, "The Queen Consort and the Struggle for Succession to the Throne," in *La Femme dans le proche-orient antique: compte rendu de la 33e Rencontre Assyriologique Internationale (Paris, 7-10 Juillet 1986)*, 33-40. Edited by J.M. Durand. RAI 33. Paris: Éditions Recherche sur les Civilisations, 1987.

A.M. Blackman, "The Rite of Opening the Mouth in Ancient Egypt and Mesopotamia." *Journal of Ritual Studies* 6 (1992): 13-42.

E. Bloch-Smith, *Judahite Burial Practices and Beliefs about the Dead.* JSOTSup 123. Sheffield: JSOT, 1992.

G. Boccaccini, *Middle Judaism: Jewish Thought 300 BCE to 200 CE.* Minneapolis: Augsburg-Fortress, 1991.

M. Boyce, "Persian Religion in the Achemenid Age," in *The Cambridge History of Judaism.* 2 volumes. Edited by W.D.

Davies and L. Finkelstein. Cambridge: Cambridge University, 1984, 1989, 1.279-307.

E. Bresciani, "Egypt, Persian Satrapy," in *The Cambridge History of Judaism*. 2 volumes. Edited by W.D. Davies and L. Finkelstein. Cambridge: Cambridge University, 1984, 1989, 1.358-72.

F. Briquel-Chatonnet, ed. *Les relations entre les cités de la côte phénicienne et les royaumes d'Israël et de Juda*. StudPhoen 12. Leuven: Brill, 1992.

M. Broshi, ed. *The Damascus Document Reconsidered*. Jerusalem: Israel Exploration Society, 1992.

R.P. Carroll, "The Aniconic God and the Cult of Images." *StTh* 31 (1977): 51-64.

R.P. Carroll, *From Chaos to Covenant: Prophecy in the Book of Jeremiah*. New York: Crossroad, 1981.

R.P. Carroll, "Textual Strategies and Ideology," in *Second Temple Studies I: Persian Period*, 108-24. Edited by P.R. Davies. JSOTSup 151. Sheffield: JSOT, 1992.

B. Childs, *The Book of Exodus*. OTL. Philadelphia: Westminster, 1974.

C. Clermont-Ganneau, *Receuil d'archéologie orientale, vol. 8*. Paris: E. Bouillon, 1924.

D.J.A. Clines, "The Perils of Autobiography," in *What Does Eve Do To Help? and other Readerly Questions to the Old Testament*, 124-64. Edited by D.J.A. Clines. JSOTSup 94. Sheffield: JSOT, 1990.

M. Cogan, *Imperialism and Religion: Assyria, Judah and Israel in Eighth and Seventh Centuries B.C.E.* SBLMS 19. Missoula, MT: Scholars, 1974.

J.J. Collins, *The Apocalyptic Imagination: An Introduction to the Jewish Matrix of Christianity*. New York: Crossroad, 1984.

T. Combe, *Veterum populorum et regnum numi qui in Museo Britannico adservantur*. London: British Museum, 1814.

M.D. Coogan, "Canaanite Origins and Lineage: Reflections on the Religion of Ancient Israel," in *Ancient Israelite Religion. Essays in Honor of F.M. Cross*, 115-24. Edited by P.D. Miller, Jr., P.D. Hanson and S.D. McBride. Philadelphia: Fortress, 1987.

A.B. Cook, *Zeus. A Study in Ancient Religion.* (Cambridge, 1914), New York: Biblio and Tannen, 1964.

J.M. Cook, *The Persian Empire.* New York: Schocken, 1983.

S.A. Cook, "The Significance of the Elephantine Papyri for the History of Hebrew Religion." *AJT* 19 (1915): 346-82.

I. Cornelius, "The Sun Epiphany in Job 38:12-15 and the Iconography of the Gods in the Ancient Near East — The Palestinian Connection." *JNSL* 16 (1990): 25-43.

A.E. Cowley, *Aramic Papyri of the Fifth Century B.C.* Oxford: Clarendon, 1923.

P.C. Craigie, "A Reconsideration of Shamgar ben Anath (Judg 3:31 and 5:6)." *JBL* 91 (1972): 239-40.

W. Culican, "Phoenician Demons." *JNES* 35 (1976): 21-24.

S. Dalley, "Yahweh in Hamath in the 8th Century BC: Cuneiform Material and Historical Deductions." *VT* 40 (1990): 21-32.

V. Dasen, *Dwarfs in Ancient Egypt and Greece.* Oxford: Clarendon, 1993.

G.I. Davies, *Ancient Hebrew Inscription: Corpus and Concordance.* Cambridge and New York: Cambridge University, 1991.

P.R. Davies, *The Damascus Covenant: An Interpretation of the "Damascus Document."* JSOTSup 25. Sheffield: JSOT, 1982.

P.R. Davies, *In Search of 'Ancient Israel.'* JSOTSup 148. Sheffield: JSOT, 1992.

P.R. Davies, ed. *Second Temple Studies I: Persian Period.* JSOTSup 117. Sheffield: JSOT, 1991.

P.R. Davies, "The Social World of Apocalyptic Writings," in *The World of Ancient Israel*, 251-71. Edited by R.E. Clements. Cambridge: Cambridge University, 1989.

J. Day, "Asherah in the Hebrew Bible and Northwest Semitic Literature." *JBL* 105 (1986): 385-408.

J. Day, *God's Conflict with the Dragon and the Sea.* University of Cambridge Oriental Publications 35. Cambridge: Cambridge University, 1985.

P.L. Day, "Anat: Ugarit's 'Mistress of Animals.'" *JNES* 51 (1992): 181-90.

J.A. Dearman, ed. *Studies in the Mesha Inscription and Moab.* ASOR/SBL Archaeology and Biblical Studies 2. Atlanta: Scholars, 1989.

M. Dietrich, and O. Loretz, "Ugaritisch *ṣrrt ṣpn, ṣrry* und hebräisch *jrktj ṣpwn*." *UF* 2 (1990): 79-86.

W. Dietrich, and M.A. Klopfenstein, eds. *Ein Gott allein? JHWH Verehung und biblischer Monotheismus im Kontext der israelitischen und altorientalischen Religionsgeschichte.* OBO 139. Freiburg: Universitätsverlag and Göttingen: Vandenhoeck & Ruprecht, 1994.

P.E. Dion, "La lettre araméene passe-partout et ses sous espèces." *RB* 89 (1982): 528-75.

P.E. Dion, "YHWH as Storm-god and Sun-god. The Double Legacy of Egypt and Canaan as Reflected in Psalm 104." *ZAW* 103 (1991): 43-71.

C. Dohmen, *Das Bilderverbot: seine Entstehung und Entwicklung im Alten Testament.* BBB 62. Bonn: Hanstein, 1985.

M. Douglas, *Purity and Danger: An Analysis of Concepts of Pollution and Taboo.* London: Routledge and Kegan Paul, 1966.

G.R. Driver, "Reflections on Recent Articles." *JBL* 73 (1954): 125-36.

J.I. Durham, *Exodus.* WBC 2. Waco, TX: Word Books, 1987.

D.V. Edelman, "Doing History in Biblical Studies," in *The Fabric of History: Text, Artifact and Israel's Past*, 13-25. Edited by D.V. Edelman. JSOTSup 127. Sheffield: JSOT, 1991.

O. Eissfeldt, "Ba'alshamem und Jahwe." *ZAW* 16 (1939): 1-31.

J.A. Emerton, "New Light on the Israelite Religion." *ZAW* 94 (1982): 2-20.

J.W. Epstein, "Glossen zu den aramaische Papyrus und Ostraka." *ZAW* 16 (1912): 128-38.

J.W. Epstein, "Weitere Glossen zu den aramaische Papyrus und Ostraka." *ZAW* 33 (1913): 138-50.

T.C. Eskenazi, *In an Age of Prose: A Literary Approach to Ezra-Nehemiah.* SBLMS 36. Atlanta: Scholars, 1988.

C. Evans, "Mishna and Messiah 'In Context': Some Comments on Jacob Neusner's Proposals." *JBL* 112 (1993): 267-89.

H.J. Fabry, "Studien zur Ekklesiologie des Alten Testaments und der Qumrangemeinde." Ph.D. dissertation, University of Bonn, 1979.

H.J. Fabry, "swd. Der himmlische Thronrat als ekklesiologisches Modell," in *Bausteine Biblischer Theologie. Festgabe für G. Johannes Botterweck zum 60. Geburtstag dargebr. von seinen*

Schülern, 99-126. Edited by H.J. Fabry. BBB 50. Koln: Hanstein, 1977.

J. Faur, "The Biblical Idea of Idolatry." *JQR* 69 (1978): 1-15.

J.A. Fitzmyer, and S.A. Kaufman, eds. *An Aramaic Bibliography Part I: Old, Official and Biblical Aramaic*. Baltimore: Johns Hopkins University, 1992.

G. Fohrer, *History of Israelite Religion*. Translated from German by D.E. Green. Nashville: Abingdon, 1972.

C.A. Fontela, "La esclavitud a través de la Bible." *EstBib* 43 (1985): 99-104.

G. Fuchs, *Mythos und Hiobdichtung: Aufnahme und Umdeutung altorientalischer Vorstellungen*. Stuttgart: W. Kohlhammer, 1993.

C.J. Gadd, "Inscribed Prisms of Sargon II from Nimrud." *Iraq* 16 (1954): 173-201.

K. Galling, *Studien zur Geschichte Israels im Persischen Zeitalter*. Tübingen: JCB Mohr, 1964.

P. Gardner, *Catalogue of Greek Coins. The Seleucid Kings of Syria*. Bologna: Arnaldo Forni, 1963.

J.C.L. Gibson, *Textbook of Syrian Semitic Inscriptions*. 3 volumes. Oxford: Clarendon, 1971-1982.

M. Gilula, "To Yahweh Shomron and his Asherah." *Shnaton la-Miqra* 3 (1978-79): 129-37. Hebrew. English summary, xv-xvi.

M. Görg, *Beiträge zur Zeitgeschichte der Anfänge Israels: Dokumente, Materialien, Notizen*. ÄAT 2. Weisbaden: O. Harrossowitz, 1989.

M. Görg, "Jahwe — ein Toponym." *BN* 1 (1976): 7-14.

E. Gombrich, "The Limits of Convention," in *Image and Code/ Ernst H. Gombrich*, 11-41. Edited by W. Steiner. Michigan Studies in the Humanities 2. Ann Arbor: Horace Rackham School of Graduate Studies, 1981.

E.R. Goodenough, *Jewish Symbols in the Greco-Roman World*. 13 volumes. Bollingen Series 37, 1-13. New York: Pantheon Books, 1953-1968.

M.D. Goodman, *The Ruling Class of Judaea*. Cambridge: Cambridge University, 1987.

L.L. Grabbe. *Judaism from Cyprus to Hadrian: Sources, History, Synthesis*. 2 volumes. Minneapolis: Augsburg-Fortress, 1991.

G.B. Gray, "The Foundation and Extension of the Persian

Empire," in *The Cambridge Ancient History*. 12 volumes. Edited by J.B. Bury, S.A. Cook *et al*. Cambridge: Cambridge University, 1924-1939, 4.1-25.

J. Gray, *I & II Kings: A Commentary*. 2nd edition. OTL. Philadelphia: Westminster, 1970.

A. Green, "Beneficent Spirits and Malevolent Demons." *Visible Religion* 3 (1984): 80-105.

W.S. Green, ed. *Judaisms and their Messiahs in the Beginning of Christianity*. New York: Cambridge University, 1987.

E. Gubel, *Phoenician Furniture*. StudPhoen 7. Leuven: Peeters, 1987.

H. Gunkel, *The Psalms: A Form-Criticial Introduction*. Translated from German by T.H. Horner. FBBS 19. Philadelphia: Fortress, 1967.

A.C. Gunter, *Investigating Artistic Environments in the Ancient Near East*. Washington, DC: Arthur Sackler Gallery/Smithsonian Institute, 1990.

H.H. Guthrie Jr., *Israel's Sacred Songs; A Study of Dominant Themes*. New York: Seabury, 1966.

J. Gutmann, "The 'Second Commandment' and the Image in Judaism." *HUCA* 32 (1961): 161-74.

J.M. Hadley, "Kuntillet 'Ajrud: Religious Centre or Desert Way Station?" *PEQ* 125 (1993): 116-24.

J.M. Hadley, "Some Drawings and Inscriptions on Two Pithoi from Kuntillet 'Ajrud." *VT* 37 (1987): 180-213.

J.M. Hadley, "Yahweh's Asherah in the Light of Recent Discovery." Ph.D. dissertation, St, John's College, Cambridge University, 1989.

W.W. Hallo, "Texts, Statues and the Cult of the Divine King," in *Congress Volume 1986*, 54-66. Edited by J.A. Emerton. VTSup 40. Leiden: Brill, 1988.

L. Handy, *Among the Host of Heaven: The Syro-Palestinian Pantheon as Bureaucracy*. Winona Lake: Eisenbrauns, 1993.

L. Handy, "The Authorization of Divine Power and the Guilt of God in the Book of Job: Useful Ugaritic Parallels." *JSOT* 60 (1993): 107-18.

L. Handy, "Dissenting Deities or Disobedient Angels: Divine Hierarchies in Ugarit and the Bible." *BR* 35 (1990): 18-35.

L. Handy, "Hezekiah's Unlikely Reform." *ZAW* 100 (1988): 111-15.

L. Handy, "A Realignment in Heaven: An Investigation into the Ideology of the Josianic Reform." Ph.D. dissertation, University of Chicago, 1987.

L. Handy, "A Solution for Many *mlkm*." *UF* 20 (1988): 57-59.

L. Handy, "Sounds, Words and Meanings in Psalm 82." *JSOT* 47 (1990): 51-66.

P.D. Hanson, *The Dawn of Apocalyptic*. Philadelphia: Fortress, 1975.

M. Haran, "The Shining of Moses' Face: A Case Study in biblical and Ancient Near Eastern Iconography," in *In the Shelter of Elyon. Essays on ancient Palestinian Life and Literature in Honor of G.W. Ahlström*, 159-73. Edited by W.B. Barrick and J.R. Spencer. JSOTSup 31. Sheffield: JSOT, 1984.

E.W. Heaton, *Solomon's New Men: The Emergence of Ancient Israel as a National State*. New York: Pica, 1974.

J. Hehn, *Die biblische und die babylonische Gottesidee: Die israelitische Gottesauffassung im Lichte der altorientalischen Religionsgeschichte*. Leipzig: J.C. Hinrich, 1913.

R. Hendel, "The Social Origins of the Aniconic Tradition in Early Israel." *CBQ* 50 (1988): 365-82.

M. Hengel, *Judaism and Hellenism*. 2 volumes. Translated from German by J. Bowden. London: SCM, 1974.

W. Herrmann, "Das Aufleben des Mythos unter den Judäern während des babylonischen Zeitalters." *BN* 40 (1987): 97-129.

W. Herrmann, "Wann wurde Jahwe zum Schöpfer der Welt?" *UF* 23 (1991): 165-80.

G.F. Hill, *Catalogue of the Greek Coins of Palestine (Galilee, Samaria, and Judaea)*. Oxford: Horace Hart, 1914.

G.F. Hill, *Historical Greek Coins*. Argonaut Library of Antiquities. Chicago: Argonaut, 1966.

D.R. Hillers, "Analyzing the Abominable: Our Understanding of Canaanite Religion." *JQR* 75 (1985): 253-69.

G. Hoffmann and H. Gressmann, "Teraphim, Masken, und Winkelorakel im Aegypten und Vorderasien." *ZAW* 40 (1922): 75-137.

K. Hoglund, *Achaemenid Imperial Administration in Syria-Palestine and the Missions of Ezra and Nehemiah*. SBLDS 125.

Atlanta: Scholars, 1992.

T.A. Holland, "A Study of Iron Age Baked Clay Figurines, with Special Reference to Jerusalem: Cave 1." *Levant* 9 (1977): 121-55.

S.W. Holloway, "Kings, Book of 1-2," in *Anchor Bible Dictionary*, 6 volumes. Edited by D.N. Freedman. New York: Doubleday, 1992, 4.79-80.

S.W. Holloway, "What Ship Goes There: The Flood Narratives in the Gilgamesh Epic and Genesis Considered in Light of Ancient Near Eastern Temple Ideology." *ZAW* 103 (1991): 328-55.

R.A. Horsley, *Jesus and the Spiral of Violence. Popular Jewish Resistance in Roman Palestine*. Minneapolis: Fortress, 1987.

F.L. Hossfeld, *Der Dekalog: seine späten Fassungen, die originale Komposition und seine Vorstufen*. OBO 45. Freiburg: Universitätsverlag and Göttingen: Vandenhoeck & Ruprecht, 1982.

C. Houtman, *Der Himmel im Alten Testament: Israels Weltbild und Weltanschauung*. OTS 30. Leiden: Brill, 1993.

T. Jacobsen, "The Graven Image," in *Ancient Israelite Religion: Essays in Honor of Frank Moore Cross*, 15-32. Edited by P.D. Miller, Jr., P.D. Hanson and S.D. McBride. Philadelphia: Fortress, 1987.

D.W. Jamieson-Drake, *Scribes and Schools in Monarchic Judah: A Socio-Archeological Approach*. JSOTSup 109=SWBAS 9. Sheffield: JSOT, 1991.

B. Janowski, "Keruben und Zion," in *Ernten, was man sät. Festschrift K. Koch*, 231-64. Edited by D.R. Daniels *et al.* Neukirchen-Vluyn: Neukirchener, 1991.

B. Janowski, *Rettungsgewissheit und Epiphanie des Heils 1: das Motiv der Hilfe Gottes "am Morgen" im Alten Orient und im Alten Testament*. WMANT 59. Neukirchen-Vluyn: Neukirchener, 1989.

B. Janowski, "Tempel und Schöpfung." *JBTh* 5 (1990): 37-69.

G.K. Jenkins, *Ancient Greek Coins*. New York: G.P. Putnam's Sons, 1972.

G.K. Jenkins, "The Monetary Systems in the Early Hellenistic Time, with Special Regard to the Economic Policy of the Ptolemaic Kings," in *The Patterns of Monetary Development in*

Phoenicia and Palestine in Antiquity. Proceedings of the International Numismatic Convention, Jerusalem, 27-31 December, 1963, 53-72. Edited by A. Kindler. Tel Aviv: Schocken, 1967.

A. Jirku, "Die Gesichtsmaske des Mose." *ZDPV* 67 (1945): 43-45.

W. Johnstone, *Exodus*. Old Testament Guides. Sheffield: JSOT, 1990.

P. Joüon, *A Grammar of Biblical Hebrew*. Rome: Pontifical Biblical Institute, 1993.

H.W. Jüngling, *Der Tod der Götter: Eine Untersuchung zu Psalm 82*. SBS 38. Stuttgart: Katholisches Bibelwerk, 1969.

L. Kadman, *The Coins of the Jewish War of 66-73 A.D.* Corpus Nummicorum Palaestiniensium 3. Tel Aviv: Schocken, 1960.

E. Käsemann, "The Beginnings of Christian Theology (ET)." *Journal of Theology and Church* 6 (1969): 17-46.

B. Kanael, "Ancient Jewish Coins and their Historical Significance." *BA* 26 (1963): 38-62.

A.S. Kapelrud, *God and his Friends in the Old Testament*. Oslo: Universitetsforlaget, 1979.

P. Katz, "The Meaning of the Root קנה." *JJS* 5 (1954): 126-31.

Y. Kaufmann, *The Religion of Israel: From Its Beginnings to the Babylonian Exile*. Edited and translated from Hebrew by M. Greenburg. Chicago: University of Chicago, 1960.

O. Keel, *Jahwe-Visionen und Siegelkunst: eine neue Deutung der Majestätsschilderungen in Jes 6, Ez 1 und 10 und Sach 4*. SBS 84/85. Stuttgart: Katholisches Bibelwerk, 1977.

O. Keel and C. Uehlinger, *Göttinnen, Götter und Gottessymbole: neue Erkenntnisse zur Religionsgeschichte Kanaans und Israels aufgrund bislang unerschlossener iknographischer Quellen*. QD 134. Freiburg: Herder, 1992.

R. Kessler, *Staat und Gesellschaft im vorexilischen Juda. Vom 8. Jahrhundert bis zum Exil*. VTSup 47. Leiden: Brill, 1992.

H. Kienle, *Der Gott auf dem Flügelrad: Zu den ungelösten Fragen der "synkretischen" Münze BMC Palestine S. 181, Nr. 29*. Göttinger Orientforschung VI, 7. Wiesbaden: O. Harassowitz, 1975.

A. Kindler, *Coins of the Land of Israel*. Jerusalem: Keter, 1974.

A. Kindler, "The Greco-Phoenician Coins Struck in Palestine in the Time of the Persian Empire." *INJ* 2 (1963): 25-27.

H. Kippenberg, *Religion und Klassenbildung im antiken Judäa: eine religionssoziologische Studie zum Verhältnis von Tradition und gesellschaftliche Entwicklung.* SUNT 14. Göttingen: Vandenhoeck & Ruprecht, 1978.

R. Kittel, *Die Bücher der Könige: übersetzt und erklärt.* Göttingen: Vandenhoeck & Ruprecht, 1900.

C. Kloos, YHWH's *Combat with the Sea.* Amsterdam and Leiden: Brill, 1986.

E.A. Knauf, "From History to Interpretation," in *The Fabric of History: Text, Artifact, and Israel's Past,* 26-64. Edited by D. Vikander Edelman. JSOTSup 127. Sheffield: JSOT, 1991.

E.A. Knauf, *Ismael: Untersuchungen zur Geschichte Palästinas im 1. Jahrtausend v. Chr.* 2nd edition. ADPV. Wiesbaden: In Commission bei O. Harrassowitz, 1989.

E.A. Knauf, "King Solomon's Copper Supply," in *Phoenicia and the Bible,* 167-86. Edited by E. Lipiński. StudPhoen 11; OLA 44. Leuven: Peeters, 1991.

E.A. Knauf, *Midian. Untersuchungen zur Geschichte Palästinas und Nord-arabiens am Ende des 2. Jahrtausends V. Chr.* ADPV. Wiesbaden: O. Harrassowitz, 1988.

E.A. Knauf, "The Migration of the Script, and the Formation of the State in South Arabia." *PSAS* 19 (1989): 79-91.

E.A. Knauf, "'You Shall Have No Other Gods'. Eine notwendige Notiz zu einer überflüssigen Diskussion." *DBAT* 26 (1989/90): 238-245.

E.A. Knauf, "Zur Herkunft und Sozialgeschichte Israels." *Bib* 69 (1988): 155-56.

K. Koch, "Ashera als Himmelskönigin in Jerusalem." *UF* 20 (1988): 97-120.

C. Kraay, *Archaic and Classical Greek Coins.* Berkeley and Los Angeles: University of California, 1976.

E.G.H. Kraeling, *The Brooklyn Museum of Aramaic Papyri.* New Haven: Yale University, 1953.

D. Kraemer, "On the Relationship of the Books of Ezra and Nehemia." *JSOT* 59 (1993): 73-92.

H. Kreissig, *Die sozialökonomische Situation im Juda zur Achämenidenzeit.* Schriften zur Geschichte und Kultur des alten Orients 7. Berlin: Akademie, 1973.

J.K. Kuan, "Third Kingdoms 5.1 and Israelite-Tyrian Relations during the Reign of Solomon." *JSOT* 46 (1990): 31-46.

B. Lang, "The Yahweh-Alone Movement and the Making of Jewish Monotheism," in *Monotheism and the Prophetic Minority: An Essay in Biblical History and Sociology*, 13-56. Edited by B. Lang. SWBAS 1. Sheffield: Almond, 1983.

A. Lemaire, "Prières en temps de crise: Les inscription de Khirbet Beit Lei." *RB* 83 (1976): 558-68.

A. Lemaire, "Who or What was Yahweh's Asherah?" *BAR* 10 (1984): 42-51.

N.P. Lemche, *The Canaanites and Their Land: The Tradition of the Canaanites*. JSOTSup 110. Sheffield: JSOT, 1991.

N.P. Lemche, "The Development of the Israelite Religion in the Light of Recent Studies on the Early History of Israel," in *Congress Volume Leuven 1989*, 97-115. Edited by J.A. Emerton. VTSup 43. Leiden: Brill, 1991.

N.P. Lemche, "Det Gamle Testamente som en hellenistk bog." *DTT* 55 (1992): 81-101.

N.P. Lemche, "The Old Testament — A Hellenistic Book?" *SJOT* 7 (1993): 163-93.

C. Levin, "Joschija im deuteronomistischen Geschichtswerk." *ZAW* 96 (1984): 351-71.

B.A. Levine and J.M. de Tarragon, "'Shapshu Cries Out in Heaven': Dealing with Snake-Bites at Ugarit (KTU 1.100, 1.107)." *RB* 95 (1988): 481-518.

I. Lévy, "Dieux siciliens." *RevArch* 34, III (1899): 256-81.

J. Limburg, "Psalms, Book of," in *Anchor Bible Dictionary*. 6 volumes. Edited by D.N. Freedman. New York: Doubleday, 1992, 5.522-36.

J. Lindenberger, *Ancient Aramaic and Hebrew Letters*. SBL Writings from the Ancient World 4. Atlanta: Scholars, 1994.

E. Lipiński, "קנה," in *Theologisches Wörterbuch zum Alten Testament*. 8 volumes. Edited by G.J. Botterweck and H. Ringgren. Koln: W. Kohlhammer, 1971-1991. 7.63-71.

A. Lods, *Isräel des origines au milieu du 8e Siècle*. Paris: Renaissance du Livre, 1930.

P.K. McCarter Jr., "Aspects of the Religion of the Israelite Monarchy: Biblical and Epigraphic Data," in *Ancient Israelite Religion: Essays in Honor of Frank Moore Cross*, 137-55. Edited by P.D. Miller, Jr., P.D. Hanson and S.D. McBride. Philadelphia: Fortress, 1987.

W.O. McCready, "Sectarian Separation and Exclusion — the Temple Scroll: A Case for Wholistic Religious Claims," in *Origins and Method: Towards a New Understanding of Judaism and Christianity: Essays in Honour of John C. Hurd*, 360-79. Edited by B.H. McLean. JSNTSup 86. Sheffield: JSOT, 1993.

H. MacCoby, *Revolution in Judaea: Jesus & the Jewish Resistance*. 2nd edition. New York: Taplinger, 1980.

F. Madden, *History of Jewish Coinage and Money in the Old and New Testament*. London: Bernard Quartich, 1864.

W.A. Maier, "Baal-Zebub," in *Anchor Bible Dictionary*. 6 volumes. Edited by D.N. Freedman. New York: Doubleday, 1992, 1:554.

R. Marcus, ed. *Jewish Antiquities, Books IX-XI*. Cambridge: Harvard University, 1966.

M.L. Margolis, "The Elephantine Documents." *JQR* 2 (1911-12): 419-43.

D. Mendels, "Hecataeus of Abdera and a Jewish 'patrios politeia.'" *ZAW* 95 (1983): 96-110.

Y. Meshorer, *Ancient Jewish Coinage*. 2 volumes. Dix Hills, NY: Amphora Books, 1982.

Y. Meshorer, "Ancient Jewish Coinage. Addendum 1." *INJ* 11 (1990-1991): 104-32.

Y. Meshorer, *Jewish Coins of the Second Temple Period*. Tel Aviv: Am Hassefer, 1967.

T.N.D. Mettinger, "Aniconism — a West Semitic Context for the Israelite Phenomenon?," in *Ein Gott allein? JHWH-Verehung und biblischer Monotheismus im Kontext der israelitischen und altorientalischen Religionsgeschichte*, 159-78. Edited by W. Dietrich and M.A. Klopfenstein. OBO 139. Freiburg: Universitätsverlag and Göttingen: Vandenhoeck & Ruprecht, 1994.

T.N.D. Mettinger, *No Graven Image? Israelite Aniconism in Its Ancient Near Eastern Context*. Stockholm: Almqvist & Wiksell, 1995.

T.N.D. Mettinger, *The Dethronement of Sabaoth: Studies in the Shem and Kabod Theologies*. ConBOT 18. Lund: CWK Gleerup, 1982.

T.N.D. Mettinger, "The Veto on Images and the Aniconic God in Ancient Israel," in *Religious Symbols and their Functions: Based on Papers read at the Symposium on Religious Symbols and their Functions, held at Abo on the 28th-30th of August 1978*, 15-29. Edited by H. Biezais. Scripta Instituti Donneriani Aboensis 10. Stockholm: Almqvist & Wicksell, 1979.

T.N.D. Mettinger, "YHWH SABAOTH — The Heavenly King on the Cherubim Throne," in *Studies in the Period of David and Solomon and Other Essays: Papers read at the International Symposium for Biblical Studies, Tokyo, 5-7 December, 1979*, 109-38. Edited by T. Ishida. Winona Lake, IN: Eisenbrauns, 1982.

M. Metzger, "Eigentumsdeklaration und Schöpfungsaussage," in *"Wenn nicht jetzt, wann dann?" Aufsätze für Hans-Joachim Kraus zum 65 Geburtstag*. Edited by H. Geyer. Neukirchen-Vluyn: Neukirchener, 1983.

M. Metzger, *Königsthron und Gottesthron: Thronform und Throndarstellung in Ägypten und im Vorderen Orient im dritten und zweiten Jahrtausend vor Christus und deren Bedeutung für das Verständnis von Aussagen über den Thron im Alten Testament*. AOAT 15/1-2. Kevelaer: Butzon & Bercker and Neukirchen-Vluyn: Neukirchener, 1985.

J. Meyshan, *Essays in Jewish Numismatics*. Numismatic Studies and Researches 6. Jerusalem: Israel Numismatic Society, 1968.

T. Middendorp, *Die Stellung Jesu ben Siras zwischen Judentum und Hellenismus*. Leiden: Brill, 1973.

L. Mildenberg, "Yehud: A Preliminary Study of the Provincial Coinage of Judaea" in *Greek Numismatics and Archaeology. Essays in Honor of Margaret Thompson*, 183-96. Edited by O. Mørkholm and N.M. Waggoner. Wetteren: Cultura, 1979.

J. Milgrom, *Leviticus 1-16: A New Translation with Introduction and Commentary*. AB 3. New York: Doubleday, 1991.

J.M. Miller, "Is it Possible to Write a History of Israel without Relying on the Hebrew Bible?" in *The Fabric of History: Text, Artifact and Israel's Past*, 93-102. Edited by D. Vikander Edelman. JSOTSup 127. Sheffield: JSOT, 1991.

J.M. Miller, "Solomon: International Potentate or Local King?" *PEQ* 123 (1991): 28-31.

J.G. Milne, *Ancient Greek Coins*. Oxford: Clarendon, 1931.

W.J.T. Mitchell, *Iconology: Image, Text, Ideology*. Chicago:

University of Chicago, 1986.

W.J.T. Mitchell, *Picture Theory: Essays on Verbal and Visual Representation*. Chicago: University of Chicago, 1994.

S. Mittmann, "A Confessional Inscription from the Year 701 BC Praising the Reign of Yahweh," *Acta Academia* 21 (1989): 15-38.

R.W.L. Moberly, *At the Mountain of God: Story and Theology in Exodus 32-43*. JSOTSup 22. Sheffield: JSOT, 1983.

O. Mørkholm, "The Monetary System of the Seleucid Kings until 129 B.C.," in *The Patterns of Monetary Development in Phoenicia and Palestine in Antiquity. Proceedings of the International Numismatic Convention, Jerusalem, 27-31 December, 1963*, 75-86. Edited by A. Kindler. Tel Aviv: Schocken, 1967.

G. Molin, "Die Stellung der Gebira im Staate Juda." *TZ* 10 (1954): 161-75.

J.A. Montgomery, *A Critical and Exegetical Commentary of the Books of Kings*. Edited by H.S. Snyder. ICC 10. Edinburgh: T. and T. Clark, 1951.

J.C. de Moor, *The Rise of Yahwism: The Roots of Israelite Monotheism*. BETL 91. Leuven: Peeters, 1990.

S. Morenz, *Egyptian Religion*. Ithaca: Cornell University, 1973.

S. Mowinckel, *The Psalms in Israel's Worship*. Nashville: Abingdon, 1962.

D.H. Müller, "Die Korrespondenz zwischen der Gemeinde von Elephantine und den Söhnen Sanballats." *Wiener Zeitschrift für die Kunde des Morgenlandes* 21 (1907): 416-19.

H.P. Müller, "Kolloquialsprache und Volksreligion in den Inschriften von *Kuntilet 'Agrud* und *Ḥirbet el-Qom*." *ZAH* 5 (1992): 15-51.

E.T. Mullen, *The Divine Council in Canaanite and Early Hebrew Literature*. HSM 24. Cambridge: Harvard University, 1980.

O. Negbi, *Canaanite Gods in Metal*. Tel Aviv: Institute of Archaeology, 1976.

J. Neusner, "The Mishna in Philosophical Context and Out of Canonical Bounds." *JBL* 112 (1993): 291-304.

J. Neusner, *Testament to Torah*. Englewood Cliffs, NJ: Prentice-Hall, 1988.

E.W. Nicholson, *God and His People*. Oxford: Oxford University, 1986.

H. Niehr, *Der höchste Gott: Alttestamentlischer JHWH-Glaube in Kontext syrisch-kanaanäischer Religion des 1. Jahrtausend v. Chr.* BZAW 190. Berlin and New York: Walter de Gruyter, 1990.

H. Niehr, "God of Heavens," in *Dictionary of Deities and Demons in the Bible*. Edited by K. van der Toorn, B. Becking and P. van der Horst. Leiden: Brill, 1995.

H. Niehr, "Host of Heavens," in *Dictionary of Deities and Demons in the Bible*. Edited by K. van der Toorn, B. Becking and P. van der Horst. Leiden: Brill, 1995.

H. Niehr, "JHWH als Arzt." *BZ NF* 35 (1991): 3-17.

H. Niehr, "JHWH in der Rolle des Baalsamem," in *Ein Gott allein? JHWH-Verehung und biblischer Monotheismus im Kontext der israelitischen und altorientalischen Religionsgeschichte*. Edited by W. Dietrich and M. Klopfenstein. OBO 139. Fribourg: Universitätsverlag and Göttingen: Vandenhoeck & Ruprecht, 1994, 307-26.

H. Niehr, "ספר V 7/8," in *Theologisches Wörterbuch zum Alten Testament*, in press. 8 volumes. Edited by G.J. Botterweck, H. Ringgren and H.J. Fabry. Stuttgart: Kohlhammer, 1970-1991.

H. Niehr, "Zaphon," in *Dictionary of Deities and Demons in the Bible*. Edited by K. van der Toorn, B. Becking and P. van der Horst. Leiden: Brill, 1995.

K. Nielsen, *Incense in Ancient Israel*. VTSup 38. Leiden: Brill, 1986.

H.M. Niemann, *Herrschaft, Königtum und Staat: Skizzen zur soziokulturellen Entwicklung im monarchischen Israel*. FAT Tübingen: J.C.B. Mohr, 1993.

C.R. North, "The Essence of Idolatry," in *Von Ugarit nach Qumran: Beiträge zur alttestamentlichen und altorientalischen Forschungen. Otto Eissfeldt zum 1 September 1957*, 151-60. Edited by J. Hempel. BZAW 77. Berlin: A. Topelmann, 1958.

R. North, "Yahweh's Asherah," in *To touch the Text: Biblical and Related Studies in Honor of Joseph A. Fitzmeyer*. Edited by M.P. Horgan and P.J. Kobeliski. New York: Crossroad, 1989.

A.T. Olmstead, *History of the Persian Empire*. Chicago: University of Chicago, 1948.

S.M. Olyan, *Asherah and the Cult of Yahweh in Israel*. SBLMS 34.

Atlanta: Scholars, 1988.

R. Patai, *The Hebrew Goddess*. New York: Avon Books, 1978.

C. Petersen, *Mythos im Alten Testament: Bestimmung des Mythosbegriffs und Untersuchung der mythischen Elemente in dem Psalmen*. BZAW 157. Berlin and New York: Walter de Gruyter, 1982.

R.J. Petty, "Asherah: Goddess of Israel?" Ph.D. dissertation, Marquette University, 1985.

R.H. Pfeiffer, "The Polemic against Idolatry in the Old Testament." *JBL* 43 (1924): 229-40.

E.J. Pilcher, "A Coin of Gaza, and the Vision of Ezekiel." *Proceedings of the Society of Biblical Archaeology* 30 (1908): 45-52.

O. Plöger. *Theocracy and Eschatology*. Translated from German by S. Rudman. Oxford: Blackwell, 1968.

T. Podella, "Der Chaos-kampfmythos im Alten Testament. Eine Problemanzeige," in *Mesopotamica-Ugaritica-Biblica. Festschrift für Kurt Bergerhof zur Vollendung seines 70. Lebensjahre am 7. Mai, 1992*, 283-329. Edited by M. Dietrich. AOAT 232. Kevelaer: Verlag Butzon & Bercker and Neukirchen-Vluyn: Neukirchener, 1993.

R.S. Poole, *A Catalogue of Greek Coins in the British Museum: The Ptolemies, Kings of Egypt*. Bologna: Arnaldo Forni, 1977.

B. Porten, "Aramaic Letters: A Study in Papyrological-Reconstruction." *JARCE* 17 (1980): 39-75.

B. Porten, "Aramaic Papyri and Parchments: A New Look." *BA* 42 (1979): 74-104.

B. Porten, *Archives from Elephantine: the Life of an Ancient Jewish Military Colony*. Berkeley: University of California, 1968.

B. Porten, "Elephantine Papyri," in *Anchor Bible Dictionary*. 6 volumes. Edited by D.N. Freedman. New York: Doubleday, 1992, 2. 445-55.

B. Porten, "The Jews in Egypt," in *The Cambridge History of Judaism*, 2 volumes. Edited by W.D. Davies and L. Finkelstein. Cambridge: Cambridge University, 1984, 1989, 1.372-400.

E. Posner, *Archives in the Ancient World*. Cambridge: Harvard University, 1972.

M.J. Price, *Coins and the Bible*. London: V.C. Vecchi & Sons, 1975.

J.B. Pritchard, ed. *Ancient Near Eastern Texts Relating to the Old Testament*. 3rd edition. New Haven: Yale University, 1969.

J.D. Purvis, "The Samaritans and Judaism," in *Early Judaism and its Modern Interpreters*, 81-98. Edited by R.A. Kraft and G.W.E. Nickelsburg. Philadelphia: Fortress and Atlanta: Scholars, 1986.

U. Rappaport, "The Emergence of Hasmonaean Coinage." *A.J.S. Review* 1 (1976): 171-86.

A. Reifenberg, *Ancient Jewish Coins*. 4th edition. Jerusalem: R. Mass, 1965.

R. Rendtorff, "El, Ba'al und Jahwe." *ZAW* 78 (1966): 277-292.

D.M. Rhoads, *Israel in Revolution: 6-74 C.E. A Political History Based on the Writings of Josephus*. Philadelphia: Fortress, 1976.

M. Robertson, *A History of Greek Art*. 2 volumes. Cambridge: Cambridge University, 1975.

J. Robinson, *The Second Book of Kings*. CBC 11. Cambridge: Cambridge University, 1976.

W. Röllig, "On the origin of the Phoenicians." *Ber* 31 (1983): 79-93.

J.F. Romano, "The Bes-image in Pharaonic Egypt." 2 volumes. Ph.D. dissertation, New York University, 1989.

F. Rosenthal, *A Grammar of Biblical Aramaic*. Wiesbaden: O. Harrassowitz, 1963.

H. Rouillard and J. Tropper, "*TRPYM*, rituels de guérison et culte des ancêtres d'après 1 Samuel XIX 11-17 et les textes parallèles d'Assur et de Nuzi." *VT* 37 (1987): 340-61.

H.H. Rowley, "Zadok and Nahushtan." *JBL* 58 (1939): 136-37.

K. Rupprecht, *Der Tempel von Jerusalem: Gründung Salomos oder jebusitisches Erbe?* BZAW 144. Berlin and New York: Walter de Gruyter, 1976.

E. Sachau, *Aramäische Papyrus und Ostraka aus einer jüdischen Militärkolonie zu Elephantine: Altorientalische Sprachdenmäler des 5 Jahrhunderts vor Christus*. 2 volumes. Leipzig: Heinrichs, 1911.

E.P. Sanders, *Judaism, Practice and Belief 63 BCE-66 CE*. London and Philadelphia: SCM and Trinity Press International, 1992.

E.P. Sanders, *Paul and Palestinian Judaism. A Comparison of Patterns of Religion*. London: SCM, 1977.

B. Sass and C. Uehlinger *Studies in the Iconography of Northwest*

Semitic Inscribed Seals. OBO 125. Freiburg: Universitätsverlag and Göttingen: Vandenhoeck & Ruprecht, 1993.

J. Sasson, "Bovine Symbolism in the Exodus Narrative." *VT* 18 (1968): 385-87.

G. Savran, "1 and 2 Kings," in *The Literary Guide to the Bible*, 146-64. Edited by R. Alter and F. Kermode. Cambridge, MA: Belknap, 1987.

L.H. Schiffman, *From Text to Tradition: A History of Second Temple and Rabbinic Judaism.* Hoboken, NJ: KTAV, 1991.

B.B. Schmidt, *Israel's Beneficent Dead: Ancestor Cult and Necromancy in Ancient Israelite Religion and Tradition.* FAT 11. Tübingen: JCB Mohr [Paul Siebeck], 1994.

B.B. Schmidt, "The Moon God," in *Dictionary of Deities and Demons in the Bible.* Edited by K. van der Toorn, B. Becking and P. van der Horst. Leiden: Brill, 1995.

W.H. Schmidt, *The Faith of the Old Testament.* Philadelphia: Westminster, 1983.

L.A. Schökel, *Treinta Salmos: Poesia y Oracion.* 2nd edition. Madrid: Ediciones Cristiandad, 1986.

S. Schroer, *In Israel gab es Bilder. Nachrichten von darstellender Kunst im alten Testament.* OBO 74. Freiburg: Universitätsverlag and Göttingen: Vandenhoeck & Ruprecht, 1987.

E. Schürer, *The History of the Jewish People in the Age of Jesus Christ.* 3 volumes. Revised and edited by G. Vermes, F. Millar and M. Goodman. Edinburgh: T. & T. Clark, 1986.

D. Schwartz, *Studies in the Jewish Background of Christianity.* Tübingen: JCB Mohr, 1992.

L. Schwienhorst-Schönberger, *Das Bundesbuch (Ex 20,22-23,33): Studien zu seiner Entstehung und Theologie.* BZAW 188. Berlin & New York: Walter de Gruyter, 1990.

E. Sellin and G. Fohrer, *Introduction to the Old Testament.* Translated from German by D. Green. Nashville: Abingdon, 1968.

C. Seltman, *Greek Coins. A History of Metallic Currency and Coinage down to the Fall of the Hellenistic Kingdoms.* 2nd edition. Methuen's Handbooks of Archaeology. London: Methuen & Co., 1965.

H. Seyrig, "Antiquités syriennes 29. A propos du culte de Zeus à Séleucie." *Syria* 20 (1939): 296-301.

K.A.D. Smelik, "The Use of the Hebrew Bible as a Historical Source," in *Converting the Past. Studies in Ancient Israelite and Moabite Historiography*, 1-34. Edited by K.A.D. Smelik. OTS 28. Leiden: Brill, 1992.

M. Smith, "The Dead Sea Sect in Relation to Ancient Judaism." *NTS* 7 (1961): 347-60.

M. Smith, "Jewish Religious Life in the Persian Period," in *The Cambridge History of Judaism*. 2 volumes. Edited by W.D. Davies and L. Finkelstein. Cambridge: Cambridge University, 1984, 1989, 1.219-78.

M. Smith, *Palestine Parties and Politics that Shaped the Old Testament*. New York: Columbia University, 1971.

M.S. Smith, "Divine Travel as a Token of Divine Rank." *UF* 16 (1984): 359.

M.S. Smith, *The Early History of God: Yahweh and the Other Deities in Ancient Israel*. San Francisco: Harper & Row, 1990.

M.S. Smith, "Kothar wa-Hasis, the Ugaritic Craftsman God." Ph.D. dissertation, Yale University, 1985.

M.S. Smith, "The Near Eastern Background of Solar Language for Yahweh." *JBL* 109 (1990): 29-39.

H. Spieckermann, *Heilsgegenwart: eine Theologie der Psalmen*. FRLANT 148. Göttingen: Vandenhoeck & Ruprecht, 1989.

H. Spieckermann, *Judah unter Assur in der Sargonidenzeit*. FRLANT 129. Göttingen: Vandenhoeck & Ruprecht, 1982.

H.P. Stähli, *Solare Elemente im Jahweglauben des Alten Testaments*. OBO 66. Fribourg: Universitätsverlag and Göttingen: Vandenhoeck & Ruprecht, 1985.

E. Stern, ed. *Greek and Latin Authors on Jews and Judaism*. 3 volumes. Jerusalem: Israel Academy of Sciences and Humanities, 1974-1984.

F. Stolz, "Monotheismus in Israel," in *Monotheismus im Alten Israel und seiner Umwelt*, 163-82. Edited by O. Keel. BibB 14.Freiburg: Schweizerisches Katholisches Bibelwerk, 1980.

A. Tångberg, "A Note on Ba'al Zebub in 2 Kgs 1,2.3.6.16." *SJOT* 6 (1992): 296.

J.G. Taylor, *Yahweh and the Sun: Biblical and Archaeological Evidence for Sun Worship in Ancient Israel*. JSOTSup 111.

Sheffield: JSOT, 1993.

D.W. Thomas, *Documents from Old Testament Times*. London: T. Nelson, 1958.

T.L. Thompson, *Early History of the Israelite People: From the Written and Archaeological Sources*. SHANE 4. Leiden: Brill, 1992.

T.L. Thompson, *The Historicity of the Patriarchal Narratives: The Quest for the Historical Abraham*. BZAW 133. Berlin: Walter de Gruyter, 1974.

T.L. Thompson, "A New Attempt to Date the Patriarchal Narratives." *JAOS* 98 (1978): 76-84.

J.H. Tigay, *You Shall Have No Other Gods: Israelite Religion in the Light of Hebrew Inscriptions*. HSM 31. Atlanta: Scholars, 1986.

S. Timm, *Die Dynastie Omri: Quellen und Untersuchungen zur Geschichte Israels im 9. Jahrtausend vor Christus*. FRLANT 124. Göttingen: Vandenhoeck & Ruprecht, 1982.

K. van der Toorn, "Anat-Yahu, some other Deities, and the Jews of Elephantine." *Numen* 39 (1992): 80-101.

K. van der Toorn, "The Babylonian New Year Festival: New Insights from the Cuneiform Texts and Their Meaning Bearing on Old Testament Study," in *Congress Volume Leuven 1989*, 331-44. Edited by J. Emerton. VTSup 43. Leiden: Brill, 1991.

K. van der Toorn, "The Nature of the Biblical Teraphim in the Light of the Cuneiform Evidence." *CBQ* 52 (1990): 203-22.

C.C. Torrey, *Ezra Studies*. Chicago: University of Chicago, 1910.

E. Tov, *Textual Criticism of the Hebrew Bible*. Minneapolis: Fortress and Assen: Van Gorcum, 1992.

C. Uehlinger, "Northwest Semitic Inscribed Seals, Iconography and Syro-Palestinian Religions of Iron Age II: Some Afterthoughts and Conclusions," in *Studies in the Iconography of Northwest Semitic Inscribed Seals*, 257-88. Edited by B. Sass and C. Uehlinger. OBO 125. Freiburg: Universitätsverlag and Göttingen: Vandenhoeck & Ruprecht, 1993.

J.C. VanderKam, "Ezra-Nehemiah or Ezra and Nehemiah?," in *Priest, Prophets and Scribes. Essays on the Formation and Heritage of Second Temple Judaism in Honour of Joseph Blenkinsopp*, 55-75. Edited by E. Ulrich *et al.* JSOTSup 149. Sheffield: JSOT, 1992.

J. Van Seters, *In Search of History: Historiography in the Ancient World and the Origins of Biblical History*. New Haven: Yale University, 1983.

J. Van Seters, *The Life of Moses: The Yahwist as Historian in Exodus-Numbers*. Louisville: Westminster/John Knox, 1994.

J. Van Seters, *Prologue to History: The Yahwist as Historian in Genesis*. Louisville: Westminster: John Knox, 1992.

R. de Vaux, *Ancient Israel*. 2 volumes. New York: McGraw-Hill, 1965.

B. Vawter, "Yahweh: Lord of the Heavens and the Earth." *CBQ* 48 (1986): 461-67.

A. Vincent, *La Religion des judéo-araméens d'Éléphantine*. Paris: Geuthner, 1937.

M. Vogelstein, "Bakshish for Bagoas?" *JQR* 33 (1942): 89-92.

T.C. Vriezen. *The Religion of Ancient Israel*. Translated by H. Hoskins. Philadelphia: Westminster, 1967.

M.K. Wakeman, *God's Battle with the Monster*. Leiden: Brill, 1973.

N.H. Walls Jr., "The Goddess Anat in Ugaritic Myth." Ph.D. dissertation, Johns Hopkins University, 1991.

J. Weinberg, *The Citizen-Temple Community*. JSOTSup 151. Sheffield: JSOT, 1992.

M. Weinfeld, *Deuteronomy 1-11: A New Translation with Introduction and Commentary*. AB 5. New York: Doubleday, 1991.

H. Weippert, *Palästina in vorhellenistischer Zeit*. Munich: C.H. Beck, 1988.

M. Weippert, "Geschichte Israels am Scheideweg." *ThRu* 58 (1993): 71-103.

M. Weippert, "Jahwe" in *Reallexikon der Assyriologie und vorderasiatischen Archäologie*. 8 volumes. Edited by E. Ebling and B. Meissner. Berlin/Leipzig: Walter de Gruyter, 1928-1994, 5.246-53.

M. Weippert, "Synkretismus und Monotheismus," in *Kultur and Konflikt*, 143-79. Edited by J. Assmann and D. Harth. Edition Suhrkamp N.S. 612. Frankfurt am Main: Suhrkamp, 1990.

P. Welten, *Die Königs-Stempel: ein Beitrag zur Militärpolitik Judas unter Hiskia und Josia*. ADPV. Wiesbaden: O. Harrassowitz, 1969.

C. Westermann. *Genesis 1-11: A Commentary.* Translated from German by J.L. Scullion. Minneapolis: Augsburg, 1984.

F.A.M. Wiggerman, *Mesopotamian Protective Spirits.* Groningen: Styx & PP, 1992.

S.A. Wiggins, *A Reassessment of "Asherah": A Study according to the Textual Sources of the First Two Millennia B.C.E.* AOAT 235. Kevalaer: Butzon & Bercker and Neukirchen-Vluyn: Neukirchener, 1993.

V. Wilson, "The Iconography of Bes with Particular Reference to the Cypriote Evidence." *Levant* 7 (1975): 77-103.

I.J. Winter, "'Idols of the King': Royal Images as Recipients of Ritual Action in Ancient Mesopotamia." *Journal of Ritual Studies* 6 (1992): 13-42.

U. Winter, *Frau und Göttin: exegetische und ikonographische Studien zum weiblichen Gottersbild im alten Israel und in dessen Umwelt.* OBO 53. Fribourg: Universitätsverlag and Göttingen: Vandenhoeck & Ruprecht, 1983.

G.E. Wright, *The Old Testament against its Environment.* SBT 2. London: SCM, 1950.

P. Xella, "Ugarit 3. Culture ugaritique et phénicienne," in *Dictionnaire de la civilisation phénicienne et punique,* 482-84. Edited by E. Lipiński. Turnhout: Brepols, 1992.

A. Yardeni, "Remarks on the Priestly Blessing on Two Ancient Amulets from Jerusalem." *VT* 41 (1991): 176-85.

J. Zahle, "Religious Motifs on Seleucid Coins," in *Religion and Religious Practice in the Seleucid Kingdom,* 125-39. Edited by P. Bilde *et al.* Studies in Hellenistic Civilization 1. Aarhus: Aarhus University, 1990.

I. Zeitlin, *Ancient Judaism: Biblical Criticism from Max Weber to the Present.* Cambridge: Polity, 1984.

Z. Zevit, "Yahweh Worship and Worshippers in 8th-Century Syria." *VT* 41 (1991): 363-66.

W. Zwickel, *Räucherkult und Räuchergeräte: exegetische und archäologische Studien zum Räucheropfer im Alten Testament.* OBO 97. Freiburg: Universitätsverlag and Göttingen: Vandenhoeck & Ruprecht, 1990.

Index of Biblical Citations

Index of Authors Cited